Iraqi Women

Untold Stories from 1948 to the Present

NADJE SADIG AL-ALI

ZED BOOKS
London & New York

Iraqi Women was published in 2007 by
Zed Books Ltd, 7 Cynthia Street, London N1 9JF, UK,
and Room 400, 175 Fifth Avenue, New York, NY 10010, USA

www.zedbooks.co.uk

Designed and typeset in Monotype Joanna
by illuminati, Grosmont, www.illuminatibooks.co.uk
Cover designed by Andrew Corbett
Printed and bound at the Gutenberg Press, Malta

Distributed in the USA exclusively by Palgrave Macmillan, a division of
St Martin's Press, LLC, 175 Fifth Avenue, New York, NY 10010, USA

A catalogue record for this book is available from the British Library
Library of Congress Cataloging-in-Publication Data available
Library and Archives Canada Cataloguing in Publication Data available

ISBN 978 1 84277 744 2 Hb
ISBN 978 1 84277 745 9 Pb

Contents

Acknowledgements

This book would not have been possible without the trust, generosity, time and support of the many Iraqi women I interviewed. I am deeply grateful for and will be forever touched by their memories, stories and experiences. While it is not possible to thank everyone by name, I would like to single out a number of people who have facilitated this project and provided me with logistic support: the al-Banna family, especially Umm Faez and Faeza in Detroit who hosted me very generously. Sonia Sharrak helped me to make contacts with Iraqi women; her mother Clare not only opened her house to me and drove me to numerous meetings, but also cooked the most delicious food, converting me even to liking *pacha*. Ali Ramadan also 'chauffeured' me around the Detroit area and set up several appointments. I hope he will get a well-deserved long holiday. Najwa Jawad was extremely generous with her time, knowledge and contacts. I thoroughly enjoyed meeting her and her family and learned a great deal from all of them. I am happy to have met and connected with Dunya Mikhail, a wonderful poet and very special person. Thanks a lot for letting me use 'Inanna' in my book. Deborah al-Najjar was incredibly helpful in terms of putting me in touch with people and organizing meetings at her house, but also helping with valuable comments on several chapters. I am thankful for her trust and for letting me become a colleague, friend and soulmate. Lamis Al-Dulaimy in San Diego kindly organized a meeting with several Iraqi women at her house. I am grateful to Hala Fattah and Zeinab Mahdi in Amman, who shared their contacts and networks with me. Thanks to the Qashu family, especially Azza, Nael and Nida, for hosting me during one of my field trips to Amman. In London, I am particularly grateful to Souad Al-Jazaery and Maysaloun Faraj, who shared their insights, their contacts and their sparkling positive energies. I would also like to thank Suad al-Attar for an unforgettable journey into the past and a preview of her new work, dazzling and moving as all of her art. Mubajel Baban generously shared her stories and photographs. I am grateful to Ibtesam Al-Tahir for sharing several accounts of women describing their everyday realities which she gathered during a visit to Iraq in 2006. Many thanks to Leila Kubba for letting me use her painting 'War and Peace' for the book's cover.

I am grateful for the institutional support I received to be able to finish this book. The field research for this project was largely supported by a grant from the British Academy. I thank Zed Books for putting trust in me and my proposed project. Special thanks to my editors Susannah Trefgarne and Lucy Morton. I am indebted to members of staff of the Kurdish Human Rights Organization in El Cajon who facilitated my research amongst Kurdish women in the San Diego area. The Institute of Arab and Islamic Studies, University of Exeter, provided me with a semester-long study leave which allowed me actually to sit down and write. I am thankful to Professor Tim Niblock, who encouraged me to apply for the leave. I feel grateful to my colleagues and friends Kamil Mahdi and Mohamed-Salah Omri: Kamil for sharing his experiences, expertise and insights related to Iraq; and Mohamed-Salah for making a difference by being there, reading and commenting on parts of this book and for nurturing breakfasts at Juice Moose.

Several friends and colleagues read some chapters and provided me with invaluable insights and lots of encouragement. I would like to thank Yasser Alwan, Jill Hubbard, Jenny Morgan, Kim Longinotto and Sami Zubaida. I am indebted to Peter Sluglett, who generously read several chapters and provided very useful comments. Nadia Bagdadi, always friend and mentor, was very helpful in terms of content and finding the right tone. I am grateful to my sisters from Act Together: Women's Action for Iraq – Caroline Simpson, Jenny Morgan, Kim Longinotto, Emma Sangster and Maysoon Pachachi – for creating a safe political space and for their passion and support over the years. Particular thanks to Maysoon, who read and commented on most of my chapters and has been a loyal and caring friend. Thanks also to Rashad Salim for appreciating 'honorary sisterhood', turning pavements into works of art, and sharing landscapes – real and imagined. Cynthia Cockburn's wisdom, politics and friendship added positive vibes and inspiration. Nicola Pratt has been a great colleague and friend to work with. Her reliability, commitment and insights have been amazing and uplifting.

As always, I am grateful to my parents Dagmar and Sadig Al-Ali, who encouraged me to go out into the world, travel and find my own way and voice. Thanks a lot for being such wonderful grandparents and providing a second home to Alhena, especially during numerous field trips. Alhena, my daughter and sunshine, I thank you so much for bringing me so much happiness, even in dark and depressing times. And thanks for being so loving and patient even if Mami is busy working far too much. Finally, thanks to the continuous loving support of my husband Mark Douglas, for his inputs in terms of style and genre and for being such a wonderful father to our daughter.

Preface

I am dedicating this book to the memory of two very special women who have been important to my life and the lives of many others: my Aunt Salima Al-Ali and my mentor and friend Cynthia Nelson. The two women were of the same generation but their lives could not have been any more different.

My Aunt Salima, who passed away in Baghdad three days after President Bush declared the end of combat operations on 1 May 2003, was in some ways very untypical of the many Iraqi women I interviewed for this book. Falling blind as a young girl in the late 1940s, Aunt Salima did not receive any formal education and never worked outside the house. She did not get married and had no children of her own. Yet, in so many ways, my aunt symbolizes for me the incredible strength, steadfastness, courage, patience, resourcefulness and warmth that I have admired in many of the Iraqi women I met over the years. Despite her blindness, she not only ran a whole household after my grandmother passed away, including doing the daily chores of cooking and cleaning, but also kept the family together. Aunt Salima raised a number of children of various aunts, uncles and cousins, mediated during numerous fights and tensions between increasingly stressed-out family members and became the centre of gravity for both our extended family and people living in the neighbourhood.

Her wisdom was humbling. It was not rooted in books, or in any formal education. But somehow Aunt Salima was able to dig deep inside her eternal darkness to reach for a well of light: thoughts, advice, views and emotions that always rang true and made sense. Sightless, she would often see much clearer than the rest of the family, who, affected by the increasingly difficult living conditions, political repression, economic deterioration, wars and sanctions, occasionally gave in to envy, personal grudges and bickering. Aunt Salima was not imr une to it all and herself liked to engage in a good gossip once in a while. I felt pity for those who angered her and became the targets of her resentment. Yet she had a profound sense of justice, fairness and a big heart that could easily forgive if given the chance.

A passionate sense of justice and empathy towards those treated badly was also at the core of Cynthia Nelson's life. She became my professor at the American University in Cairo, where she taught for over forty years before passing away in February 2006 after battling with cancer. It is through Cynthia that my own passion for anthropology, feminism and writing developed. Sitting in her classes, listening to her eloquent and intricate stream of thoughts (uttered with her eyes closed in full concentration), being encouraged to open up my mind and think deeply, engage, analyse and stretch the boundaries of my imagination, I felt challenged and inspired. I did not always agree, especially later on as she generously and gracefully let me become a colleague and friend and not only one of her students. Cynthia was open to rethinking her ideas, but her constant was her strong commitment to Egypt, to the Arab world, to justice and to good-quality work. Deeply outraged by US foreign policy, she would often engage in slightly polemical outbursts which seemed to contradict her otherwise nuanced and complex approach as a scholar. I often wondered how difficult it must have been for someone of US background to live for so long in the region, make it her home, and watch political leaders in the USA engage in disastrous policies which hurt the people she grew to love.

Although Aunt Salima and Cynthia Nelson never met, I always imagined how such an encounter would have turned out. They were both no-nonsense women, strong-willed, interested and curious about the world around them. They would have learned about each other's lives, would have shared stories, laughed and cried together. With this book, I hope to honour the memory of both Salima and Cynthia, thanking them for having touched my life and for inspiring me to gain the wisdom, courage and strength that connected them despite being worlds apart.

Introduction

This book tells numerous hitherto untold stories by Iraqi women about their country between 1948 and 2006. It is not about Saddam Hussein, or the many wars Iraqi men, women and children have lived through. Neither is it another book about Islam and the plight of Muslim women. Instead, the study puts the life stories and experiences of Iraqi women at the centre and attempts to construct an alternative history or histories. Of course, given recent Iraqi history, political repression, coups and revolutions, wars and occupation are certainly at the core of many of the narratives selected and reproduced here. However, the women I talked to are not mere passive victims of circumstance: they have been resourcefully, creatively and actively trying to adapt to rapidly changing situations; they have resisted political oppression; and they have been trying to keep together and sustain their families and society despite the deterioration of infrastructures, lack of security and harsh everyday living conditions.

Rather than providing a linear chronological account of the political, social and economic changes that Iraqi women have experienced from the late 1940s until today, I try to show how different women have experienced specific historical periods. And difference, as is one of my central arguments in this book, is not necessarily defined in ethnic and religious terms – that is, whether a woman is Shi'i, Sunni, Kurd or Christian, for example. It is important to emphasize that these are relatively new paradigms for classifying Iraqis. For until very recently, difference has been experienced largely in relation to social class, place of residence, urban or rural identity, professional background, political orientation and generation.

This book is based on the premiss that all histories and memories are constructed. My starting point is the experiences, life stories and oral histories of Iraqi women, interwoven with more conventional published histories as well as my own anecdotes, experiences and observations. Trying to put together a complex puzzle, juggling different personal experiences, narratives and official accounts, is not a mere narrative technique. Processes of construction and selection have already begun at the level of the women's own narratives. Memories, whether individual or collective, are not static and frozen in time, but are alive, rooted in the present as much as in the past, and linked to aspirations as much as actual experiences.

Different accounts and interpretations of events are also linked to particular world-views and frames of mind. For example, I grew up being told by my father that his younger sister, my Aunt Salima, lost her eyesight as a young girl in 1948, the year of the mass demonstrations later called al-Wathba (the Leap) and the establishment of the state of Israel. According to my father, young Salima was playing with other children of the neighbourhood near a building site with unslaked lime. Some children started throwing the lime at each other and my Aunt Salima got some into her eyes, subsequently becoming blind. Yet, when researching for this book, I discovered that there were other stories about this loss of eyesight circulating within the family. My relatives appear to agree that Salima had been blessed with beautiful big black eyes. According to one of my uncles, the big eyes were a trademark of the whole family, prompting the children of the neighbourhood to sing a little tune every time one of the Al-Ali children passed by: 'Min jaybe ayunak? Min beit Al-Ali! – Where did you get your eyes from? From the Al-Ali house!' According to my grandmother, it was the 'evil eye' that was to blame. One day, Salima, who was only 8 years old at the time, had taken a bath, and washed her beautiful long black hair, when a strange woman passed by and exclaimed: 'Oh, what beautiful eyes!' A few days later, as my late grandmother would tell the story, Salima's left eye became redder and redder. Several doctor's visits were in vain and she soon lost sight in one eye and later in the second one.

My eldest uncle, Salem, on the other hand, a retired judge, mentioned an eye disease that was common in the late 1940s in Iraq and brought blindness to many children. According to him, my aunt lost both eyes to the disease. I suspect that I will never know how exactly my aunt became blind, although my own world-view and set of experiences lead me to discard the 'evil eye' version. Unfortunately I did not have the chance to discuss this version of events with my grandmother as she passed away in the early 1980s. But I can also see how her story, and the versions told by my uncle or my father, might not necessarily be mutually exclusive.

On a philosophical level, I am interested in the relationship between experiences, memory and truth. Studying the role of public non-academic history, Jeremy Black asks a poignant question which is also central to this book: 'Do people who live through dramatic events feel that their experiences give them a special knowledge and understanding, and that therefore what they say when recalling them is the plain unvarnished truth?' (Black, 2005: 10). For me, one of the biggest challenges in writing this book has been to recognize that experience, memory and truth do not necessarily overlap, that there might be multiple truths about an event without diminishing either the significance of memory or the importance of finding out what 'really' happened in terms of political developments, repression, wars and social changes. The question is how to acknowledge the validity of contesting subjective truths without falling into the postmodern trap of nihilistic relativism. 'Everything goes' is not good enough when recounting stories of repression, suffering, torture, flight, and attempts to remain alive when violence reigns. It is also not good enough in a context when distortions, partial truths, outright lies and propaganda have serious and far-reaching implications for people living inside Iraq.

This book is about the past, about how history is constructed and how it is used. It is also very much about the present. In the context of the aftermath of the invasion in 2003, the escalating violence and sectarian tensions, contestations about power and national identity, history becomes a very important and powerful tool. Contesting narratives about what happened in the past relate directly to different attitudes towards the present and visions about the future of the new Iraq. They relate to claims about rights, about resources, and about power. More crucially, the different accounts of the past lay down the parameters of what it means to be Iraqi, who is to be included and who is to be excluded. History justifies and contains both narratives of unity and narratives of divisions and sectarianism.

While I point to differences on the level of experiences and memory among women, I am also trying to delineate a series of different trends and developments that have affected everyone, even if in distinct ways, as well as aiming to provide a historical context to the current crisis. About a year after the invasion of Iraq in March 2003, I was approached by Zed Books to write a book about Iraqi women in the present situation. It was certainly an interesting and challenging proposal. But, after thinking about it for a while, I declined, feeling strongly that a general Western readership would not be able to grasp the full extent to which women are losing out in the present period without being familiar with the broader historical context. I could see how a description and analysis of what is happening to women in the post-Saddam Hussein era could all too easily be misconstrued in terms of culture, tradition or religion, raising familiar questions like 'Isn't this just another instance of a Muslim country oppressing its women?' Hence, the idea for another book emerged, and I returned to Zed with a new proposal.

Over the past decade, I have worked both as an academic and as an activist to document the various ways in which Iraqi women and gender relations have been changing in the context of political repression under the Ba'th regime, changing state policies towards women, a series of wars, as well as economic sanctions. I decided to build on this earlier work, extend the historical frame to include the period before the thirty-five years of the Ba'th regime (1968–2003), looking back to the transition from monarchy to republic (the 1950s through the revolution of 1958 to the early 1960s), and to deepen my understanding by interviewing a greater number of women over a period of a couple of years. In addition to the interviews with about eighty women I had carried out earlier, I talked to over a hundred women in different locations in the run-up to writing this book, in London, Amman, Detroit and San Diego. Although most women have lived outside Iraq for a while – some have been away for more than forty years while others have only left recently – I also managed to speak to women who still live inside Iraq but were just spending some time abroad, mainly in Amman but also in London. In Chapter 1, I map out the different locations for my fieldwork and explain the rationale for choosing these particular sites.

The women I talked to were of different generations, varying ethnic and religious backgrounds: some were more secular, others more religious. I talked to those who have been politically active and those not, women associated with different political orientations and parties, professional women, housewives, mothers, happily married women, divorced women, women in unhappy relationships, women who had settled fairly comfortably in their new home countries, and those who were eternally homesick for Iraq. Yet the majority of the women I talked to were educated middle-class women from urban backgrounds. It is important to stress the limitation of this specific sample in terms of its representativeness. Hence, while there has been a relatively large urban middle class since the economic boom of the 1970s, this book does not explore the lives of women of the poorest strata of society nor women who were living in the countryside. In terms of places of origin, most women I interviewed were from the capital, Baghdad, but I also spoke to women from other major cities and towns such as Basra, Najaf, Karbala', Mosul, Babylon, Kirkuk, Irbil and Dohuk.

As many of the excerpts of women's narratives touch on sensitive political, social and personal issues, I have decided to use pseudonyms throughout the book to ensure the anonymity of everyone I interviewed. This unfortunately has the disadvantage of not allowing me to document the important cultural, social, professional, economic and political contributions specific women have made. A history acknowledging these contributions is certainly needed and hopefully will be undertaken by writers more qualified for this challenge than me. I should also state that throughout this book, I opted to mention the ethnic and religious affiliation of a woman only if it appears to be of relevance to her narrative and views.

Due to the worsening security situation inside Iraq and the arrival of my baby daughter a few months before the invasion, I did not travel to see my relatives in the post-2003 period. I had visited my family in Baghdad regularly as a child and teenager and continued to do so, if less frequently, when I started university. My father had left Iraq in 1958, long before the Ba'th or Saddam Hussein came to power. He travelled in order to study in Germany and only ended up staying after marrying my German mother. So, unlike most of my friends and the Iraqi refugees and asylum seekers I got to know over the years, who were not able to go back as long as Saddam Hussein was still in power, we were able to visit our relatives every so often during holidays. On one of my trips to Iraq in July and August of 1990, my father and I were trapped on the way out because of the invasion of Kuwait. My last journey to Iraq was in 1997, when economic sanctions had already left an ugly mark on society.

This last visit to Iraq was a turning point in my personal, professional and political life. As with so many other second-generation Iraqis living abroad, it was the increasing recognition of the human suffering inside Iraq, triggered by political repression, wars and economic sanctions, that pushed me to a closer relationship with the country my father had left almost four decades before. I was humbled by my cousins, who did not show any sense of envy of my ability to come and go, spending my Easter or summer holidays for family visits to Baghdad but then being able to leave the country while they had to stay behind. Nor did I sense any resentment of my privileges and freedoms, having been able to travel to many places and having obtained an education in Germany, the USA, Egypt and the UK. Instead I felt that my cousins, at least those closest to me in age, appeared to be curious about my life, and, to my great astonishment, genuinely happy for me. It was during that last trip in 1997, as I saw how the country's infrastructure had deteriorated beyond belief, in addition to the ongoing political repression, that I promised myself to use my freedom, my education and my skills more purposefully. I wanted to increase public consciousness not only about what had been happening to Iraqi women, but also regarding the transformation in Iraqi society at large. Initially, my focus was the devastating impact of economic sanctions, while always recognizing and stressing the dreadful impact of the repressive regime of Saddam Hussein. More recently I have been focusing on the impact of the recent invasion and the ongoing occupation. As I will describe in greater detail in the next chapter, I have found political homes and safe spaces with Women in Black London – part of a worldwide network of women campaigning against war and violence and for peace with justice – and Act Together: Women's Action for Iraq, an Iraqi–British organization that I co-founded in 2000.

In terms of my academic interests and writings as a social anthropologist, one of my principal concerns has been women and gender relations in the context of the Middle East, particularly Egypt and Iraq. More recently, I have studied the role of refugees and migrants in situations of reconstruction and political transition, as well as wider questions of diasporic mobilizations, focusing on Bosnia–Hercegovina in addition to Iraq. Throughout my research and writings, I have always been interested in exploring the relationship between individual lives and wider historical trends, or what social theorists have coined agency and structure. Influenced by my own trajectory as someone of Iraqi–German origin, who has lived in multiple places and inhabited different spaces, my work attempts to circumvent essentialized and generalized notions of 'the other', polarized visions of the world and its peoples, as well as simplistic black-and-white depictions of events. I see my writings as contributing to a post-colonial scholarship that recognizes ongoing and even deepening injustices and inequalities but also acknowledges cultural entanglements, creative encounters as well as complicities and resistances that cut across nation-states.

My academic work and my political activism are rooted in feminism, a thoroughly unfashionable and almost dirty word, not only in the context of Muslim societies in which feminism is often constructed as something alien and imposed from the outside, but also within Western societies where the association tends to be with man-hating radical women. Yet feminism for me, as for many thousands of women and men across the globe, is based on the recognition of and struggle against inequalities based on gender as well as intersecting inequalities and injustices related to class, race, ethnicity and religion. Feminism is an analytical tool with which one can study societies, explore social changes, and explain complex social phenomena. For example, feminist theories and concepts provide me with the analytical tools to discuss the relationship between state policies, economics and changing ideologies about how men and women should behave and relate to each other. In other words, feminist theories and concepts point to the interrelationships and intersections between what is happening inside families in the so-called 'private sphere' and what is happening outside people's homes, on the street, at workplaces, in the media, in the political sphere and so on. Feminist scholars have also explored both historically and in different cultural contexts how women's dress codes, mobility and comportment are so central to constructing identities and communities, especially in conflict situations. At the same time, feminism refers to a social and political movement that tries to address the inequalities and injustices that seem to pervade our lives. It gives birth to political practices, which differ depending on specific interpretation and political leaning. I associate my own political practices as a feminist with the struggle against all inequalities, whether they are rooted in sexism, racism, class or Islamophobia, and the attempt to find non-hierarchical and non-violent ways of resisting.

Social histories of marginalized people – whether women, people of colour, peasants, workers, ethnic or religious minorities – have increasingly challenged previously prevailing accounts of human history with a single narrative thread, usually told from the perspective of a white Western middle-class man. One important aspect of feminist research is the attempt to enable women to participate in the production of knowledge and to use experiences and 'the subjective' as part of the research process.

The term 'oral history' refers to a method of gathering historical information related to specific events, experiences, memories and ways of life. It includes various forms of in-depth interviews, such as life stories, personal narratives and accounts of specific historical events. Oral histories allow for a holistic approach to the past and the present by allowing people not only to provide accounts of specific events, but also reflect on their own roles, their interpretations of events and their emotions. I approached the research as an interactive process, in which I didn't simply ask questions to elicit information and listen, but also engaged, discussed and occasionally argued with the women I interviewed. Although oral histories in the broadest sense should ideally be recorded, I only managed to record about half of my interviews; I took detailed notes of the other half. Despite my reassurance about the anonymity of the interviews, some respondents felt nervous about being tape-recorded, which is not surprising given the level of political repression inside Iraq as well as legal insecurities in the diaspora.

My narrative in this book begins with the history of the Iraqi dispersal and the mapping out of the different sites of my research (Chapter 1), before moving into the various historical and personal accounts related to developments inside Iraq. Relying mainly on women's personal life stories and oral histories, I decided that the late 1940s was as far back as I could go, given that the oldest women I talked to were in their late seventies. Central to Chapter 2 is the question of how different women experienced the period leading up to the revolution of 1958, the actual events related to the revolution and its aftermath, including the first Ba'th–nationalist coup in 1963. In Chapter 3, I explore the first decade of the Ba'th regime (1968–1979) prior to the presidency of Saddam Hussein (1979–2003). Accounts of women reveal both the effects of state repression as well as the 'days of plenty' associated with a booming economy and an expanding middle class. In Chapters 3 and 4, I also look at the various ways changing state policies affected not only women but also gender ideologies and gender relations. The impact of the Iran–Iraq war (1980–1988) on society in general and women in particular is the focus of Chapter 4. In Chapter 5, I share different experiences related to thirteen years of the most comprehensive sanctions regime ever imposed on a country (1990–2003). In the last chapter, the events since the invasion in 2003 and its immediate aftermath take the story up to the present period of escalating violence, sectarianism and systematic diminution of women's spaces and rights (2003–06).

For the reader not familiar with the history of Iraq, a few words about the period before 1948 are in order, as the women introduced in Chapter 2 will have inherited from this pre-1948 period. Before the First World War, what is now Iraq consisted of the three Ottoman provinces of Baghdad, Basra and Mosul. In October 1914, Britain, sensing that the Ottomans would probably side with Germany in the coming conflict, sent a force from India to the head of the Persian Gulf which landed and took Basra. After initial successes, the campaign in 'Mesopotamia' dragged on for two years before Baghdad was taken in March 1917 and Mosul at the very end of the war in 1918. Since most of the British officials who came with the forces had been trained in India, a civil administration on Indian lines was set up as the army advanced northwards. At the Paris peace conference in 1919–20, and under the terms of the Treaty of San Remo in April 1920, the victors of the First World War decided that the former Ottoman territories now under British and French control should be assigned to Britain and France as 'mandates'. Under the general umbrella and supervision of the newly created League of Nations, Iraq, Palestine and Jordan were placed under British control, and Syria and Lebanon under French control.

A few months later, Iraqis of all ethnic and religious backgrounds responded to this news with a major uprising, known as the Great Rebellion of 1920. The British responded forcefully, using security forces and intelligence services (Abdullah, 2003: 129; Farouk-Sluglett and Sluglett 2001: 11; Tripp, 2000: 42–4). Having brutally suppressed the rebellion, the British government decided that this form of colonial control was too expensive to maintain, and that direct colonial rule should be replaced with indirect rule, creating an Iraqi government that was at least to have the appearance of being 'constitutional, representative and democratic' (Abdullah, 2003: 130). It was decided to establish a kingdom in Iraq and to offer the throne to Faysal, the son of Sharif Husayn of the Hijaz, the exiled king of Syria and the leader of the British-sponsored Arab revolt against the Ottomans during the First World War. An Iraqi government was to rule with the help of 'British advisers' (whose advice had to be taken) and Britain continued to administer directly the defence and internal security of the country and to have a right of veto in military and financial matters (Abdullah, 2003: 131; Farouk-Sluglett and Sluglett, 2001: 11). Based on stereotypical and simplistic assumptions about Iraqi society, the British relied heavily on securing the loyalty of tribal chiefs and giving 'official' recognition to their authority, thereby radically changing the previous relationship between tribal sheikhs and their tribal followers (Dodge, 2003). When order seemed to break down, or resistance to the British and their puppet government became open and dangerous, the RAF would be called to use its new technologies and British airplanes would bomb areas known for dissent (Sluglett, 1976: 259–72). By 1930, with an agreement to develop Iraqi oil signed between the Iraqi government and a company in which the British government had a majority, and the dispute over Iraq's northern frontier settled in Iraq's favour, Britain announced that it would support Iraq's admission to the League of Nations in 1932, which duly took place. Thus Iraq became nominally independent, but British military and economic control as well as internal meddling by British 'advisers' continued, promoting a narrow urban Arab Sunni political elite supported by 'loyal' tribal sheikhs. In fact, the Sunni Arabs, who represented perhaps 17–20 per cent of the population – then as now – continued to monopolize public office (although under changing political circumstances) until the overthrow of Saddam Hussein in 2003.

As in most of the rest of the world at the time, women were almost completely excluded from formal political institutions and processes, but from the 1920s onwards established a growing number of philanthropic, social and political organizations that were part of an emerging Iraqi 'civic order' (Kamp, 2003). Baghdadi elite women embraced the idea of 'the new woman' in the first Iraqi women's movement called Women's Awakening (Nahda al-Nisa') during the 1920s. Women's education, the need for enlightened mothers and housewives, suffrage and entry into the labour force became subjects of debate. Mostly male reformers also addressed the subject of the veil which they perceived to be a major symbol of cultural backwardness and subordination. During the 1930s, women's associations set up charitable organizations, including shelters for orphans and health centres, to address the growing 'social question' and lack of state welfare provision (Kamp, 2003) – issues that were only seriously debated in Western Europe after World War II. While women of elite background were encouraged by their families to obtain an education, neither the Iraqi state nor its British advisers actively promoted women's education or women's rights.

Against this broadly sketched historical background, much of what is unfolding post-2003 might trigger a reaction of déjà vu. However, it is beyond the scope of this book to consider the detail of parallels between British colonial rule in the early part of the twentieth century and the early-twenty-first-century occupation of Iraq by American and British forces.[1] Instead this book focuses on the period between these two historical junctures, illuminating, on the one hand, women's great achievements, the positive developments with respect to their status and the increase in their social, political and legal rights, and, on the other, the continual obstacles, repression and immeasurable human suffering in their lives. The book ends by exploring the current situation in an attempt to shed new light on events, developments and debates by providing context, historical depth and the untold perspectives of Iraqi women.

ONE

Living in the Diaspora

For decades, Iraq has not only existed inside the territorial boundaries of the nation-state but has also stayed alive within the numerous migrant and exile communities dispersed throughout the world. Iraq has been living in the hearts of diaspora Iraqis and has filled their imaginations. Alienation, nostalgia and depression are chronic and widespread amongst Iraqis abroad, whether living in one of the neighbouring countries in the Middle East, or further away, in Europe, the Americas, Australia or the Far East; speaking to them one often senses a great sadness. Yet, diasporic communities have also been great sources of hope, of political mobilization, of humanitarian and financial assistance as well as creative synergies.

Iraqi women and men have been leaving in significant numbers since the 1940s for a variety of reasons. The vast majority had to leave due to political repression or fear of persecution. Others left to escape war and destruction. Economic betterment as well as the wish to pursue higher education abroad have also been amongst the reasons why Iraqis have migrated. During the period of economic sanctions (1990–2003), simple categories of voluntary versus forced migration did become blurred as hundreds of thousands of Iraqis left in the context of a severe economic crisis and ongoing political repression.

When my father left Iraq in 1958 to study in Germany, along with a number of his contemporaries, he did not think about leaving for good. Even when he married my German mother in 1966, he was still eager to return to Baghdad and she was adventurous enough to agree. Yet by the time my father finished his studies and training, the Ba'th Party had come to power in a second *coup d'état* (1968) and the political situation inside Iraq started to look unsettling. For a long time, my father and his Iraqi Turkmen friend Hashem from Kirkuk were among a very small number of Iraqis in the German town I grew up in. Some bigger cities had more substantial communities of Iraqi refugees and migrants. However, in the aftermath of the Gulf War in 1991, even my small home town of Krefeld saw a steady growth of a community of Iraqi refugees and asylum-seekers, duplicating the mushrooming of Iraqi communities in many countries and cities throughout the world.

During my last visit to Baghdad in 1997, my Aunt Salima pleaded with my father and my mother to find a way to get one of my cousins out of the country and into Germany – to what she imagined must be a better life. She had raised my cousin Hamid after his father had been killed by the regime of Saddam Hussein, which left his mother too distressed to cope. Although, or maybe because, she was extremely attached to Hamid and treated him as her son, she wanted him to leave, hoping that he would have a better chance elsewhere. After many years of struggle, finally my cousin managed to emigrate to Germany, soon followed by his wife, his sister (my cousin Iba), her husband and two children. Yet their experience of leaving Iraq and starting anew in a foreign country could not have been more different from that of my father, who left voluntarily. Instead of the opportunities, open labour markets and relatively warm welcome extended to the small numbers of students from Arab countries that my father found in the 1960s in Germany, my cousins have found themselves in the midst of an economic crisis, high unemployment rates, a pervasive suspicion of asylum-seekers, and widespread Islamophobia. Entering into this milieu, carrying the baggage of their own traumas and anxieties related to their upbringing inside Iraq, they have become part of a generation of Iraqi refugees and migrants who are in a continuous state of limbo: suspended between the harsh economic and social realities facing migrants and asylum-seekers in Western countries and the worsening situation inside Iraq, which prevents most from returning to what they still perceive to be home.

In this chapter, I will explain the historical circumstances that have led to the dispersal of more than 4 million Iraqis (out of approximately 24 million) throughout the world. I will map out my main sites of research for this book – London, Detroit, San Diego and Amman – explaining the different migration trajectories of Iraqi communities in each location and the specific conditions they find themselves in today, and sharing my own travels and observations. Before delving into the different layers and sites of dispersion as well as specific historical circumstances that resulted in the migration and flight of millions of Iraqis, I will clarify my use of concepts and my understanding of the terms 'diaspora' and 'exile'.

Diaspora and Exile

Although the term 'diaspora' has traditionally been used in the context of the tragic Jewish and Armenian experiences, the Greek origins of the word refer to a more mixed bag of forced and voluntary migration (Cohen, 1995: 6). I work with the more open perspective adopted here:

> First, the population is dispersed from a homeland to two or more territories. Second, the presence abroad is enduring, although exile is not necessarily permanent, but may include movement between homeland and new host. And third, there is some kind of exchange – social, economic, political or cultural – between or among the spatially separated populations comprising the diaspora. (van Hear, 1998: 6)

Much of the Iraqi dispersal is tragic both in terms of the conditions that forced people to flee from Iraq and in terms of the circumstances of flight and the living conditions in the country of settlement. Yet, there are also many stories of success, achievements and flourishing of communities abroad. Aside from differences related to social class, educational background and professional qualifications, the specific circumstances and time of migration and the economic, social and political conditions within the host country have very much shaped the experiences of Iraqis abroad. Gender is one among many variables that have contributed to a diversity of experiences. While some Iraqi women have become more dependent on male family members, suffered from the loss of support networks and lived through an acute sense of isolation, others have managed to thrive and benefit from the opportunities and possibilities connected to their new surroundings.

While the term 'diaspora' encompasses a whole range of voluntary and forced migration patterns, the term 'exile' refers more specifically to the condition of having left one's home country due to political repression, persecution or oppositional politics. Iraqi women of all ethnic and religious backgrounds have become exiled due to their own political activism inside Iraq. Others experienced exile because of the persecution due to their ethnic and religious affiliation, especially as Kurds and Shi'is. And many women ended up in exile due to their affiliation, either as wives or relatives, with male political activists.

Aside from the physical and material realities and hardships related to living in a strange place away from home, exile also refers to a state of mind and being. Received notions and ideas as well as set practices and traditions are unsettled when people are forced to leave the known and the familiar behind. While many of those exiled face a 'crisis of meaning', others fervently and desperately hold on to the past and everything they knew and did before. Among the women I interviewed, exile came to mean different things depending on their socio-economic positions, their educational and political backgrounds and their wider social relationships and networks within the place that became their new physical home.

Yet the notion of Iraqi exile itself has transformed in the aftermath of the downfall of Saddam's regime. Thousands of Iraqis were initially able to go 'home' for the first time in decades after the invasion in 2003. Most went for a short visit only, but many among them were hoping to return for good. Their experiences varied from emotional homecomings to encounters with a land and people that had become utterly alien to them. As I sit here writing, more than three years after the end of the dictatorship, Iraqis abroad are once more unable to return to their home country, fearing the violence, lack of security and rampant kidnappings inside Iraq. Meanwhile hundreds of thousands of Iraqis are trying to escape the deteriorating living conditions and spiralling violence, adding a new phase and new layers to Iraqi diasporic communities throughout the world.

Becoming Iraqi in London

My own initiation into Iraqi diasporic life started in the mid-1990s when I moved from Cairo to London to do my Ph.D. During my childhood I often felt embarrassed about the things that marked me and my family as 'different': my name, visitors speaking Arabic, and different foods. I still feel a pang of shame remembering the moment when some friends visiting our home asked me about the picture of my grandmother, sitting on the floor wearing the traditional black garment called *abaya*. Just as I told them that I did not know who the person in the photo was, my father stuck his head through the door and heard what I said. He never commented on it but I could sense his hurt. Later on as a teenager my sense of embarrassment turned into a defiant pride in my 'difference', although German society's lack of multiculturalism at the time did not allow for much expression of it. It was during my five-year stay in Cairo that I gave up trying so hard to be *Deutscher als die Deutschen* (more German than the Germans) and eagerly explored and asserted my 'Arab roots'.

I began to develop a sense of 'Iraqiness' in the context of the Gulf War in 1991 and the unfolding humanitarian crisis due to economic sanctions. But it was in London that I 'became Iraqi', in terms of both an ascribed identity as an academic and activist and in the way I started identifying myself. Due to my own mixed background and voluntary moving between different countries, I have been attracted to cosmopolitan places like London. Yet, over the past decade this cosmopolitanism has been living side by side with a growing political, cultural and emotional attachment to Iraq, or at least to my particular vision of it. I have also been feeling something of the mounting pain, maddening anger and, at moments, utter helplessness that so many Iraqis have felt as a result of repression, destruction and escalating violence.

Initially it was just a matter of socializing with Iraqi opposition intellectuals and artists at a particular café in Camden, within walking distance of my rented room in Kentish Town. Between writing my Ph.D. on the Egyptian women's movement and working as a postgraduate teaching assistant at the university, I would eagerly seek out their company, and listen to the stories about their lives inside and outside Iraq. We would also discuss novels, films and exhibitions, philosophize about this and that, and sometimes exchange news and gossip. I never had to arrange a meeting as I knew that I would always find one of my friends at the café. The actual café changed several times throughout the period I lived in north London, but the regulars did not.

Sometimes my friends would take me along to concerts, poetry readings, talks, dinners and parties, and slowly my circle of Iraqi friends and acquaintances grew. Many of the Iraqis I knew were struggling to make ends meet, working as journalists or freelance writers, occasionally selling their artworks or making some money interpreting. Most of my friends were living in council flats at the time and some were getting income support. I often tried to imagine how it must feel to have had a career, a certain status, and then being forced into a new place where one's skills and abilities are not appreciated or not needed. I also became painfully aware of my own privilege as someone holding a German passport being free to come and go and travel all over the world, while many of my friends were, even after years of residency in the UK, still waiting to obtain citizenship. As it turned out, my circle of friends ended up doing quite well and managed to re-establish their lives and careers in London, but many other Iraqis continue to struggle despite being highly qualified, and there are many whose legal status remains insecure.

One of the most active venues for cultural activities was the Kufa gallery in West London, an institution that, as I was shocked to find out, recently closed down. I used to attend events there regularly, always feeling fascinated by the numbers of Iraqis interested in culture and intellectual issues. At some point I must have had the impression that all the Iraqis I met in London were writers, poets, artists, journalists or intellectuals in the widest sense. Through my father's acquaintances I had also come across an older generation of Iraqi professionals and business people. Later on as I started to become politically active in the context of anti-sanctions and anti-war activism, I met with Iraqi exiled political activists of different political orientations. It was only when I started to document the impact of economic sanctions on women and gender relations that I started to meet the more recently arrived refugees and asylum-seekers, who were not attending the cultural events frequented by my friends, but were either socializing among themselves or occasionally attending events organized by the Muntada al-Iraqi (the Iraqi Community Association) in Hammersmith, West London.

Historically, London has been home to vibrant communities of Iraqi migrants, intellectuals, artists, exiled political activists, journalists, wealthy and poor business people as well as professionals, especially medical doctors. Although Iraqis can also be found in some other major cities in the UK, mainly Birmingham and Manchester, as well as in the home counties of Surrey, Essex and Kent, the vast majority have settled within the Greater London area. Since the 1980s, but especially in the aftermath of the Gulf War in 1991, thousands of refugees and asylum-seekers of all ethnic, religious and class backgrounds have added new layers to the already heterogeneous Iraqi communities. While there are no statistics available, migrants and refugees of Iraqi origin were estimated to number about 70–80,000 in the early 1990s (Al-Rasheed, 1994: 204). As the UK has been one of the main destinations for Iraqi refugees within Western Europe over the past decade, one can safely assume that over 100,000 people of Iraqi origin currently live in the country. Iraqis can be found scattered throughout London, with notable clusters in West London, especially Ealing, Acton and Hammersmith and Fulham, as well as in North London, particularly Brent and Camden.

There is a clear division between the various communities, cutting across ethnic and class boundaries. One of the earliest communities started in the 1950s by a small group of Assyrian Iraqis, who had worked in the levies in Habbaniya, north of Baghdad, before the British withdrawal from Iraq (Al-Rasheed, 1994: 207). The community, numbering now over 4,000, is concentrated in Ealing (West London) and is rather self-contained, not mingling much with Iraqis of different ethnic and religious backgrounds.[1]

Similarly, the Iraqi Kurdish community is relatively separate from the other Iraqi communities, although, on an individual basis, a number of Iraqi Kurdish intellectuals, activists and artists do mingle with Iraqis of Arab origin. Since the 1970s, the UK has been a significant host for Kurdish students and later refugees from Iraq. There are no reliable statistics, but the Kurdish community overall is estimated to be about 50,000. Among those, the Iraqi Kurds make up the largest group, exceeding the numbers of Kurds from Turkey and Iran (Wahlbeck, 1998: 217).

Iraqis of Arab origin, both Sunni and Shi'i, are divided in terms of social class background, political orientation, profession, time of arrival and current living conditions. The earliest wave of refugees was associated with the revolution in 1958 and consisted mainly of Sunni upper-class professionals, politicians and landowners, who made up the main bulk of the bureaucracy and state apparatus under the monarchy. Later on, as the Ba'th came to power, Iraqis of different ethnic, religious and social class backgrounds fled government repression. While London saw a particularly large influx of Iraqi communist exiles, many other opposition groups and parties found refuge in the British capital as well, including Arab nationalists, non-Saddamist Ba'this, democrats and Shi'i Islamists. In the aftermath of the uprising in 1991 after the Gulf War, it was mainly Iraqi Shi'is and Kurds who made up most of the numbers of refugees arriving in the UK.

Although some of the cultural and political events organized by Iraqis in London are male-dominated, Iraqi women have been actively involved in the rich cultural scene and political mobilizations. In the context of my own activism as a member of Women in Black – a worldwide network of women campaigning against war and for peace with justice – I had met a number of Iraqi women who were trying to raise consciousness about the plight of women, suffering not only from the dictatorship of Saddam Hussein but also from the most comprehensive sanctions regime ever imposed on a country. These women were members of political parties, of women's groups linked to parties, of independent women's organizations or individual activists.[2] Some of the women I met in the context of our activism became friends, and we soon started thinking about trying to bridge the gap between British anti-sanctions and peace groups on the one side and Iraqi activism on the other. In 2000, a group of us came together and established a mixed group of Iraqi and British women activists who were trying to work together across political differences, stressing both the atrocities of the previous regimes and those linked to US and UK policies on Iraq, particularly with respect to sanctions and war.

As an active member of Act Together: Women's Action for Iraq,[3] I became more attuned to the complex political landscapes of Iraqi diaspora mobilization in London and elsewhere. A thriving civil society of Arab dissidents and intellectuals as well as a strong anti-war and peace movement and a diverse women's movement, have constituted the backdrop against which Iraqi women's organizations and individual activists have flourished in London. Significantly, Iraqi diaspora activism in the UK is extremely varied in terms of specific attitudes towards the recent war, the occupation and ongoing political developments inside Iraq.

Many of the interviews I conducted in London were among Iraqi women who have led active cultural and political lives within the diaspora. However, I also spoke to many women who had never been involved in politics, although most had some sort of interest in Iraqi culture, literature or art. I visited many family homes scattered throughout London (but would often end up either in Ealing or Acton), while other interviews took place in cafés or offices. Aside from individual interviews, I attended numerous meetings, seminars, day-schools and demonstrations in which Iraqi women activists participated.

One of the many women I met during these events was an older woman by the name of Siham M., who is an active member in the UK branch of the Iraqi Women's League (IWL).[4] Siham's story of dispersal might not be representative of a large number of Iraqis in London. Of Iraqi Jewish origin, she was forced to leave Iraq earlier than most of the other women I talked to in London. Yet, moved by her continuing sense of belonging to Iraq and her resolve, I decided to share her story and thereby also shed light on one of the tragic moments of Iraq's history.

Siham's Story: The Jewish Exodus

When I met Siham and listened to her life-story I was aware that her feelings and experiences do not reflect the majority of Iraqi Jewish experiences. After all, the vast majority had settled in Israel and had become Israeli despite continuing cultural ties to Iraq. Yet

I was not only very moved by her personal story and her genuine continuing sense of loss where Iraq is concerned, but I also felt that Siham's story showed that, historically, political orientation and affiliation often superseded ethnic and religious divisions. Without ever denying her Jewish roots, Siham was first and foremost Iraqi, then a communist and, later on in her life, women's rights activist.

We met in a café in London's King's Cross Station – not the most comfortable of surroundings, sitting on hard gaudy plastic chairs, with noise and movement all around us – but as her story unfolded, I forgot our situation and became totally absorbed. 'I was only 13 years old when I was forced to leave Iraq in 1949. Until today I feel this was the worst day in my life. Now I am almost 70 years old and my homeland has been denied to me for most of my life. Not a day passes by when I don't think about Iraq.'

The 1948 Arab–Israeli war had left great bitterness among the Iraqi population as the Iraqi government had sent only a token force which had not been able to assist fellow Arab armies effectively in the war against Israel (Abdullah, 2003: 150). Trying to divert attention from domestic problems, especially concerns with social and political reforms, but also from the utter failure in Palestine, the Iraqi government contributed to the stoking of anti-Jewish sentiments among the Iraqi population (Shiblak, 2005: 90–91). In this, it was inadvertently colluding with the pan-Arabists affiliated with the Hizb al-Istiqlal (Independence Party), who accused the local Jewish community of supporting Zionism (Davis, 2005: 89). And Zionism, in the eyes of right-wing nationalists and pan-Arabists, was perceived to be a by-product of communism. Siham and her two older sisters had been active in the Iraqi Communist Party (ICP) for a number of years, when the general crackdown started to affect her family in dramatic ways:

> When I grew up in the late 1930s and 1940s, I lived in a multi-cultural society. We had equal opportunities in school and with jobs. I never thought that being Jewish meant being different. My family was traditional Jewish. We were proud of being Iraqi and

of being Jewish. We were living in Karrada, a mixed neighbourhood in Baghdad. I had three sisters and four brothers. Even in
'48, when Israel was established, most Iraqi Jews refused to go. But
when they started to harass people and sack them from their jobs,
they started to think about leaving. In 1949, they arrested my elder
sister, my middle sister and one of my brothers, because of their
communist ideology and activism rather than because they were
Jewish. Both of my sisters had studied, one medicine and the other
one civil engineering, but both ended up in prison. One of them
was imprisoned for life, but she was released after the revolution
in '58.

The Iraqi Jewish community had been relatively well integrated
and had generally prospered before the establishment of the state of
Israel. Siham's account is paralleled by Zeynab B., a Shi'i sympathizer
of the Dawa Party who now lives in Dearborn, USA:

> We were all friends. We celebrated holidays together. When we
> had the celebration in commemoration of Imam Husayn, they
> came with us. Even Jews and Christians joined us. We never
> thought about race, religion or anything else. Schools were open
> to everybody. In schools, we had Jewish, Christian, Sunni and
> Kurdish classmates. There were no bad feelings towards anyone. I
> myself came from a very conservative family. We wore *abaya* and
> long dresses. But when I look at some family pictures, some of my
> cousins had sleeveless shirts and short skirts. I tried to put pressure
> on my dad so that we could do what my cousins were allowed to
> do. But the king's mother and sister were covered like us. We never
> saw them. Religion was part of the country. Religion was reflecting
> the mosaic of our country. We had lots of celebrations on religious
> holidays and we would celebrate each others' holidays whether
> they were Muslim, Jewish or Christian.

Despite the general integration and peaceful co-existence, there
had been problems and tensions before. The most serious of these
events took place in 1941, during the short period of the anti-British
and pro-German Rashid 'Ali government, a pogrom known as *farhud*
accounted for the deaths of between 150 and 180 Jews, as well as
a large number of Muslims who had tried to protect their Jewish

neighbours and friends. However, it was only after the establishment of Israel in 1948 that the systematic harassment of the Iraqi
Jewish community took place: their movements and travels abroad
were increasingly restricted, people were sacked from government
positions, business licenses were refused, and political activists were
arrested and imprisoned.

By the summer of 1949 the situation seemed to be improving
slightly for Iraqi Jews, yet the Zionist campaign inside Iraq gained
momentum. The discovery of a Zionist network by the Iraqi secret
police led to more arrests and restrictions among the Jewish community. When Siham's mother was contacted by the secret police in
1949, she was given the alternative of having her daughter deported to
Israel or having her arrested and put into prison. The mother agreed
to deportation, yet Siham was desperate to stay in Iraq:

> They took me by force from home. I tried three times to run away
> from them. First they took me to Basra and then in a very terrible
> boat to Ahwas in Iran. It was winter. When I arrived in Basra it
> was very cold. They took us by bus from Ahwas to Tehran. There
> were other people with us. Some older people and some children
> died on the way. Israeli agents and the Iranians worked together.
> When I ran away from the camp in Tehran, the Iranian police
> brought me back. I begged them to bring me back to Iraq but they
> sent me back to the camp. The same day, an airplane took me to
> Israel. In the boat there were five or six people, but in the camp
> there were hundreds of people who wanted to go to Israel. The
> Zionist movement worked very hard and so many people believed
> that they were going to paradise.

Living conditions in Israel were very hard. And Siham, as other
Mezrahim (Oriental) Jews, experienced the prejudice of Ashkenazi
(European) Jews, who treated them as second-class citizens:

> In Israel, they put us in a camp and we lived in tents. They sprayed
> us with DDT when we arrived. I stayed for the first three months
> in a camp called Shaar Aliya near Haifa. I was actually in a very
> difficult situation until I met my brother who came later. Once he
> told me that there is a very important person to see me. It was a

communist who wanted to go to Russia. I went with him to the Communist Party in Israel and stayed in a youth camp established by the party. It was a very difficult life. After a year and a half, my father came with my youngest sister and brother. I left the communist youth camp to be with them, so we lived in a tent again. For about three years we lived in a tent. Then they put us in wooden accommodation. They asked us, 'Do you know how to eat with a fork and a knife?' Although our community was the most educated community of all refugees. One of our friends, who was a solicitor, had to take an exam before his degree was recognized. He went to Jerusalem and died of starvation.

When a law allowed all Iraqi Jews to renounce their citizenship and leave for Israel in 1950, the majority of the community felt too insecure to remain inside a country that was no longer guaranteeing their citizenship and economic rights. By 1952, only a few thousand Jews remained from the previously estimated 130,000-strong Jewish community, out of a total population of about 4.5 million Iraqis (Shiblak, 2005: 33–5). While the majority of Iraqi Jews left for Israel, there are substantial communities of Iraqi Jewish origin in London, the New York metropolitan area and Los Angeles. There are also small communities scattered in Connecticut, Florida, Massachusetts and New Jersey (Shiblak, 2005: 162).

Unable to make herself and her family feel at home as she was witnessing the dwindling influence of the Israeli Communist Party on the Israeli political landscape, and worried about her son having to serve in the Israeli army, Siham sent the son to one of her brothers living in France in 1972. She herself left for the UK shortly afterwards. By 1977, her whole family had been reunited in London, where they have been living ever since. However, Siham's hardship did not stop here:

> We bought a house in London from our savings, and we wanted to open a printing shop in Arabic and Hebrew. The British authorities gave all of us permanent residence. Our solicitor was very surprised it went through so quickly. After four months we got a letter from the Home Office stating that we have to leave. Our

solicitor asked if we had committed any crime. We said: 'No.' Then
he asked us if we were communists. Imagine, we stayed for eleven
years without papers.

Siham and her family finally managed to obtain permanent leave
to remain. After some years of hardly any political involvement,
Siham, as many other Iraqi exiles in London, tried to expose the
atrocities of the Saddam Hussein regime during the 1980s, although
very few people in Britain were ready to listen: 'They did not believe
us. Even when we went to a group of women MPs to speak about
Halabja,[5] they did not believe us.' In the 1990s, Siham was active in
the anti-sanctions movement and later on became involved in the
Iraqi Women's League. Before the recent war in 2003, the IWL in
London played an important role in providing financial, practical and
emotional support for recently arrived Iraqi refugee women. After
2003, members of the IWL shifted their focus to developments inside
Iraq and have been trying to fund-raise to support IWL branches
inside Iraq as well as support women's rights activists there. Despite
her age and frail health, Siham continues to be active and closely
follows the unfolding events inside Iraq.

Detroit: American Dream?

Given the role of the United States in the current developments in
Iraq, I decided it was important to explore the range of experiences
and attitudes among Iraqi women living in the USA. Metropolitan
Detroit, in the state of Michigan, was an obvious choice, as the home
of the largest Arab community in the States, but I had also learned of
its sizeable Iraqi community. Other than that I knew very little about
the city. Once the buzzing centre of the automobile industry, mainly
associated with Henry Ford, it had experienced a drastic decline and
had become one of the most impoverished cities in the USA with
one of the highest crime and murder rates. During my several visits
to Detroit, I in fact only twice visited the inner-city area as the Iraqi

communities are mainly spread in suburbs and surrounding areas. I was shocked by the level of poverty visible on the street, the number of clearly homeless people and the physical signs of deterioration, although I was told that the city centre had received a facelift and looked much better than before.

Not knowing quite where to start in terms of making contacts, I recruited my father as a research assistant and asked him to find out whether our family and friends in Baghdad knew of Iraqis living in the Detroit area. He graciously obliged and soon provided me with a list of names and phone numbers. However, except for a family that he had himself known in Baghdad and kept in contact with, all other names were of Iraqis scattered throughout the USA. Yet, as I called each name on the list, I was generously given the details of people who were actually living in the Detroit area. Iraqis I knew in London also started to put me in touch with relatives and friends. I then contacted various community organizations, such as the Arab Community Centre for Economic and Social Services (ACCESS), the Arab and Chaldean Council, the Chaldean National Congress, the Iraqi–American House and the Karbala Islamic Education Center. By the time I arrived in Detroit on Easter Monday of 2005, I was equipped with a long list of names and numbers.

I had made contact with the Iraqi family that my father had known in Baghdad, and indeed visited himself about a decade ago when he was on a work-related trip to the USA. Umm Redwan and her daughter Samira insisted that I should stay with them for at least part of my visit. One of Umm Redwan's sons was waiting for me with his own young son Steven at the airport. Both were extremely welcoming and Redwan asked me lots of questions about my parents and our family in Baghdad. Driving from the airport to Southfield, where the family was living, I was too involved in conversation to gain much of a sense of the outside world. Only as our car pulled up in front of a small three-bedroom house in a suburban neighbourhood, did I notice that most front gardens featured colourful Madonnas as well as Easter and even remaining Christmas decorations. I subsequently learned that I was staying in a largely lower-middle-class Chaldean neighbourhood where it was more common to hear Aramaic or Iraqi dialect than English spoken on the streets.

My father may or may not have mentioned that the family was Christian; belonging to a generation of Iraqis who didn't think in categories of ethnic and religious affiliation, he would not have considered it important. I was therefore little prepared for the degree of segregation characteristic of Detroit, not only between the Iraqi Chaldean and Shi'i communities but also along class and race lines.[6] Unlike most other Chaldeans I met during my visit, Umm Redwan's family spoke Arabic at home, not a dialect of Aramaic, the language spoken by the majority of Chaldeans in the USA. Speaking Aramaic is mainly a way of distinguishing themselves from Arabs and Muslims and of stressing their ancestral roots in ancient Babylonia. Chaldeans, unlike Assyrians, are Roman Catholics who converted from Nestorianism in about 1830.

In Umm Redwan's house, however, Iraqi and Arab identity did not seem to contradict a strong sense of their Chaldean culture and roots. I was not sure how much was for the benefit of my presence, but several family members stressed to me on numerous occasions their strong emotional and social ties to Iraq and the Arab world, regardless of their religious and ethnic background. The younger of two brothers, Roni, was particularly outspoken and stressed his disapproval of Bush's policies on Iraq. As the family used to live in cosmopolitan Baghdad in a mixed neighbourhood, they did not seem to have experienced persecution as Christians before they left in 1977: 'The main reason we left was because my husband did not want our sons to do military service and be killed in a war or some sort of fighting', says Umm Redwan. Other relatives had already settled in Detroit, and helped the family obtain the necessary papers to enter the USA. One month after the family's arrival, the father had a stroke, which was a big setback for the family, who had neither health insurance, nor proper jobs. Consequently, they struggled economically for the first years of their stay. Nevertheless they managed to find their feet, get jobs and buy homes. However, without proper health insurance the family continues to struggle to cover all the medical bills for Umm Redwan, who herself had a stroke a couple of years ago and has also been suffering from serious dental problems.

Most Iraqi Chaldeans, who started coming in small numbers to the USA at the beginning of the twentieth century for economic or religious reasons, came from the village of Tal Kayf in the northern Iraqi province of Mosul, near the ruins of the ancient city of Nineveh. Indeed, the vast majority of the 70–80,000 Chaldeans living in the Detroit area can trace their origin to this specific location. The first migrants triggered a chain migration of Chaldeans to the USA, specifically to Michigan and California. Many of the older Iraqi Chaldean women I interviewed in Detroit had left Iraq in the 1950s and 1960s. Most mentioned mainly economic reasons as well as family unification, although some women also talked about the pressures of having been a minority religious group within a predominantly Muslim society. Those Chaldeans who had emigrated more recently reported to me that they started to experience more systematic discrimination and open persecution in the aftermath of the Gulf War in 1991 as many Muslim Iraqis started to associate Christianity with US imperialist policies.

I had been offered lodging by another Iraqi Chaldean family, through a tenuous family connection – via a friend of a friend of an uncle in Baghdad. I decided to spend a few days with this family who had not only offered me a place to stay but had also been extremely helpful in putting me in touch with some Chaldean women who were very active within the community, mainly doing charity work helping recently arrived Chaldean refugees. Several women were also involved in humanitarian assistance, collecting money, medicines and clothes and shipping them to Iraq.

Rita, the energetic mother, who had excellent cooking skills, took me under her wing for the brief time of my stay and fed me the most delicious traditional Iraqi dishes, starting with *gamer* (buffalo cheese) and *dibbes* (date syrup) for breakfast then later *bamiya* (a dish made from okra) and even a version of *pacha* (stuffed intestines) that I liked. She would scold me for 'eating like a bird' after I had eaten my third cooked meal in a day. I had told her of my dislike of *pacha* as a child, cooked by my grandmother or one of my aunts. The version I knew was based on the cooked head of a sheep. It became Rita's mission to show me that her *pacha* – she jokingly referred to it as 'Chaldean *pacha*' – was better and more delicious than that of my childhood. She did, in the end, succeed in this mission.

Despite sharing the same ethnic and religious background, these two families were very different. Rita and her family were living in West Bloomfield, one of the most expensive upper-middle-class neighbourhoods in the entire United States. I was stunned by the huge villa-like houses, with their large gardens and well-kept lawns, the residential area surrounded by woods and small streams. Rita and her husband Samir had both migrated to the USA in the late 1950s, some twenty years before Umm Redwan and her family. They had started out working for very little money in relatives' grocery stores. Many of the early Chaldean migrants worked as retailers, opening grocery and liquor stores and later on petrol stations. After their marriage, the couple managed to open a store on their own. For decades, Rita worked as a cashier in the growing business. By the time I met the family, Rita had stopped working, but all four children were involved in the family business, which now owned and managed seven petrol stations. For Rita and her husband the American dream had become a reality: having arrived from Iraq with almost nothing, they had managed to accumulate considerable wealth. Other Chaldean women living in the same area were from educated professional backgrounds, mostly also having arrived in the 1950s, 1960s and 1970s from Iraq.

Rita not only fed me the most delicious dishes, she also arranged for meetings at her house, inviting some of her friends and acquaintances for my benefit. I was very moved by her kindness and generosity and that of her whole family. She also volunteered to drive me to numerous meetings and interviews. On one occasion we were going to a Lebanese restaurant in Dearborn, the other side of town, home to a sizeable well-established Lebanese Shi'i community and a newer growing Iraqi Shi'i community. I encouraged Rita to join me in a meeting of women activists of different religious and ethnic backgrounds organized by a member of a secular US-based Iraqi women's organization.

Due to heavy traffic, we were about twenty minutes late for the meeting, and arrived at the restaurant with everyone else already present. About twenty-five women were sitting around the table obviously waiting for my arrival. I went around, greeting everyone individually and then sat down next to Mona B., the organizer of the event. I suggested to her that I should get up and tell everyone what my research was about. But before I had the chance to do so, the oldest woman, Zeinab J., dressed in a tight headscarf and long dress, started addressing everyone in a very loud and authoritarian manner. She reminded us that we were there for business and that we should start the meeting and stop chatting. Looking at me in a rather suspicious manner, she asked in a loud voice with a clearly hostile undertone what I was doing, why I was doing it and who was funding me. These were obviously all very legitimate questions that I usually address anyway when introducing my project. However, the tone and manner in which I was asked reminded me of an interrogation and was seriously intimidating. Most of the other women present looked quite embarrassed and some tried to intervene, only to be scolded by Zeinab. After I explained the purpose of my research, and answered more questions from Zeinab and some of the other women, Zeinab started to relax and be more friendly, before she finally smiled and said: 'Well, I had to make sure that you were not a Ba'thi spy.'

Even two years after the downfall of Saddam Hussein, Zeinab and some of the other women present were seriously worried about remnants of the past regime. I initially found this hard to understand, but when I got to know Zeinab and her sister Fatima better, and heard their stories, I understood their fears. They, in common with other Iraqi women I talked to, had suffered from Ba'thi repression and persecution in the 1980s, even while studying in the USA. Indeed, when the other women activists around the table introduced themselves it became clear that what united these women – who difffered not only in terms of generation, social class and religious background but also in political orientation – was their hatred of the previous regime. With the exception of one Chaldean woman, who expressed concern about developments in Iraq, all seemed to be strongly in favour of the invasion in 2003, and indeed most women were still optimistic about Iraq's future in March 2005.

Shi'i Dearborn

The Lebanese restaurant we were meeting in was in the heart of Dearborn's busy high street, with its numerous Lebanese and Iraqi restaurants, cafés, grocery shops, bakeries, clothes shops and community centres, such as ACCESS,[7] and the Karbala Islamic Education Centre. This was clearly a buzzing area trying to absorb the continuous flow of new migrants and refugees. Since the Gulf War in 1991, over 3,000 Iraqis a year have arrived (directly from Iraq or via a third country) in the Detroit area (Abraham and Shryock, 2000). Although the refugees are of all ethnic and religious backgrounds, the vast majority who arrived after 1991 are Iraqi Shi'is from the south. Most came after 1992 from Rafah refugee camp in Saudi Arabia, where they had spent months or even years in tents suffering extremely difficult living conditions. Many had been part of the intifada (uprising) after the Gulf War in 1991, which I will discuss in greater detail in Chapter 5. These refugees largely settled in the Dearborn area where there already existed Shi'i communities of Lebanese and Iraqi refugees and migrants. The vast majority of recently arrived refugees are from rural or impoverished backgrounds, have little formal education, struggle with the English language and 'American culture', and thus tend to work in low-income jobs. The older generation of Iraqi

Shi'i refugees, in contrast, tend to be highly educated, professional and well versed in Iraqi Shi'i history and tradition as well as 'the American way of life'.

One of the political and religious centres for Iraqi Shi'i in Dearborn is the Karbala Islamic Education Centre (*Markaz Karbala'*) on West Warren Street, directed by Sheikh Hisham Al-Husainy. Fatima M., Zeinab's younger sister, took me there the first time we met. A researcher at Wayne State University had put me in contact with Fatima, who was extremely helpful and generous with her time throughout my numerous research trips. That day, outside in the car, she had helped me to transform my scarf into a *hijab* (headscarf) so that I could enter the *Husainiya*[8] and meet with Imam Al-Husainy, who welcomed me warmly. It was the day of *Arbaeen* (the commemoration of the fortieth day after *Ashura*, which marks the martyrdom of the Shi'i Imam Husayn [d. 680]) in Karbala') and hundreds of men and women dressed in black had gathered in front of the building – men on one side of the street; women on the other. A few minutes later the police blocked off the main street in Dearborn and the procession started with some men beating drums, chanting and rhythmically beating their chests. A few women were crying but in general it did not seem to be an overly sad event. There was quite a bit of chatting and general socializing going on as we marched down Warren Street. After a couple of hours of marching, Fatima took me to her home for tea and told me about her political activism:

> We moved to Dearborn from Kansas where I studied in 1985. There were lots of Shi'i Lebanese and some *muhajirun* [emigrants] – Shi'i Iraqis who had been kicked out by Saddam in the 1980s as they were accused of being of Iranian origin. Most of our discussions were about what happened in Iraq and Lebanon and what might possibly happen in the future. Because we were very few Iraqis, our connections were mainly with the Lebanese. We had a weekly women's gathering talking about Islam. Later on, we ran an Iraqi women's group for five or six years. I started to give speeches and talk about Iraq. But then some of us got married and had children and stopped being involved. I got busy with an organization called

the Iraqi-Islamic Organization in America, which was established
in 1986. I was the only woman in that organization. We were a
small group, and we worked very hard. The first time we organized a conference, we did not realize how big the Ba'thi presence
was. We did not only invite Islamists but also other Shi'i and some
Sunni. The Ba'this came and there was a physical fight. They were
violent and we had to call the police.

Both Fatima and her sister Zeinab spoke of the harassment and
intimidation carried out by Ba'thi students and officials throughout
the 1980s. The sisters, who were not members of any political party
but sympathetic to the Islamist Dawa Party, were both systematically threatened while they were pursuing their Ph.D.s at American
universities. Later on, the threats continued in the context of anti-
government events organized by the Islamic groups that Fatima
and Zeinab were involved with. The fear, intimidation, verbal and
physical threats experienced by the sisters resonates with the accounts
of other women I talked to in Dearborn, London and Amman. The
secret police and thugs affiliated with the regime of Saddam Hussein
were not only terrorizing people inside Iraq, but also penetrated the
various locations where Iraqis were studying or hoping to find refuge
from political repression.

Being part of an earlier generation of Iraqi refugees to the USA,
Fatima has an ambiguous relationship to the more recently arrived
refugees. On the one hand she feels sorry for the repression and
hardship they have been through inside Iraq and later on in refugee
camps, especially in Saudi Arabia. But she also thinks of them as
more materialistic and easily seduced by the American way of life:

When the refugees came in the 1990s, they were not at all into
organizations. They just wanted a house and a good life. They said
that they wanted to go back but it was clear that it was not true.
I told them that the way they behave, buy houses, they will stay.
People would attack us: 'You did not do enough for us. You have
forgotten about Iraq. We come fresh from Iraq and we are the real
Iraqis.' I told them: 'I give you five years and we will see about
your identity.' They get indulged in this life. They have become

materialistic. For a long time, we did not buy a house. Because buying a house means that you will stay. It took us thirteen years to decide finally to buy a house. Now I find it very difficult to move back after twenty-five years. Now where I am living, I find that the people I am associating with, Iraqis and Lebanese, are supporting my identity. If I had not come to Dearborn, I would have left the States.

Fatima becomes very emotional when speaking about the decision finally to buy a house. Despite the comfort and stability of owning a home that houses three of her four children, her daughter-in-law and often her small granddaughter, the moment of buying a house in the USA actually represents a moment of defeat as well as a betrayal of what she perceives to be her 'real home', Iraq. Her sister Zeinab has also been uncomfortable about getting too settled in the USA:

When a person leaves a country, one type wants to forget their country, the other type wants to keep their links, their roots. I have resisted. I emphasize: I resist blending into this country. I have had the opportunity to do it the American way during my time here. But my intention was to keep myself the way I was and the way I am. I like who I am. I like my culture, my morals. Everything is rooted in my country. Everything. My body, my blood. I do not want to have to change my feelings towards my country. This is what made me very active here. I tried to serve my country. I thought the road back was blocked. I was trying to do my best to open this road and clear it so that I could go back. That made me active politically. At university there were students who had similar opinions: Iranians, Pakistanis, Indonesians, Malaysians. It does not matter where they came from. We had the same principles. I tried to build my roots through these groups. Any activity we could engage in through the university we did: demonstrations, exhibitions, talks on twlevision and radio, organize seminars... Anything that could absorb my anger. We did not want to blend in. We wanted to take advantage of being here to strengthen our roots. You are lonely over here. You have to find people you can relate to and work with them.

A few days later I was invited to meet with a group of refugee women who had come more recently in the aftermath of the Gulf

War and *intifada* in 1991. Khadija B., a community activist, researcher and member of the Islamist Dawa Party, had helped to facilitate a meeting with a group of young women in the Karbala Education Centre. Khadija had been imprisoned and tortured under the previous regime, and had also lost her husband, who was executed for membership of the Dawa Party. As someone of an older generation, a heart-wrenching history of suffering and physical signs of torture all over her body, Khadija was clearly perceived as a spiritual and political leader among the group of young women sitting around the table. Some of the bolder ones took turns in telling me their stories: how they lived in Iraq and the circumstances of their flight. These were stories of disappearing brothers, fathers and husbands, of relatives killed in war or by the regime, of systematic harassment, arrests, torture, and of economic hardship. Many of the women present spent time in Rifah refugee camp in Saudi Arabia before coming to the USA, and their suffering and terrible stories continue there: there was little in terms of shelter, not enough food, inadequate sanitary facilities, no electricity. All of the women are angry and bitter about their experience at the camp.

As I talked to the group of young women refugees, it became evident that at least this group of recently arrived women had a very strong sense of their roots and identity, both as Iraqis and as Shi'is. Emphasis on the particular plight and suffering of Iraqi Shi'is involved a strong sense of entitlement in terms of rights and privileges in the new Iraq. It also entailed a very strong and, for me personally, disturbing sectarianism that was directed not only at Sunni Iraqis but also at Iraqi Chaldeans. Khadija, just like Fatima and her sister Zeinab, criticized Iraqi Chaldeans for having been supporters of the previous regime and for failing to engage in anti-government activities in previous years. I was puzzled by this sweeping generalization and condemnation of the Chaldean community. Although several Chaldeans I talked to had clearly appreciated the generally secular nature of the previous regime, especially before 1991, which allowed for the relative religious freedom of minorities, many of the more

established and well-to-do Chaldean families have been active supporters of the Bush government and his war on Iraq.

Stereotypes and sectarian sentiments were commonplace among
members of both communities living in the Detroit area. Yet I also
found a few women who refused to think in sectarian and com-
munalist terms. Not only were they trying hard to hold on to multicultural and inclusive notions of Iraqiness, but they also challenged
simple divisions into Western and Arab, appropriating both terms in
hyphenated identities. These women, both the older generation and
young second-generation Iraqi Americans, were consciously reaching
out, risking being branded traitors for challenging widely accepted
'truths' and refusing easy answers.

Kurdish Women in San Diego County

After the rather unpredictable and cold Michigan weather, I was
happy to fly to sunny California to interview mainly Iraqi Kurdish
women in the outskirts of San Diego. Most of the 8,000-plus Iraqi
Kurds in San Diego county reside in East County and the South Bay
area, making up the second largest Iraqi Kurdish community in the
USA after Nashville. The first wave of Kurdish refugees to live in and
around San Diego arrived around 1976 after fierce fighting with the
Iraqi regime. Most entered as refugees or under family reunification
programmes. While Kurdish refugees came throughout the 1980s in
small numbers, more substantial numbers arrived at the beginning of
the 1990s in the aftermath of the Gulf War and the uprisings in 1991.
San Diego County is also home to about 18,000 Chaldeans, many
of whom also arrived post-1991. As in the Detroit area, Chaldeans
in California tend to run grocery and liquor shops as well as petrol
stations. Other Iraqi refugees and migrants living in the area are of
Shi'i and Mandean[9] origins.

I had made contact with a Kurdish community organization based
in El Cancun, a town on the outskirts of San Diego with a large
immigrant community and home to many Iraqi Kurds. As I arrived

in the middle of the night after a 45-minute cab drive from the
airport, it soon became obvious that El Cancun was rather different
to the affluent and touristic San Diego that I had visited myself on
numerous occasions while an undergraduate student at the University
of Arizona in Tuscon in the 1980s. The morning after my arrival, I set
out walking from my rather dismal motel next to a big intersection
and a petrol station to find the Kurdish Community Centre. I soon
realized that, despite the sunshine, this was one of many US cities
in which the only people who walk on sidewalks tend to be the
homeless and impoverished. I made my way to the centre, where I
was warmly welcomed by several of the women working there.

The centre had clearly transformed from its initial conception as a
Kurdish human rights organization to being a wider centre for service
provision, training, counselling and community liaison work. The
centre provides English and citizenship classes, computer training,
health and hygiene awareness programmes, translation services, legal
advice, job placement and immigration services. Saheena J., who
arrived in the USA in 1992 with most of her family, except for her
grandparents, who went to France, has been working at the centre
for several years. Her family had to leave Dohuk to escape Saddam
Hussein's Anfal campaign and ended up in a refugee camp in Turkey
for four years with some 6,000 other Kurdish refugees. Saheena told
me about the history of the centre called Kurdish Human Rights
Watch (KHRW):

> I think we are the only organization here that serves Arabs,
> Kurds and Chaldeans. The organization was founded in 1989. In
> the beginning, it was mainly lobbying around Kurdish human
> rights, but then it expanded into social services. No one is turned
> away, including Mexicans and Somalis who live in the area. It
> has turned into an international office. If you need help, it does
> not matter who you are. Our headquarters are in Fairfax, but we
> have offices across the USA, in Dallas, Seattle and Nashville. We
> even have offices in Kurdistan. The aim is basically to help people
> to become self-sufficient. There are tensions between Kurds and

Chaldeans, and there are tensions between generations. There are
a lot of runaway Kurdish youngsters, and lots of problems with
drugs. Among male youth there are gang-type groups within the
Chaldean and Kurdish communities, who often fight each other.

Community relations and sectarian tensions were clearly an
issue, especially among male youth but also among other members
of the community. Although most people working at the centre
were of Kurdish origin, there were also a couple of Iraqi Shi'is
employed. Saheena stressed the non-sectarian nature of the centre
and acknowledged that it was only after arriving in the USA that
she learned about the plight of other Iraqis who had suffered
under Saddam:

> I was 11 when we had to escape to Turkey. My brother was
> paralysed. He was hit by a bomb. The government gave us fifteen
> days to bring my brother back. We fled to the mountains during
> that time. We were in Dohuk and then moved to the mountains
> for three years in the mid-1980s. We had to move every day to
> avoid being bombed. In the end when the bombs exploded, I did
> not even move anymore. My mind was so tired of everything.
> You die once, but this was like dying every day. It made me hate
> everyone who is not Kurdish. I didn't hate just the government, but
> all people – all Arabs. I was never aware of the suffering of other
> Iraqis until I came here when I was 16 years old. I never thought
> anyone else had been persecuted by the regime.

As I was talking to Saheena, a group of about a dozen young
women emerged from a room at the back of a centre. 'They just
had an English class', Saheena informed me as she tried to negotiate
between talking to me and answering the busy phone. Her colleague
Nada, who had recently been promoted to programme director, was
comforting her eight-month-old baby, who appeared to be at home
in the centre with everyone showing affection and helping to look
after it. When I asked Nada how she managed with the baby and
her work, she replied:

It is difficult, but I somehow manage. Everyone here helps. Last
week we organized a Halabja event, and before that a Nourouz
event, so I put in many extra hours. The Halabja event was to
commemorate the victims of that crime and also to raise consciousness and to educate the public about what happened. Every
year we organize this. We invite people from Congress, the chief
of police, the mayor etc. Most of the time, they come. We work
closely with the police department, because many of our youth
get into trouble at school, so we mediate, because when people
see the police they get very scared. So there is much to do all the
time.

Saheena and Nada are also members of a Kurdish Women's Association that is closely affiliated with the Kurdish community centre.
They put me in touch with one of the founding members, Runak
G., who was among the first generation of Iraqi Kurdish refugees
in San Diego:

We started in 1992 as Kurdish women who had already lived in
the USA for quite some time. We felt that we needed to do something for women. I felt responsible. I have been here for thirty
years. My husband was the president of the Kurdish community
centre. We were successful business people and we wanted to
help people out. We raised money and I myself took it back to
Kurdistan. We mainly raised money through concerts and took
it to an orphanage. All of us who were very active initially had
been here for quite some time. We did this on a voluntary basis.
Lots of Kurds came here in the early 1990s and they were suffering from culture shock. We tried to help women to familiarize
themselves with the system here, to find jobs, to help them with
schools, and to learn English. When they had babies we went to
hospital with them. We have a pot-luck once a month to bring
women together, so that they can socialize. Many women just
stay at home while their husbands work. During these monthly
meetings, we talk to the women to try to find out what their
needs are. We also help them when they have family problems.
We go to their homes and help them financially and emotionally.
We raise funds and organize festivals to show our culture to the
American community.

As with the Chaldean and Shi'i communities in Dearborn, the Kurdish community in the San Diego area is divided in terms of socio-economic background, with the older generation of refugees and migrants being generally well established, while the more recently arrived refugees tend to struggle economically as they adapt to the lifestyle and culture of the USA.

After talking to several women involved in the centre and the Women's Association, it became clear that community associations were the first port of call for the US military trying to recruit Iraqi women. Runak herself has been employed by the Department of Defense since 2004, having worked with the US Army in Kirkuk:

> I brought all the women's associations together: Turkmen, Kurdish, Chaldean, Assyrian and Arab. I worked very hard to bring them all together. We even brought women from Sulamaniyya and Irbil. I was in Kirkuk for a year and a half after the liberation of Iraq. We tried to get buildings for women's centres. We visited women in their homes. In our compound we brought everyone together. They were happy about the involvement of women from the outside. Women from Irbil have been active since the Gulf War, but unfortunately women in Kirkuk had not been able to be active under Saddam. They were very happy for women of other cities to come in. You would think they would hate each other, but they worked very well together. I worked with a female US sergeant and she was very much pro-women. I have been offered a job in Germany, but I am not sure whether I should take this or go back to Iraq. My husband is still in Iraq. My immediate family is still here. I was 16 when I left Kurdistan. To me it is like my duty.

Most of the Kurdish women I talked to in El Cancun were either members of or sympathetic to the Kurdish Democratic Party of Mas'ud Barzani, and viewed the US government and army as liberators. It was also evident that despite paying lip service to the unifying experience of having suffered under Saddam Hussein, the Kurdish women in El Cancun, just like the majority of Kurdish women inside Iraq and in the diaspora, were aspiring to an autonomous if not independent Kurdistan.

Amman: Ambiguous Neighbourly Relations

The Amman I knew from childhood visits and brief trips as a graduate student in Cairo was quite different from the city I experienced during my research trips in 2005 and 2006. What any visitor to the Jordanian capital notices first nowadays are the crowded streets and the heavy traffic. Driving in taxis, I frequently heard complaints about 'all these rich Iraqis having arrived since the invasion in 2003', allegedly inflating house prices. Yet it is not the rich and well-to-do Iraqis but the impoverished ones that walk the streets of downtown Amman, peddling almost anything to survive, begging and, in the case of some women, engaging in prostitution. In addition to the struggling refugees and the rich Iraqis who were either close to the regime or part of the upper-class elite, there are tens of thousands of middle-class families trying very hard to get by and maintain a tolerable standard of living. It was mainly women from this background that I met and interviewed for my research, although I also interviewed a number who were clearly struggling economically. In addition, I spoke to a small number of women of well-known family backgrounds as well as a handful whose husbands or who themselves had been closely affiliated to the previous regime.

Palestinian friends of my parents kindly put me up in their home in the summer of 2005 and provided not only a base but also an introduction to Amman's buzzing nightlife. Many new cafés, restaurants, bars as well as galleries, bookshops and cultural centres had sprung up since my last visit. The city had changed from the rather sleepy and provincial town I used to visit in the 1980s and 1990s to a crowded, expanding cosmopolitan place that was trying hard to absorb the numerous and diverse populations that had entered, travelled through and settled in Jordan over the past fifteen years. Palestinian and Iraqi refugees of different socio-economic backgrounds, foreign aid-workers, employees of international organizations and NGOs, and journalists all contribute to a rather crowded but vibrant Amman. Jordan has not only become one of the most important countries of safe haven and transit in the region, but is also hosting increasing numbers of people belonging to the 'international community' involved in reconstruction, political transition and development work, albeit from a safe distance and rather ineffectively in light of the worsening security situation inside Iraq.

Until 1991, Iraqi refugees made up only a small number of Jordan's high refugee population. Jordan had mainly provided a haven for Palestinian refugees in the region, beginning with the establishment of Israel in 1948. After the Gulf War in 1991, thousands of Palestinians with Jordanian citizenship had to leave the Gulf countries and migrated to Jordan. According to UNRWA's figures for June 2003, Palestinian refugees and their descendants registered with the UN agency account for over 1.7 million of Jordan's total population of 5.5 million (Chatelard, 2004). However, numbers might be much higher as many established well-to-do Palestinian families are not registered with UNRWA and have become difficult to distinguish from the rest of the Jordanian population.

At the same time as great numbers of Palestinians added to the existing refugee population in Amman, a substantial wave of Iraqi migrants and refugees entered the Jordanian capital during and after the Gulf War of 1991, in flight from government repression in the aftermath of the 1991 intifada, as well as in response to the humanitarian crisis produced by economic sanctions. Before the invasion in 2003, the number of resident Iraqis in Amman was estimated to be about 300,000.[10] Yet in 2002, only 20,000 Iraqi individuals had obtained long-term residence permits renewable for one year (Chatelard, 2002). Others had to renew their residence permit every six months initially and then every three months, being forced to leave the country before every renewal, or, if failing to do so, risking being fined by the Jordanian authorities.

As became evident in my interviews with Iraqi women living in Amman, and as charted by Géraldine Chatelard (2002, 2003), who has been closely monitoring and analysing the changing situation of Iraqi refugees in Jordan over a period of several years, the

Jordanian government has been ambiguous towards Iraqi refugees: allowing them to enter Jordan but depriving them of legal status and humanitarian assistance, thereby encouraging Iraqis to use Jordan only as a place for transit to a third country (Chatelard, 2002). In the aftermath of the war in 2003 and the ongoing violence, the numbers of Iraqi refugees hoping to find temporary refuge, transit elsewhere or to settle permanently has reached a million, according to estimates, and is increasing daily.

Aside from Iraqis having settled in Amman or in transit to a third country, there are at any given time thousands of Iraqi women and men visiting the Jordanian capital for a short period. I managed to speak to a number of these women who had made the dangerous journey to Jordan in order to get some respite from the harshness of life in Iraq, visit friends and family, obtain medical treatment, attend conferences or check out possibilities for earning a living abroad and leaving the country. The first women I met were members of my own family, my Aunt Azza and cousin Miriam, who had travelled to escape the unbearable summer heat for a couple of weeks, but also to find respite from the deteriorating living conditions, increasing violence, and sectarian tensions. Like many Iraqi families, they had rented an overpriced apartment and were spending their days enjoying being able to walk on the streets, going shopping, sitting in cafés and not having to worry about US snipers or suicide bombers. When I met them in a busy shopping mall, it was clear they were exhausted and stressed. I had last seen them a couple of years ago at my aunt's sister's house in London: two years of hardship were painfully written on both women's faces. They tried to be cheerful and to take an interest in my life and work. Nevertheless I could sense their bewilderment when I spoke about my project and my passion for the plight of Iraqi women – a plight they obviously wished they could escape.

I met other women who were just visiting Amman – we met in their rented accommodation, in cafés, in hotel lobbies. Several expressed a wish to stay and not return to Iraq, but others made it clear that they wanted to go back as they strongly felt they had a role to play in the new Iraq, either through their professions as teachers, university professors, medical doctors and lawyers, or through their involvement in charities, humanitarian assistance or women's rights organizations. I also talked to a number of women who initially had wanted to stay in Iraq but by the summer of 2005 had decided not to return.

One woman who had resisted leaving despite her husband's decision to move to Amman in 2003 was Claire M. An Iraqi friend in Germany had put me in contact with Claire, who had been his former colleague and close friend. Claire left Iraq at the end of 2004. As with so many women I met, Claire was trying to make the best of her new situation, but was clearly distressed by the events in Iraq and by being away from home:

> I did not want to leave Iraq. I tried to stay and to be part of the changes. I was even engaging with the old middle classes who came back after the fall of Saddam. I used to go to their meetings. I discovered that they did not come back because they care about our country… I felt they were just after power. The way Iraqi expatriates are dealing with everything made me suspicious. They get involved in these corrupt deals, they cheat, draw up contracts for millions which only cost a fraction of this. When things got really bad last year, I joined my husband in Amman. It is much better here than it used to be. Amman progressed a lot. I remember in the 1970s, it was a tiny town which ended in the third circle.[11] Iraqis came and brought with them their culture, art and their wealth. But the Jordanian government forced back many of the poor, begging Iraqis who came in the 1990s during the sanctions period.

Claire was also critical of the large numbers of well-to-do Iraqis who were trying to re-create a lifestyle of high living and socializing in Amman, while the situation in Iraq was deteriorating:

> Many women just totally live in their own worlds. It is very difficult to find women here who are willing to do something. There are some charitable organizations, but most Iraqis I know are just

busy with their own lives. And the government here does not like Iraqis to be politically active.

Even before the suicide bombs in Amman, the Jordanian government was worried about the multiple levels and causes of violence inside Iraq spilling into neighbouring Jordan. As Widad K. explained to me: 'We help privately, donate money, but there are no official organizations. The government here is worried. They are afraid of the Zarqawis of the world.' In a bid to maintain internal political stability in a generally volatile region, the Jordanian government has not been encouraging grassroots activism or civil society mobilization by Iraqis on its soil. It has also been balancing the high number of Iraqis who were closely affiliated with the previous regime and those who opposed it.

Most of the handful of Iraqi women I met who had been closely affiliated with the Ba'th live in relative isolation and keep a low profile. I heard stories about members of the former Ba'thi elite leading lavish lifestyles and engaging in conspicuous consumption. Yet the women I met must have been lower down in the hierarchy or their husbands had been less able to stash away wealth and possessions. They came across as depressed, defeated and apologetic, distancing themselves from the crimes and atrocities of the previous regime, while clearly showing signs of nostalgia for a 'better time'.

An economic elite of Iraqi professional and business people has managed to maintain a relatively high standard of living, and appears to be using Amman mainly as a base for their worldwide travels and connections. I spent one morning in the apartment of Nour K., an upper-class woman whose husband worked as a surgeon before retirement. Nour's family was dispersed between Iraq, Jordan, the USA, the UK and Portugal and she travelled frequently to stay in touch with relatives and friends. However, that morning as I was interviewing her, the whole world seemed to descend on her. Female relatives and friends dropped in briefly, having arrived from Baghdad, London, or various US cities. Nour explained:

Amman during the summer has become the main meeting point for all Iraqis. This is the place where Iraqis from inside Iraq can meet up with their relatives who live in England or the USA, or anywhere else in the world. When I am here during the summer I constantly have visitors coming to see me, or I go and see people. It is very busy. We have social gatherings and invitations every evening. I like people to come to my house during the day though. I don't like the traffic and the crowded streets. But this summer I will have to go to Beirut to do some shopping for the wedding of my son.

As I was interviewing Nour, several of the visiting women chipped in, and soon a lively discussion ensued about women's social and love lives in the 1960s in Baghdad. Between drinking tea and nibbling biscuits, the women giggled as they told each other and me about their boyfriends, fiancés and husbands.

That same afternoon I went to see Hana A., a successful architect and the mother of two boys. We met in her apartment. Although Hana had planned to leave Amman to migrate to Canada, she ended up settling and putting down roots in Jordan:

In 1991, we were there during the war, but we left at the end of the year. I almost had a nervous breakdown after what happened during the war. Our house was hit by a missile. I did not feel that any of the wars were justified so I did not want to be part of them. I did not want my sons to go into the army. I managed to convince my husband. So we came here to Amman. My husband is a surgeon and found a teaching position here at the university. Our eldest son was 16, the younger one 14. They started school here. I started working. Then we applied for immigration to Canada. In 1996, I and the boys went to Toronto. The boys went to college. We rented an apartment for them. I was planning to stay with them and to continue my studies in interior design. But about a month after I arrived in Canada, my mother had a stroke; she was paralysed. She was in Amman. My husband was also in Amman, because he was not allowed to work in Canada. They did not need doctors at the time. So I had to come back and leave the boys alone. I spent two years taking care of my mother before she passed away in 1998. By then we had Jordanian nationality. My husband was allowed to have his own clinic. Then we got more attached to Jordan. My own work here was getting better as well. The boys graduated. One is still in Canada, the other one is in Qatar.

I asked Hana about her legal status, as this has been a great obstacle to feeling settled in Amman for many of the women I talked to. Hana and her husband were among the few lucky ones to actually obtain Jordanian citizenship:

It is very difficult for an Iraqi to become a Jordanian citizen. We had a big *wasta* [connection]. My husband's relatives used to be in the government under the monarchy, so they had a good relationship with the late King Hussein. Other people have to leave every three months. It is very difficult. My father still lives in Iraq. He goes back and forth. He has a green card. He is a lawyer and has a law firm. He does most of the work from here. It is almost useless to be in Baghdad, because even if you have to go to court, there are many obstacles, like curfews.

Hana herself has not been back to Iraq after 2003 and is very worried about her father travelling back and forth. Other women I talked to had visited once or twice since the downfall of the previous regime. Yet, by the summer of 2005 many would no longer risk the journey, as the violence had escalated and kidnappings and killings were reportedly rampant. Several of the women I interviewed had initially been eager to get involved in emerging civil society initiatives or women's organizations inside Iraq. However, not all were welcomed with open arms and many experienced open resentment, even from their own families and friends who had remained in Iraqi throughout. Najwa R., a middle-aged professional woman who had been living in exile for over thirty years, first in London and then Amman in order to be closer to Baghdad, her home town, told me:

Many Iraqis who lived outside wanted to come inside to help rebuild the country, but we faced this hatred, this anger: 'You did not see it! You did not live it! Why should you come now?' They are very bitter about it. I even felt it with my own family. There is a bitterness towards those of us who did not live through the misery. I understand their position. I always thought that those who go back should not look for positions, but should go as advisers.

Others were much less understanding in their account of their experience inside Iraq. Many women I spoke to in 2005 and 2006 were feeling very disillusioned and giving up, either because their efforts were not appreciated by people inside Iraq or simply because things had gone from bad to worse.

In turn, several women who are still living inside Iraq complained to me in Amman about the expatriate Iraqi women who lived outside for a long time but then tried to tell Iraqi women what to do. Many, though by no means all, diaspora women are perceived to be patronizing and detached from realities on the ground. Dr Hala K., a pharmacist who lives in Baghdad, was invited to participate in one of the numerous workshops and conferences in Amman organized by various international bodies and organizations to discuss the Iraqi constitution in the summer of 2005. Hala is a co-founder of a woman's organization based in Baghdad and Fallujah providing literacy and English classes, computer training, as well as Qur'anic recitation classes, mainly to widows and young women. I went to see her in a modest hotel in a quiet part of town where she had stayed on after the conference, waiting anxiously for relatives from Baghdad to arrive. She complained:

> There was a big problem in the workshop: most of the women who participated are women who have lived outside for forty years. This was the first time I have spoken about this subject with Iraqi women who had been abroad. I was surprised to hear what they were saying. They said women had no rights before. They have not been to school, not to university. I asked them whether they lived in Iraq. Most had just returned after forty years. I told them: 'Look, all the women here are over 35 years old. We all have college degrees, our education was free. I was in the college of pharmacy. In that college, women were in the majority.' They were saying all

the bad things about Saddam. I said: 'We have to tell the truth. Not everything was bad.'

Some pro-war diaspora women have been involved in a widely publicized campaign supported by the US government stressing the previous regime's poor record on women's rights. Without wanting to play down the atrocities of Saddam Hussein and his regime, some of the alleged claims contradict the accounts of the majority of women I interviewed. One especially absurd example is the assertion of some pro-war activists that women were not allowed to enter university under Saddam.

Moving from the five-star hotels, where many of the workshops and conferences were held, to the downtown area of Amman, where large numbers of Iraqi refugees try to survive as street vendors, cleaners, painters, domestic workers and seamstresses, I could get a fleeting sense of the gaps and divisions that must exist inside Iraq, not only between the Green Zone and the rest of the country, but also between an educated urban middle- and upper-middle-class and the vast majority of impoverished Iraqis.

Layers of Dispersal

Throughout my research for this book, I met and talked to Iraqi women who not only helped to construct an alternative vision of the modern history of Iraq but also revealed to me the various layers of the widespread and diverse Iraqi diaspora. I was only able to visit a few locations that are home to substantial Iraqi communities. Nevertheless Iraqis can be found in almost every country in the world today. The majority live in neighbouring countries, especially Iran, Jordan, Turkey and Syria. There are also considerable communities in Yemen, Lebanon and the Gulf states. Although the bulk of Iraqis have found asylum in Iran, in 2000 Iraqis were the second largest group of asylum applicants in the main industrialized countries (Chatelard, 2002: 1). In Western Europe, Iraqis are mainly living in the UK, Germany, the Netherlands and Sweden. In the USA, Iraqis are scattered throughout the country, but considerable communities can be found in Detroit, Chicago, Nashville, Los Angeles and San Diego. The Iraqi dispersion has also extended to Canada, Australia, New Zealand, Indonesia and Malaysia.

From the 1940s onwards, Iraqis of all religious and ethnic backgrounds have travelled to Western Europe and the USA to pursue higher education and economic betterment. Most students have been male, although a small but growing number of female students have also obtained degrees abroad. While the majority of Iraqi students returned home after completing their degrees, some ended up staying and became successful in their respective professions. Iraqi men who remained in Europe or the USA would either return home to find themselves an Iraqi wife or – just like my own father – marry a national of the country they settled in.

Many of the earliest Iraqi migrant communities abroad, such as the Chaldean and Assyrian communities, started as all-male communities, but eventually some members of each community decided to settle permanently in Europe or the USA and brought their families over. In the 1950s, 1960s and 1970s, they were joined in a classic chain migration by relatives who felt encouraged by the economic success of the first generation. From the late 1950s onwards, economic migrants and students were joined by political exiles. Many Iraqis among the elite associated with the monarchy left after the revolution of 1958. Later on, mainly communists fled the persecution, arrests and executions by Ba'this following the coups in 1963 and 1968. Throughout the Ba'th period (1968–2003), male and female opposition activists of all ethnic and religious backgrounds and across the political spectrum, including communists, Nasserites, democrats and Islamists, had to flee from government repression. Many of the women I interviewed for this book have been in political exile, due either to their own or to their husbands' opposition politics.

One of the first victims of systematic Ba'thi repression and Arabization policies were the Fayli Kurds, who represent a minority within a minority: as Kurds within a predominantly Arab state and as Shi'is among otherwise Sunni Kurds. From 1969 onwards, tens of thousands of Fayli Kurds who were living in the southern section of the Zagros mountains near the Iraq–Iran border were deported to Iran. This forceful deportation of Fayli Kurds preceded the large-scale deportation of Iraqi Shi'is in the 1970s and 1980s on the pretext that they were of Iranian origin. Hundreds of thousands of Shi'i were forced to leave their homes during the *zamn al-tasfirat* (time of deportations) because of their alleged *tabaiya iraniya* (Iranian nationality). I will discuss the plight of Iraqi Shi'is in the context of forced deportations in greater detail in Chapter 4.

Iraqi Kurds have suffered a long history of repression and dispersion. During the mid-1970s, as there was open war between the Iraqi regime and the Kurdish movement under the leadership of Mustafa Barzani, some 200,000 Kurds fled for Iran while thousands of others were displaced to the south. In the 1980s, during the Iran–Iraq war, the atrocities against the Kurds were stepped up, eventually culminating in the Anfal campaign, and the destruction of villages and gassing of thousands. Large numbers of Iraqi Kurds have escaped to Iran, Turkey and Syria – some temporarily, many never to return. I highlight the specific plight of Kurdish women in Chapters 3 and 4.

The majority of Iraqi refugees and asylum-seekers living abroad today left Iraq during or after the Gulf War in 1991. Mainly Iraqi Kurds and Shi'is escaped after their failed uprisings against the regime of Saddam Hussein in 1991. Many of the Iraqi Shi'i women I interviewed in Dearborn for various chapters of this book were part of the more recent wave of refugees after 1991. The drainage of the marshlands in the south worsened the general hardship and repression endured by the Marsh Arabs and led to more dispersals, especially to Iran. Displacement and forced resettlement were elements of the regime's strategy to undermine political opposition, to punish and subdue the Marsh Arabs and to secure valuable economic resources.

Thirteen years of the most comprehensive sanctions system ever imposed on a country (1990–2003) led to a deterioration in economic conditions and a humanitarian crisis. Throughout the 1990s and the first three years of the twenty-first century, Iraqis migrated due to a mixture of economic and political factors (Chatelard, 2002: 1). During and in the aftermath of the invasion in 2003, there has been an ongoing flow of people escaping the rampant violence, general lack of security, kidnappings, targeted assassinations of doctors and academics, a worsening humanitarian crisis and deteriorating infrastructure. I explore the impact of economic sanctions and changing gender relations in Chapter 5.

In addition to the migrants and refugees making up the different layers of the Iraqi diaspora, Iraq has a huge population of internally displaced persons (IDPs). According to a recent report by the European Council for Refugees and Exiles (ECRE),[12] there may be as many as 800,000 IDPs throughout northern Iraq[13] and anything between 100,000 and 300,000 in central and southern Iraq. Significant numbers of Iraqis from within the country have returned to their places of origin or settled in other areas of their choice since the fall of the previous regime. However, the worsening violence and lack of security, including continued armed conflict and increasing ethnic and religious tensions, new patterns of persecution, as well as the acute lack of services and infrastructure have led to new displacements of Iraqis both inside and outside Iraq.[14]

Ongoing military operations, especially in western and northern parts of the country, continue to generate displacement and hardship for thousands of families. Between May and October 2005 several thousand Iraqis all over Iraq were displaced from their homes following a series of offensives by the US-led coalition forces against insurgents.[15] In the last chapter of this book, I will explore the various ways the recent war, occupation and escalating sectarian violence have affected women and gender relations in particular. First, though, we will consider the generally more hopeful accounts and memories of the period before and after the revolution of 1958.

TWO

Living with the Revolution

E ver since my childhood I have had vivid images of Iraq during the 1950s and 1960s. Initially my imagination was triggered by the curiosity and romanticism of a daughter listening to her father's childhood memories: stories of mischief, of an extended family, of sibling rivalry and fun times, of holidays in the countryside with a favourite aunt, of friendships and first loves, of teachers and exams, but also stories about political upheaval, a scar on the right leg as evidence of police violence during student demonstrations, a revolution... Later on as I started to study the history of Iraq and also listened to the life stories and experiences of Iraqi women of different backgrounds, my romanticism turned into a nostalgia for a past that I never lived myself but that seemed to hold so many possibilities, so much positive energy and so much hope. But even then, 'in the good old days', there was repression, there were seeds of violence, and tensions often erupted, leaving bloody traces. Already long before the Ba'th took over, people's experiences differed radically, depending on their social class background, their place of residence, their family background and their political orientations.

My grandparents had moved in the early 1960s from the traditional and predominantly Shi'i neighbourhood of al-Ja'fir in Baghdad to the more mixed and upper-middle-class area of al-Mansur. During our visits we always stayed at our grandparents' house, but would often pay a visit to the area where my father grew up. He referred to it as 'the old town', describing the traditional family house with the courtyard, the rooms surrounding the open interior, the roof where the family would spend the summer nights. My eldest aunt, Chakura, who was the only one who remained in the old town of al-Ja'fir with her husband and four sons, lived in a very modest home. I will never forget my surprise when, as a child, I noticed chickens roaming around the house. In appearance and mannerism, Aunt Chakoura always seemed much closer to my grandmother, Omi Baghdad – as my brother and I used to call her. Like my grandmother, Aunt Chakoura dressed in the traditional black garment called an *abaya*, and had blue tattoos with a slight greenish tint on her face and arms. Her appearance was very different from my father's younger sisters and my other aunts, who had mostly all been to university, and dressed in Western-style clothes. They seemed to belong to different worlds although they were members of the same family.

After she lost the sight of her left eye in 1948, my Aunt Salima spent a considerable amount of time during the 1950s and 1960s in al-Ja'fir with my father's paternal uncle, Baba Mahdi, and his children. Amme Salima, like all of her other brothers and sisters, referred to her Uncle Mahdi as *baba* (Daddy). While all my uncles and my youngest aunt went to school, Salima was deprived of any formal education. Her younger sister Widad was sent to school, but with Chakoura and Salima my grandfather did not push for the education of girls. Salima would stay at home, play with the kids in the family, learn how to cook traditional Iraqi dishes, listen to people's conversations and volunteer her characteristically insightful and measured opinions. For some reason, she preferred the ambience of the old town to the new house in al-Mansur. Maybe it was the busy life of the small alleys, the women sitting in front of their houses, drinking tea and exchanging the latest news and gossip. Maybe she felt intimidated by the unknown spaces inhabited in the new house and its surroundings?

My grandparents' house in al-Mansur was quite a contrast to
the houses we saw in al-Ja'fir. It was spacious, modern, with a nice
garden, and the only animals entering the house were the occasional
lizards or cockroaches and, far too often for me, the hungry mos-
quitoes. Since the mid-1950s, al-Mansur had become a prestigious
residential development area close to the racetrack in Baghdad and the
newly established al-Mansur Club. My grandfather, a small merchant
with a shop in an area called Alawi al-Hela, managed to buy a plot
of land cheaply from a rich relative, and over a number of years
built a house that was to accommodate the large family.

My father would tell us stories of his days at Thanawaiyat al-
Karkh, a well-known boys' high school on the east bank of the
Tigris. Like many other school and university students and teachers,
but also workers and peasants, he would regularly demonstrate
against the repressive government attached to the monarchy. The
female students from the nearby girls' high school would join them
as they marched through the streets shouting anti-government,
anti-British and anti-Israeli slogans. Only later, when interviewing
a number of Iraqi women who had been either in school or
in university during the 1950s, did I realize that my father was
part of a whole generation of young women and men who were
extremely politicized and engaged in trying to change the course
of events.

This chapter revolves around the revolution of 1958 and the
years preceding and following the beginning of the republic. I will
start by providing a range of views and experiences related to the
last years of the monarchy leading up to the revolution, before
discussing different accounts of the revolution and its aftermath. I
will present fragments of women's lives at the time: their education,
the cultural scene, their social and love lives, as well as women's
political mobilization.

Experiencing the Monarchy

Set against the background of widespread poverty, oppressive semi-feudal relations in the countryside, the extreme concentration of land-ownership,[1] increasing numbers of indebted and landless peasants, the continued influx of rural migrants into urban areas, limited industry, rising unemployment and high inflation rates, as well as a severe housing shortage in urban areas, large parts of the Iraqi population became increasingly active in opposition movements which targeted not only social injustice and oppression within Iraq but also the monarchy's continuing close ties to the British (Abdullah, 2003; Davis, 2005; Farouk-Sluglett and Sluglett, 2001; Tripp, 2000). The British had invaded the Ottoman province of Basra at the end of 1914, and received the mandate for Iraq in 1920. Despite having been granted official independence by the League of Nations in 1932, Iraq continued to be subject to British influence and meddling. The Portsmouth Treaty between the Iraqi and British governments in 1948 promised the final withdrawal of all British troops, but was to formalize and prolong British influence. The signing of the treaty sparked a huge hostile uprising, later called al-Wathba (the Leap).

The Wathba consisted of a series of strikes and demonstrations involving students, intellectuals, political activists, workers and shanty-town dwellers. The demonstrations and violent clashes with the police and military continued even after the Regent[2] announced that he would not ratify the treaty. Soraya B. was a secondary-school student during the period of the Wathba. Of Kurdish origin, she grew up in Baghdad and got involved in leftist political activism very early on:

> I and my sisters and brothers used to join in the demonstrations at the time. My parents were worried about our safety, but that did not deter us. We used to walk from Adhamiya to the Medical College, near to Bab al-Mu'adham, where everyone was meeting. There were lots of women, workers and poor people joining us. The police fired on us several times. The brother of al-Jawahiri[3]

was killed. His name was Ja'far. This made people very angry.
Al-Jawahiri read a poem to all of us. It was so powerful and
moving. After the demonstrations stopped, I joined the Ittihad
al-Taliba [Student Union]. Of course, it was underground. Well, not
really underground, because everyone knew about it, but it was not
licensed.

Although it would be another ten years until the revolution of
1958 and the end of the monarchy, the women who experienced the
Wathba agree with historians who see the events of this period as a
turning point in Iraq's history. State repression was initially more
fierce in the aftermath of the Wathba, affecting particularly senior
members of the Communist Party (ICP), which had become increasingly popular among the disenchanted population but also among
educated intellectuals. In 1949, Nuri al-Sa'id, who had held office as
prime minister on and off since 1939, took over once again, cracking
down fiercely on all opposition and imposing martial law.

Although many women I interviewed pointed to the political
repression, the social injustices and the big gap between rich and
poor as characteristics of the monarchy, a number of women (and
indeed many men of that generation) remembered the days of the
king with great nostalgia. I had expected women from the former
political elites and upper-class backgrounds to reminisce with
sadness about the 'good old days' of the monarchy. Yet perhaps
not surprisingly, considering what was to follow, many women
of more modest social backgrounds reflected on the relative social
and political freedoms people had under the monarchy. Several
women acknowledged that they had rethought their views and
attitudes towards the monarchy in light of the severe political
repression and suffering experienced over the succeeding decades.
One of the most surprising accounts came from a devout Shi'i
woman, today a sympathizer of the Islamist Dawa Party. Zeynab
B. was full of praise for the young King Faisal II, who only came
of age in 1953, and the political and social conditions during the
monarchy:

The King lived on the other side of Baghdad in Karkh, close to
the British embassy. He had a humble house. They called it Flower
Palace. We saw him every day in the morning and every day in
the afternoon. All the people really loved him. He was so cute and
so nice. He would stop by the grocery store to buy something. We
even saw the King walking in the street. People saw him every day
in an open carriage giving salute to people or walking in al-Rashid
Street. He had one servant, no one else. No guard. The palaces
had no guards. You might see one or two guards, but no more.
You did not see police or military on the street. We saw them
only once a year, during the military parade. We had democracy.
We had congressmen. We had laws. We had a parliament. We
had freedom. As I remember, we had equality. I recall that with
me in school there was the daughter of the prime minister. Other
ministers' children were with us in public school. You could see
the ministers picking up their children.

Zeynab's extremely positive account has to be understood in
the context of her strong dislike, even hatred, of the communists,
who were instrumental in turning the 1958 coup d'état by a group
of military officers into a full-fledged revolution. In her view, the
traditions associated with the monarchy were much more in line
with her family's and her own social and political attitudes than the
secular ideas propagated by the communists. While Zeynab's account
might be extreme in terms of the praise and lack of criticism about
economic exploitation and political repression during the monarchy,
I came across many other positive recollections of women's everyday
lives, socializing, their education and their involvement in public
and political life. However, what needs to be stressed is that most
older women I talked to came from a social background that allowed
for a relatively comfortable life, and that encouraged education
and a degree of freedom where social life was concerned. Their
fathers were typically lawyers, doctors or employees in government
ministries. Women of less bourgeois backgrounds had fathers who
mainly worked as teachers or government clerks. The mothers of
the women I interviewed were housewives, although some worked
as teachers and doctors.

Women's Education

At the time of the monarchy, girls' and women's education was mainly restricted to upper-middle-class and middle-class urban families. Despite the expansion of the education system in the 1950s, overall illiteracy rates were extremely high, estimated at around 85 per cent in 1958 (Abdullah, 2003: 146). Older Iraqi women from an upper-class background would frequently refer to a well-known female member of their family who had managed to obtain higher education and a position as university professor or medical doctor in the early 1950s. Sana' K., whom I met in Amman, where she moved after the Gulf War in 1991, showed me around her gallery full of Iraqi paintings, sculptures and artefacts. In her social circle in Baghdad in the 1950s, the education of girls and women was the norm rather than the exception, although there were few provisions for formal schooling for girls prior to the 1940s. In her family, it was her paternal Aunt Bassima who captured the imagination of a younger generation of women:

> My aunt graduated from Kulliyat Malika Aliya [Queen Aliya College] for girls in the early 1950s. Her friends were doctors, university teachers and so on. Her family came from Karbala'. My Aunt Bassima was educated by a teacher at home in the 1920s. Teachers at the time came from Turkey or from Iran. In Karbala' most teachers came from Iran. They would teach Persian among other things. My aunt used to write poetry in a very sophisticated language, both in Arabic and in Persian. Her daughter was educated in a school in Karbala'. Kullyat al-Tarbiyya [the College of Education] was mixed in the 1950s in Baghdad. My mother graduated there in engineering.

When Sana' was asked about the class factor in terms of access to education, she insisted that the education of girls was widespread and that at least primary-school education was not limited to a particular social class in Baghdad:

> All the women were educated in the 1950s. My mother was a teacher and then a headmistress. Girls were at school and

university. Girls of 'lower classes' also went to school. My mother was a head teacher in a school in a poor district called Nahiya. There were female teachers of that area in the school. It was a mixed school. In 1954, we moved from Adhamiyya to Sa'dun. It was a new and trendy area to live in. My mother opened another school. All the students were from a poor area, a shanty town called Shuruq, which became al-Thawra[4] after the revolution. They built houses there after the revolution.

Other women acknowledged the big gap between social classes, as well as between urban and rural areas, where the education of girls and women was concerned. The majority of the population clearly had no access to any form of education. Higher education was only available in the capital Baghdad, and most of the girls who were able to go to primary and secondary school did not pursue higher education. Some families allowed their daughters to study in Baghdad and live in university accommodation. Nuha F. left Iraq in the 1970s and now lives in London. She was one of several women who reported moving to Baghdad from cities in the south or north to enable an older sister to study at university:

> I was born in December 1945 in Mosul. I spent the first five years of my life in Mosul. Then we moved to Baghdad. My sister entered university in 1950, and my family did not allow her to stay in the halls of residence. At the time, there was only one university in Iraq. We were three girls and five boys. My father used to work for the Ministry of Education. I was not crazy about school and I was not doing well in school. Almost every year, I used to fail my English exams.

Although most women I talked to cherished their time at university, experiences at school varied greatly. Some complained about strict teachers and rigid regimes at both primary and secondary schools.

Ibtisam R. grew up in Najaf, a predominantly Shi'i city about 160 km south of Baghdad. One of the holiest cities in Shi'i Islam, Najaf is the site of the tomb of Imam Ali and has historically been a centre of pilgrimage as well as of Shi'i theology and teaching. Ibtisam's own

parents were not religious, although the larger family was. She recalls
her time in primary school as a time of fear and anxiety:

> In year two, I had a teacher called Zahra. She was very harsh.
> When we did something wrong, we had to stand on the desks and
> she said: 'You should fly into the air or I will hit your legs.' This
> really frightened me. I think it affected my character for a long
> time. I used to be scared of school. My father would bring me and
> my sister to the front entrance of the school. Sometimes, because I
> was so afraid of the teacher, I would hide in the corridor and not
> enter the classroom. One day I even ran away from school. When
> my father found out he was very upset. But when I told him about
> the teacher, he talked to the headmaster and I was transferred to
> another group.

The positive influence of fathers who were supportive and encouraged their daughters' education was a common theme among the
women I talked to. Zeynab, whose traditional and religious family
background was different from the majority of older women I talked
to, recalls how her father was extremely keen on her education,
although other family members were opposed to it:

> In the early 1950s, women just started to go to university. Life
> was much simpler. My uncle was pushing my father not to send
> us to school or to college. But my father always felt that education
> was best for women. He wanted us to have a higher degree. He
> was very religious and he always tried to talk to us softly and to
> appeal to our common sense. He never followed us around to see
> what we were up to or whether we were wearing abaya[5] on the
> street or not. He trusted us and built confidence in us. He always
> made us feel that we are doing the right thing. He really made us
> respect ourselves. Even now after he has been dead for over thirty
> years, I always see my father in front of me whenever I want to do
> something challenging.

Eman L.'s father, on the other hand, also of Shi'i background like
Zeynab's family, was not religious, which, at the time, was more the
norm than the exception among the educated middle classes. Despite

his secular views, he sent his daughter to a French missionary school for girls, associating Western education with 'quality education':

> My father was well-educated. He was a director of two important schools in Baghdad in al-Karkh and al-Markaziyya. Many of his students would take classes in the afternoon and they would work in the morning. My mother did not work. We were two boys and one girl at home. My father wanted quality education. He put me into a sisters' school. There I learned French. I spent most of my childhood in Kadhimiya and afterwards in Alawiya. I still remember all these beautiful Shi'i ceremonies in Kadhimiya. My mother left Najaf wearing an *abaya*, but she was without it in Baghdad. My father was not a believer. We were not educated with religion, but I love the ceremonies.

Most women I talked to stressed the sense of inter-communal contacts, co-education of students of different religious and ethnic backgrounds, the sharing of religious celebrations and everyday lives. More than being Sunni, Shi'i, Kurd, Christian, Mandean or Yazidi, and until the early 1950s Jewish, it was social class that would be the main marker of differences and commonalities. As Hana N., a woman of Shi'i origin put it: 'We grew up with all the ethnic and religious groups. We went to school with Jews and Christians. And we celebrated all holidays together.'

Nuha, whose family had moved to Baghdad from Mosul when she was 5, recalls:

> I only had one experience with sectarianism when I was young. When we were living in Karrada in the 1950s, our next-door neighbour invited us for dinner. The next day we saw all the plates chucked out in the back yard. My mother called my sister and they saw all the plates and the cutlery. They thought were dirty because we were Sunni. The next time, I was 20 at university. My best friend was Shi'i. I asked her: 'When are you going to stop beating yourself every year.' She asked me: 'Do you know anything about the tenth day of *Muharram*?'[16] She asked me questions and I had no idea what she was talking about. She asked me: 'Do you want to learn?' So she started telling me religious stories in great detail and I started weeping. My friend laughed.

Despite some incidents of prejudice and sectarianism, all the women I talked to were in agreement that they lived in relatively multicultural and to some extent cosmopolitan environments that encouraged education, travel abroad and cultural appreciation. The increasing opportunities in education went hand in hand with considerable accumulation of wealth and development programmes, which started in the early 1950s. Yet, once again, it is important to point out that the specifically urban and middle- and upper-class backgrounds distinguished the women I talked to from the majority of the Iraqi population at the time. Most Iraqis, especially girls and women, did not have access to education and were struggling to survive under harsh economic conditions. Social injustice and exploitation led to social unrest, and later on to the revolution, but there was also an increasingly politicized class of educated young people who wanted total independence from Britain, the former colonizer, and a more fair and just social system. At the same time as there was a strong and urgent move to change the existing political order, Iraqi intellectuals and artists were also involved in creating new cultural movements and found new expressions and forms in literature and the arts.

Cultural and Artistic Lives

A cultural effervescence was ascendant in the city in those days. It was an effervescence in which destinies mixed and enthusiasms took exciting and ever-changing political and social directions, and I found myself in its whirl perhaps at just the right historical moment. There were the young women who were itching for their freedom, and I knew many of them. There were the poets and short-story writers who were seeking to create new forms in everything they wrote. There were the painters who had returned from their study abroad and who, despite their small numbers, were able to create new theories for Arab art everywhere, out of the expression of their experiences in line and colours. There were also the persons specializing in economic, social, political, philosophical and historical thought, ranging from the extreme right to the extreme left. They were represented by a number of professors, prominent in their colleges, who were no less influential than their friends, the writers and artists, in shedding their old traditions and announcing the good news of a forthcoming modernity that would change the whole Arab world, not only in relation to political and social attitudes but also with regard to the aspirations, visions and emphatic call for freedom in all its forms that individual men and women were harbouring in their heart. (Jabra, 2005: 73–4)

The vivid description of Baghdad's cultural and artistic spirit by the famous Palestinian writer, intellectual and artist Jabra Ibrahim Jabra resonates with the stories and impressions of the Iraqi women who shared with me their experiences of the 1950s and 1960s in Iraq. Soraya, who had been extremely busy with mostly clandestine political activism throughout the 1950s and early 1960s, emphatically stressed that she and her friends would still find time to enjoy the dynamic cultural life of the time:

I used to meet my boyfriend in Café Swiss. There were always lots of intellectuals, painters and poets hanging around, drinking coffee and discussing things. Both men and women. Everybody used to know everybody. We would talk a lot about literature, art and music. I went to many many exhibitions with my friends. There were lots of new and exciting developments in the arts. I went to the first exhibition of al-Ruwwad [the Pioneers Movement]. I would also meet with friends to listen to classical music. Next to the Café Swiss was the Brazilian café. It was also full of intellectuals and artists but it was more traditional than the Swiss Café.

The Swiss and the Brazilian cafés on the buzzing al-Rashid Street were two of the many incarnations of the coffee house in which people would not only drink coffee, chat, read newspapers and play backgammon, but also spread intellectual, philosophical and political ideas. Specific coffee houses became associated with particular political and intellectual trends. Both the Swiss and Brazilian coffee houses, for example, were associated with existentialist thought (Davis, 2005: 95). The Swiss Café was one of the few coffee houses that was freely and frequently visited by women intellectuals, artists and activists.

Coffee houses were also important civil society institutions where information was shared between intellectuals and spread to illiterate people. Intellectuals and artists would read out newspapers, recite poetry, and discuss the latest literary or artistic trends, often with an implicit or even hidden political message. In other words, coffee houses became sites of resistance against the state as much as sites of cultural exchange and proliferation.

The Pioneers Movement (al-Ruwwad) referred to by Soraya emerged in the encounter between Iraqi artists and European painters who had lived in Iraq during World War II (Davis, 2005: 82). Other artists' movements and organizations included the Baghdad Association of the Friends of Art (1952), the Baghdad Association for Modern Art (1953), the Iraqi Writers Association, and a group of communist intellectuals who were associated with the magazine al-Thaqafa al-Jadida (New Culture), first published in 1953 (Davis, 2005: 82–97). Although most writers, poets and artists were male, women artists and writers, such as Naziha Salim, Madhiha Omar, Suad al-Attar, Fatina al-Laib and Nazik al-Mala'ika, participated in the various experimental movements and contributed to the opening up of new cultural, social and political spaces. Artists and writers were not only experimenting with new aesthetics and cultural expressions, but were also implicitly providing visions for a multiethnic, multicultural and democratic society (Davis, 2005: 92).

One of the first female artists and one of Iraq's most important living artists, Suad Al-Attar, started painting while in elementary school in the early 1950s, a mixed school in which well-trained arts, drama and music teachers encouraged the pupils' talents. When I met Suad on a gloomy summer's day in 2006, she (as so many of us during this time) was extremely distressed by the war in Lebanon and the deteriorating situation in Iraq. She had just received bad news about the house she used to own in Baghdad before it was appropriated unlawfully, and thirty of her paintings stolen. Yet her face lit up and her youthfulness and beauty came alive when she talked about her early career as a painter. Throughout her childhood and teenage years in the late 1940s and 1950s, she was encouraged to pursue her artistic talents by her teachers as well as her family:

> My high school gave me two rooms to show my work in an exhibition. Which school would do that nowadays? And the opening was packed. I have a photograph of a minister looking at my exhibition. I was just 16 years old. I showed forty-five oil paintings and sketches in that exhibition. My parents were very encouraging. I never forget the day my mother, who used to paint herself before she had her children, gave me her paint box. I was only 5 years old. At the age of 9, my father gave me an album with about a hundred postcards of mainly French painters. I used to copy these cards over and over again. My parents would take us children regularly to exhibitions and musical concerts. Until the age of 16, I had my own studio at home where I used to paint every day.

When I asked Suad how the other mainly male and older artists reacted to her work, she laughed and replied:

> The other painters always had doubts. They could not understand why I was so persistent. I hate to say it, but many of them felt threatened. And as I was very young and with good looks, they could not take me seriously. Jawad Salim[7] was different though. When one of my relatives showed him my work when I was a teenager, Jawad said: 'I don't think this girl needs to be taught.' When I had my first exhibition after I graduated from high school in 1957, Jawad helped me to price my work. We did it together. However, later on, the other artists started to respect me – not only my talent but my intellectual abilities as well. In 1966, the Pioneer group invited me to join them.

Despite Suad's obvious calling as a painter from an early age, she never questioned her role as mother and housewife. She got married shortly after graduating from high school, at the age of 16:

> I had three children, and they always came first. I never painted when I was needed. I always finished my duties first and then would paint at the end of the day. I painted almost every night. I feel miserable if I don't paint. Imagine the charisma and energy I had. I never behaved like a bohemian with my children.

While Baghdad was certainly the centre for cultural and artistic ex-
perimentation and new movements, other cities in Iraq were not left
unaffected by the cultural buzz that characterised the scene among
the educated middle and upper classes in the capital. Ibtesam, who
grew up in Najaf, has vivid memories of the way literature, visual
arts and music were very much part of her family's conversations:

> My father was an intellectual and my mother was a housewife.
> But she was very intellectual as well. She taught herself to read
> and write. Her older brother had helped her. She read all kinds of
> books: novels, poetry, social issues. She would discuss intellectual
> issues and new cultural movements with our family guests. My
> parents were cousins from a well-known family. The family was
> very religious. The women would cover up even inside the house.
> But my parents were both different. My father drank arak and
> played the oud. In Najaf, the houses had cellars called *sirdab*. During
> the hot summers, we used to sleep in the *sirdab*. It was really cool
> as it was deep in the basement. My father used to sit in the *sirdab*
> in the evenings, drink and play the oud. When my grandfather
> used to listen to my father singing, he thought it was the radio. My
> father subscribed to the Egyptian magazine *Huwa* and other politi-
> cal and cultural magazines. We would all read them eagerly and
> discuss what we read inside the family and with our friends.

Music, literature, art and books played a very important role in the
upbringing and socializing of all the older women I talked to. They
were obviously part of an educated and cultured elite of middle-class
and upper-class backgrounds who were open to new ideas, whether
in politics or art, and reflected a sense of cosmopolitanism and the
embrace of difference.

Much of the intellectual and artistic production at the time was
concerned with modernity and a critique of tradition. The free-
verse movement in poetry, for example, challenged conventional
and traditional rules of Arab poetry. It also challenged the idea
of a 'platform poetry' – associated with the populist poetry that
was moving people in the context of political demonstrations and
gatherings, and that linked a poet to particular political slogans and

trends (Davis, 2005: 92–3). One of the most famous free-verse poets was Nazik al-Mala'ika, who was at the forefront of a new form of avant-garde poetry, experimenting with verses outside the rigid structures of traditional poetry. Influenced by her mother, Umm Nizar al-Mala'ika, a poet herself, Nazik al-Mala'ika started writing poetry at a very young age. In the 1950s, she was among the most prominent figures of modernism, and backed the movement with her critical writings. Ardently anti-communist, she was a great admirer of Nasser and the idea of Arab nationalism. During the 1950s, 1960s and 1970s, in addition to her eloquent and prolific poetry, she published a number of important and influential works in the fields of literature and literary criticism. One of her most famous poems, entitled 'Who Am I' (Ana) reflects the modernist spirit that was prevalent in her poetry:

> The wind asks who am I?
> I am its confused spirit, whom time has disowned
> I, like it, never resting
> continue to travel without end
> continue to pass without pause
> should we reach a bend
> We would think it end of our suffering
> and then – void
> Time asks who am I?
> I, like it, am a giant, embracing centuries
> I return and grant them resurrection
> I create the distant past
> From the charm of pleasant hope
> And I return to bury it
> to fashion for myself a new yesterday
> whose tomorrow is ice.
> (Nazik al-Mala'ika, 'Who Am I', 1948)

The Political Spectrum

This generation of young and educated Iraqi women and men were divided across political lines, reflecting the wider political spectrum:

some favouring Iraqi nationalism, and others being attracted to pan-Arab nationalism. The more radical and popular wings of both trends were represented by the ICP and the Ba'th Party, the latter representing a radical wing of Arab nationalism. Other anti-monarchical yet less radical political forces were the National Democratic Party (NDP) and the Independence Party. The NDP advocated social democracy and political reform by parliamentary means, concentrating on conditions inside Iraq, including opposing continued British military presence and influence. The Independence Party, on the other hand, although largely ineffective after the Second World War, was much more interested in the promotion of pan-Arabism and denounced British influence in the context of Arab nationalism.

The major opposition force in the 1940s and 1950s was the Iraqi Communist Party, founded in 1934. Notions of social justice, egalitarianism, class struggle, anti-British Iraqi nationalism and secularism were appealing to an intellectual elite as well as to impoverished workers and peasants, shanty-town dwellers and students. Many of the older women I talked to had become politicized in the context of the student movement in the late 1940s. I met Salwa R. on a cold and grey winter afternoon in West London. She took me to a favourite café in the neighbourhood, where she told me about the beginnings of her political involvement while in high school:

> I was approached by outside students, not from our school. I
> got involved in the Ittihad al-Taliba al-'Amm (General Union of Iraqi
> Students, GUIS). It was a very strong movement in the country,
> belonging to the communist tendency. I became particularly active
> in this movement after the Mu'tamar al-Siba (the Congress of Lions)
> in 1948, which was held at a square with lion monuments during
> the time of the Wathba [the Leap]. Big personalities participated,
> such as the poet al-Jawahiri, who wrote a poem specially for this
> event Ayyam Al-Shabab' [days of the youth].

Not officially licensed by the government, members of communist-led organizations had to work underground and were regularly subjected to repression and persecution. Nevertheless they were

Demonstration during 1948 *al-Wathba*

growing in numbers. For example, the women's organization *Rabitat Difa' Huquq al-Mara'* (the League for the Defence of Women's Rights) grew considerably in the 1950s and was active in both humanitarian work and political mobilization. The ICP's inclusive nationalism was particularly popular among Iraq's minority communities, including the Kurds and the Jews.

The leftist critique of social injustice was appealing to many Kurds in the north, who, despite being unified by Kurdish nationalism and aspirations for independence, were divided in terms of 'haves and have nots', especially in terms of landowners and tribal leaders on the one side, and the impoverished majority of the population on the other. Many Kurds joined the ICP or the distinctly urban leftist parties such as the Kurdish Communist Party or *Shoresh* (Revolution) (Tripp, 2000: 115–16). The most popular nationalist party to emerge was the Iraqi wing of the Kurdish Democratic Party (KDP), later headed by Mulla Mustafa Barzani after his return from exile in the Soviet Union. Although 'conspicuously silent on questions of social

or economic reform' (Tripp, 2000: 115), the KDP supported the aim
of anti-monarchical forces and embraced the revolution in 1958.

Many contemporary commentators argue that Arab nationalism
does not appeal to the majority of the Shi'i population, who feel
alienated by a movement that is predominantly Sunni. Yet, during the
1950s, Shi'i leaders and general supporters were to be found in the
pan-Arab movements, including the Ba'th Party. However, pre-1958,
the Ba'th Party was very small, and while the first Ba'th secretary
general, Fu'ad al-Rikabi, was a Shi'i from Nasiriya, most members at
the time were his friends and kin. Rather than thinking of themselves
as Shi'i or Sunni, people identified as Arab, or alternatively Iraqi,
before anything else. With the establishment of the State of Israel,
xenophobic attitudes towards minorities were most tragically in
evidence in relation to Iraq's Jewish population, but later on also
targeted the Kurds and increasingly the Iraqi Shi'is. However, it was
only after the Ba'th *coup d'état* in 1963 that sectarianism deepened and
became institutionalized (Davis, 2005: 85).

Across the political spectrum, resentment against the established
political regime grew throughout the 1950s. In 1952, mass demonstrations initiated by student discontent, known as the *intifada* (uprising),
resulted in martial law, increased repression and mass arrests of
political leaders. In 1954, three of the opposition parties (NDP, ICP
and the Independence Party) joined forces in a National Front. The
return of Nuri al-Sa'id as prime minister for the twelfth time brought
even worse repression, including the banning of all opposition parties
and newspapers (Farouk-Sluglett and Sluglett, 2001: 45). This did not
stop people from expressing their discontent though. Salwa N., a
retired paediatrician who left Iraq for the UK during the mid-1990s,
was studying engineering at Baghdad university at the time. She
recalls the period just before the revolution:

> I was not a member of any political party, but I remember that my
> friends and I were always demonstrating against this or that. Some
> of my friends were communists and others were Arab nationalists.
> In the mid-1950s, we were protesting against the Baghdad Pact, an

alliance with Britain and the USA. We demonstrated in support of Nasser, especially in '56 when he was attacked for nationalizing the Suez Canal. Sometimes we just shouted anti-government slogans. The police were violent at times. On several occasions, people got shot at. But we would still continue. Lots of girls and women took part in these demonstrations. There was never a sense that women should not be part of these actions. On the contrary.

One of the decisive external factors influencing the course of events inside Iraq was the *coup d'état* of the Free Officers in Egypt in 1952, which brought about the end of the monarchy in Egypt. Gamal Abdel Nasser, a fervent proponent of pan-Arabism and the non-aligned movement, condemned the 1954 Baghdad Pact between Turkey, Iraq and Great Britain. It increased resentment at Iraq's dependence on the British military, among not only the Iraqi population but also the Iraqi officer corps, who established a secret Free Officers Movement themselves with the aim of overthrowing the monarchy. Anti-British and anti-government mass demonstrations erupted across Iraq – a show of solidarity with Nasser, whose regime managed to survive after an attack by France, Israel and Britain shortly after he nationalized the Suez Canal in 1956.

The 1958 Coup and the Revolution

What started out as a military *coup d'état* by a small group of Free Officers, in the early morning hours of 14 July 1958, soon turned into a full-fledged revolution. Masses of people started crowding the streets, celebrating and expressing their support after hearing one of the leading Free Officers, 'Abd al-Salam 'Arif, declaring the Republic of Iraq on radio. Memories of the day itself and the significance of the revolution differ greatly among the women I talked to, largely according to their political perspective. Members of or sympathizers with the ICP generally describe the revolution with great enthusiasm. Soraya, who earlier related her experiences during the student demonstrations at the time of the *Wathba* in 1948, left Iraq over twenty-five years ago. She has been living in London in an apartment decorated with paintings and photos from the 'good old days', including a photo of 'Abd al-Karim Qasim on one of her sideboards. Soraya is full of despair and anger about the current situation inside Iraq. Yet her facial expression changes and her eyes light up when she speaks about the days of the revolution:

> The 14th of July 1958 is the most important day of my life. The joy we had! I had my first boy. He was seven months old. We lived in al-Mansur behind Qasr al-Malik [the King's Palace]. We were sleeping on the roof as we always used to do during the hot summer nights. My son and the baby of my brother, who was married to a German woman, had woken up early and we were preparing milk for them. All of a sudden the house was shaking. Two days before, the party [Communist Party] distributed a message, saying: 'There will be big events coming soon. Be prepared!' We did not know what it would be. I said: 'Barbara, the King's house has been attacked.' She did not believe me. I took my son to my mother's and I went to the street. All of Baghdad went out. People had found out what happened by word of mouth. Later there was a radio announcement. Most people did not think it was a bad thing to pull the body of the King through the streets. I did not think it was bad at the time. But now we feel differently about it. The communists were blamed for it. But people were angry. They had been exploited and had lived in poverty and they reacted badly.

Memories of the shooting of members of the royal family, the hanging of political leaders and the display of executed members of the ancien régime evoked contrasting feelings among most of the women I talked to. It has been argued that, given the strong anti-British sentiments at the time, the violence associated with the 1958 revolution was relatively contained certainly in comparison with what was to come (Farouk-Sluglett and Sluglett, 2001: 49). Yet women across the political spectrum mentioned the violence that took place in the first days of the revolution, although several communist women, even of upper-class background, acknowledged that they did not think about it a lot at the time. 'These things happen in revolutions.' Hana R., a communist activist told me, 'It's the mob. We could not stop it at the time.' Nadia R., who had not been involved in any political activism in the 1950s, recalls: 'At 6 o'clock in the morning on the radio, we heard the news. The driver was saying in a very happy way: "They are dragging people in the streets!" I can never forget my shock. But they were wise enough to introduce a curfew and by 1 o'clock things started to settle down.'

Fatima N., who grew up in an economically stable but modest environment, has been close to Shi'i Islamist ideas ever since she left Iraq for the USA in the late 1970s. She was a teenager at the time of the revolution and became very agitated when she told me her version of events:

> Not many people were happy with the revolution. My father was very sad. He said: 'We will never see that kind of democracy again.' I thought a republic was better than a kingdom, but people lost their freedom. During the kingdom there was justice. No one could be punished like that. The only group who made problems were the communists. When the revolution happened, 'Abd al-Karim Qasim came to power. A small group of military men seized power. There was lots of violence. They killed everyone in the royal family. From the eldest to the youngest one, even the King's aunts, nephew, niece. None of them got out. It was a very barbaric way. They claimed that other people did it. Even Qasim himself rejected the violence.

Fatima's perception is clearly coloured by her Islamist anti-communist feelings, and did not reflect the perceptions of the majority of the population at the time. It is important to stress that almost all the violence and anger was directed against the main symbols of the *ancien régime* and never turned into sectarian violence or looting. Even so, I was surprised how many women expressed ambiguity and mixed feelings about the revolution. Aliya N. recalls how significant age and generation were in terms of shaping people's attitudes towards the events. In her own family, as in many other families at the time, different views coexisted:

The most vivid memory I have about the revolution was my
mother crying on the phone, wailing: 'The child! The child!' And
we thought that something had happened to my younger brother.
But my mother was talking about the King. He was only 18 at the
time. My father put in for his retirement right away. He said: 'A
government of rubbish is not worth it. I don't belong to it!' My
parents were not part of the aristocracy and they were not rich,
but they belonged to 'ahd al-ba'id ['the time gone by', meaning
'the period of the monarchy' in Iraqi terminology], while my
sister and I had become Arab nationalists. To me, the age thing
is important. My parent's generation, their friends, relatives and
neighbours, had similar views. But I remember my older sister was
extremely happy. She was twelve years older than me. I was just
excited that something was happening. I did not witness any of the
violence. The closest violence I remember happened to a friend of
my brother. He was from a very rich family in Mosul. He had a
fiancée. The girl was taken by the Communist Party in Mosul. Her
name was Hafsa. They took off her clothes, raped her and hanged
her on an electric mast at the end of 1959. My brother's friend lost
it afterwards. He was in hospital for a long time.

Aliya's views about generational differences resonates with the
accounts of several women I talked to. I got a sense of a big gap between the younger educated generation of politicized Iraqis and their
parents' generation, who were relatively happy with the monarchy
and the general status quo. Much of the contentment – or rather lack
of revolutionary spirit – relates to the specific class backgrounds of
parents living on a spectrum that ranged from 'financially stable' to
'doing very well'. For a number of women, support for the revolution
was not so much an expression of a specific political position as a
sense of having to go with the times and of 'being modern':

In 1958 we were living in Hayy al-Sa'ad in Najaf. I was 6 years
old. At the time, people who were fairly well off would buy abid
(slaves) from Saudi Arabia. In our house, we had two slaves, Fayruz
and Sabah. People often got a male and female slave so that they
would have children and that the children would work for them.
But many families did not deal with them like servants, and they
became part of the family. When Sabah said something, even my

father and mother would listen to her. What I remember about the revolution is Sabah dancing in the street. She was very happy. All the children were dancing with her. Everyone was happy. Everyone went to the statue of the King. They used rope and then pulled at the rope. Some time later, they placed a statue of 'Abd al-Karim Qasim in the new part of Najaf. They put fancy lights in the water around the statue. My family did not say anything bad about the King. They liked him. But they liked the change from malikiya (monarchy) to jumhuriya (republic). They did not hate the King, but they were very modern. My mother dressed in a very modern way. My uncle would buy her clothes from London. Nothing really changed in terms of impact on everyday life. They changed the name of the head of the country, they changed the pictures. But nothing really happened in terms of most people's everyday lives.

It seems paradoxical that the aspiration to embrace 'the modern' did not extend to questioning the idea of having slaves, even if they were well-treated and included as part of the family. Yet, while the practice of buying slaves from Saudi Arabia was no longer widespread in the 1950s, exploitative semi-feudal relations between a small percentage of wealthy landowners and the majority of landless peasants was still the norm in the countryside. Among the petty bourgeois, the peasants and workers, the aftermath of the revolution made some difference to everyday lives as progressive policies worked to boost the education system, to improve health care and labour rights, to provide affordable public housing and to start what was intended to be a far-reaching land reform (Farouk-Sluglett and Sluglett, 2001: 76).

Women's Political Activism

Throughout the 1940s and 1950s, women and girls had been involved in humanitarian assistance and welfare work, but had also participated in demonstrations, strikes, sit-ins as well as underground political activism. They were active across the political spectrum, being attracted to both leftist Iraqi nationalism in the form of the Communist Party and its associated students' and women's organizations, as well

as different trends within Arab nationalism. Salwa, who became an
important figure in the ICP and the Iraqi Women's League, recalls
how she started to get involved in student politics, before her activism shifted more to women's issues:

> At university in 1952 I was in the College of Chemistry. We were
> treated like in secondary school. We were not free at all. We had a
> very severe director. In the beginning of the second year, he issued
> a new set of by-laws for the college, which allowed him to inter-
> fere more in our affairs. We formed a committee from all classes.
> We elected representatives. I was the one representing my class.
> We tried with the director to change the by-laws. He was very
> harsh. It would have given the administration the right to look
> into our books and exams, restricting our rights more and more.
> We declared a strike. Our College of Pharmacy and Chemistry was
> close to the College of Medicine and Dentistry. We were really
> afraid of our director. We organized a delegation to go to the other
> colleges and tell them about our problem. We all assembled in the
> College of Medicine after we had solidarity from the other colleges.
> All the students went on strike.

Salwa, like all the older women I talked to, transforms into an
enthusiastic and animated person when speaking about the events at
the time. As during most of my interviews and conversations with
Iraqi women, we had started out speaking about the current situation
inside Iraq. Salwa is one of the few women I talked to in London
who remains somewhat optimistic: her hatred and resentment of the
previous Ba'th regime still outweighs her disappointment with the
USA and UK in their handling of the aftermath of the invasion. Yet
her disillusionment and sadness are evident and only leave her face
when she talks about the past. She continues:

> The prime minister was away. The acting prime minister wanted
> to see the students. His son was in the College of Medicine. He
> told us that they would abolish the by-laws. We said that it would
> not satisfy us, as our director was very harsh and that he would
> continue to make our lives difficult. The government decided to
> give him a month's holiday and said that he would not return to
> work after that. So we discussed it with the students; they accepted

and we returned to the university. But when we returned some hooligans hired by the director started to beat up students, and two members of the committee were injured. It was obvious that the director was behind it. The director was expelled. The next year, we obtained the right to form a student committee. I became the representative of my class. At the time, the Ministry of Health was responsible for us. When they learned that most of the students who were on the committee were leftists and communists, they decided to stop it. They abolished this committee in spring 1953. I passed my exams, but in September, when we had to go to our new classes, there was an announcement that four students, including me, were expelled from the College.

Salwa was forced to leave university because of her political activism and left Iraq to continue her studies in Europe. When she came back after the revolution, in 1959, she found that her friends and comrades were not obliged to work underground anymore but could be active in the open. Yet the relationship between the ICP and 'Abd al-Karim Qasim, the leading political figure, was ambiguous and went through tense periods, including accusations and arrests. Despite this, for women affiliated with the ICP, the period up to the Ba'th coup in 1963 is generally remembered as the most hopeful and dynamic time they experienced.

Some women I spoke to found it generally quite hard to admit that they were initially attracted to the Ba'th as part of their Arab nationalist orientation and admiration for the pan-Arab leader Nasser. They stressed the difference between the ideology of pan-Arabism rooted in tradition and regional solidarity and the way political leaders implemented it and acted when coming to power. Mona F. who became an outspoken critic of the Saddam Hussein regime in the 1980s and 1990s, was quite nervous in speaking about her experience, but relaxed when I reassured her that I would not reveal her identity:

At that period, in 1959, I joined the Ba'th Party. All my friends and my sister were in the Ba'th Party. This was my life, my teenage years. I was so much involved. I put all my passion, all my love into the party. My parents did not know about it. My mother once told me that someone told her that I went to someone's house. She was very angry with me. My father heard that I went to demonstrations. He took my hand and for the first time he told me: 'My whole family honour is in this hand. Please protect it. I respect you. And I don't want to question you. I trust you, but please protect our family honour.' I was attracted to the Ba'th because of Arab nationalism and Nasser. My sister brought home lots of Ba'th Party literature. She was a librarian and she had access to books. She was highly educated. She had a strong personality and was very dominating, so I would do anything she would say.

The principal ideological foundations of Ba'thism were formulated by Michel 'Aflaq, a Syrian Christian. It originated in the context of anti-colonial struggles in the post-World War II period and promoted Arab unity and independence. It was secular in nature and extremely hierarchical and centralized in organization. The creation of the State of Israel and the pan-Arab ideology of Nasser-fuelled pan-Arab sentiments and boosted the membership of the Iraqi Ba'th. Mona herself evolved into one of the student leaders during the early 1960s, although her activities were curtailed by the watchful and protective eyes of her elder brother, himself a member of the ICP.

I would lead demonstrations. My older brother had studied law abroad. He came back as a communist. We all thought that he was only theoretically socialist but did not think that he was actually involved in the Communist Party. When the Ba'th Party took over in 1963 he was arrested. The year before, I had been very active at school. The headmistress, who was also a communist, knew my brother and would call him, telling him about my activities. The moment demonstrations started she locked me in her room as she had agreed with my brother. I felt I was the leader of the Ba'th in my school. The slogans were anti-communist, and anti-government, and calling for a revolution. We were encouraged and ordered by the Ba'th Party to mix with uneducated women and to educate them. My mother was a very charitable woman. Because of her and because of the Ba'th Party, I became very humble and casual with people from the working classes. One of the stupid things that the communists did was to speak about sex and sexual relations. '*Ra's al-shahr maku mahr! Mutu ya ba'thiya!*' [The end of the month, no more gifts to the bride, wish you death, Ba'this].[8] They propagated sexual relations outside of marriage. Such a slogan and lots of their practices made the Ba'th Party much more popular. It strengthened the party.

According to another source, *Ra's al-shahr maku mahr* (By the end of the month no more gifts to the bride) culminated with: *wal-qadi n'thebba bel-nahar* (and we will throw the judge into the river), and was chanted on the occasion of the 1959 law reforms on personal status. The addition of *mutu ya ba'thiya* (wish you death, Ba'this) is seen to have been a modification. However, other women I interviewed vehemently denied that this slogan was ever used in any form. Soraya laughed as I asked her about the slogan and said, 'This is a fabrication by those who wanted to discredit the communists. We never shouted anything like that! We were so careful to touch anything religious. I was against the dowry but would not have shouted it out. When I got married I asked for 1 dinar, which was symbolic only.' All women who had been active in the Communist Party stressed that, despite the party's rhetoric about more liberal gender relations, they were very careful – almost puritanical – precisely because their opponents invoked religion and popular culture against their supposed godless immorality.

As became evident in Mona's account of her political activism, women's mobilization and involvement in public activities did not automatically challenge the prevailing ideology related to woman's honour and propriety. Mona, like many of the other politically active women I talked to, felt compelled not to disappoint her father's trust: 'I used to be very conscious of how to behave on the street, what to do and what to say, to the extent that I would not turn my head if a boy called my name.' Yet most women across the political spectrum enjoyed relatively relaxed mixed socializing and joint activities with male political activists.

Even within a single family, there existed different political orientations. What seems to have united the generation of young educated people across a range of middle-class backgrounds was their politicization rather than a specific political orientation. Mona and her elder sister left the Ba'th Party shortly after the first Ba'th *coup d'état* in 1963 in protest against the arrest and torture of their brother, who had been a leading member of the ICP:

> My brother was moved from one prison to another. He was
> tortured, despite my sister's connection in the Ba'th Party. We
> both left the party and that was the end of my political career.
> But I have no regrets. It made me read a lot. It made me think on
> a much higher level than what is usual for an ordinary teenager.
> I was thinking about the world, about the needs of people. The
> experience in the party formed my personality and made me grow
> up a lot. But leaving the party and knowing what I knew about the
> party was devastating. I suffered from depression for the first time
> in my life. I escaped into the world of books.

Despite the political differences between communists and Ba'thists at the time, both political orientations were essentially secular in nature and generally cut across ethnic and religious backgrounds, although few Shi'is and Kurds would have had much reason to be attracted to Ba'thism, however much they may have admired Nasser. Based on my interviews, I did not come across many women who had been involved in any religiously motivated activism at the time. The Shi'i Islamist organizations and parties such as the Dawa Party (the Islamic Call), which are now popular among many of the Shi'i women I talked to in Dearborn and London, only came into existence in the late 1950s. The Dawa Party was organized around the young cleric Muhammad Baqir al-Sadr – the uncle of Muqtada' al-Sadr, who since 2003 has become an important public figure, proponent of Shi'i Islamist politics and head of the militia called the Mahdi Army.

Hala K., who has been very active in an NGO helping widows and orphans in Baghdad and Fallujah, told me about a religiously based women's organization that her mother helped to found in the mid-1950s:

Three women went to the Shaykh, who was very supportive, and told him: 'We are teaching in the school, but we need a space to gather.' There were societies for men, in the name of religion and freedom, but the women wanted to start a society as well. They went to the ra'is al-'ulama [head of religious scholars], who supported them, stating that it was alright so long as they were doing it in the frame of religion. They rented a house and people accepted it. So, in 1955, they started Jam'iyat al-akhwat al-muslima [the Society of the Muslim Sisters]. The daughter of the ra'is al-'ulama, Nihal al-Zahawi, was involved in it. They started to have weekly meetings. They just read the Qur'an, discussed women's problems, got involved in charity work for women and widows. After the 1958 revolution, politics started to cause problems. Communists and Ba'thists were both against religion. Especially after 1963, the society had to decrease its activities, but the association is still in the same place. It is still active.

The Society of Muslim Sisters was not a political organization, being mainly involved in charity education and welfare, but its existence shows that a minority of women were mobilized in the context of their religious beliefs rather than political ideologies. Yet the women's organization that carried most weight in the 1950s and 1960s, and was most influential in changing women's legal rights after the revolution, was the communist-led Iraqi Women's League.

The Iraqi Women's League

As in other countries in the region, Iraqi women's political mobilization and the emergence of women's organizations were boosted by the broader political context of anti-colonial and anti-imperialist sentiments, the wider struggle for social justice and equality, and humanitarian crises and welfare needs.[9] In the 1940s, women of mainly upper-class backgrounds had been active in women's branches of charitable organizations, such as the Red Crescent Society, the Child Protection Society and the Houses of the People Society (Efrati, 2004: 167). These organizations were mainly involved in efforts to obtain the provision of better health-care services, instructions in child care, welfare for the poor, and assistance for flood and earthquake victims. But women were also active in more political organizations, such as the League against Nazism and Fascism (later the Women's League Society), which had been established to combat fascism in the context of World War II. Literacy programmes and a range of events, such as lectures, plays and discussions, aimed to raise women's cultural levels (Efrati, 2004: 168). The Iraqi Women's Union, founded in 1945, was the most important feminist organization at the time; it had been inspired by a major women's conference in December 1944 organized by the Egyptian Feminist Union, associated with Huda Sharawi (Efrati, 2004: 169).

Several of the older women I interviewed were involved in the emergence of a very active and, at some point, broad-based woman's organization that was closely linked with the ICP, *Rabitat al-Mara' al-'Iraqiya* (Iraqi Women's League). The name that was mentioned over and over again in connection with the struggle for women's rights and the emergence of the Iraqi Women's League was Dr Naziha al-Dulaymi. She was a pioneer in both her professional and political lives: as a medical doctor she was instrumental in improving public health in Iraq; as a political activist, particularly connected with women's rights, Dr al-Dulaymi inspired thousands of young women to join in the struggle for women's legal rights. She was also the first woman minister in the Arab world, becoming Minister of Municipalities in 1959.

Salwa, who had been involved in the student movement since the late 1940s, had been approached by Dr al-Dulaymi in 1951 to help start a new woman's organization:

> When I was still a student, we tried to establish *Jama'iyat Tahrir al-Mara'* [the Society for the Liberation of Women] in 1951, which was headed by Naziha al-Dulaymi. The law at the time stated that you had to present fifty names so that you could start a society or a party. We gathered fifty names of housewives and professional women. After you presented your signatures, you had one month until the government would issue their reply. During this month

you were allowed to practice legally. I worked with them as an activist and I was mainly trying to get in contact with other young women. Our demands included women's right to vote, economic rights, social rights, but we also had national aims and were fighting against imperialism. But after the month passed, we were refused permission. Among the fifty women, the majority were not communists. When we were not granted permission, the communist women decided to continue their activities underground with a different name and the same constitution. It was initially called *Rabitat Difa' Huquq al-Mara'* [the League for the Defence of Women's Rights]. Some of the fifty women did not want to continue illegally but some of us went on. We had meetings and began to contact other women. We convened a small congress with our contacts although it was illegal. About fifty women attended our first big meeting in the garden of one of the members of the League.

While Salwa was abroad continuing her studies after she had been expelled from Baghdad University for her political activities, her friend Soraya was approached by Dr Naziha al-Dulaymi in 1952:

At the time I was studying at the College for Trade and Economics. I became one of the co-founders of Rabitat. We used to celebrate secretly. About 200 women celebrated International Women's Day in Bustan in 1952. We opened a small factory for tailoring. In the factory, we were providing poor women with work and an income, But we also used the factory as our meeting place. It was close to al-Rashid Street. We would go to the countryside and distribute medicine among the women. We would ask them about their lives and their needs. We provided literacy classes. As time went by, Rabitat got bigger and bigger, mainly through word of mouth. I think we were successful because we touched on the most important things in these women's lives: their welfare, their children's health, and their problems with their husbands. They felt we cared. They all received us with respect. Rabitat became one of the strongest women's organizations. The Ba'thists and the Arab nationalists had a joint women's organization called *Nisa' al-Jumhuriya* (Women of the Republic). They had a voice, but not as strong as Rabitat. They did not do our work. In the north, there was a Kurdish women's organization. We had lots of contact with them and we organized several events together.

Obviously, the extent of their influence is a contentious issue among women across the political spectrum. As was to be expected, the Islamist and Arab nationalist women I talked to dismissed Rabitat's activities and appeal in the 1950s and 1960s, claiming that they were too radical for Iraqi society and that they alienated large parts of the population. Soraya, in turn, was critical of the lack of radicalism among members of the Union of Iraqi Women, which had been established in the 1940s and had been at the forefront of women's mobilization until the early 1950s:

> Before the Rabitat there was an organization called Ittihad al-Nisa'
> al-'Iraqi [Union of Iraqi Women]. These were mainly the wives of
> ministers and big directors. They used to sit, chat and drink coffee.
> They did some charity work. But it was pretty trivial. In 1956
> when the West attacked Nasser, we decided to join the Ittihad as
> individuals, not as a group. I joined and registered. The head was a
> friend of my mother's. We managed to convince the older ladies to
> join us in a protest against the attack on Nasser. The older women
> were shocked by us younger women, but they could not throw us
> out. After the Revolution we occupied the building of Ittihad al-Nisa'.
> The older generation did not object. Many of their men were
> imprisoned. We worked hard. We formed many committees, like a
> cultural committee and a medical committee. We organized clinics
> in poor neighborhoods. Doctors would work voluntarily after their
> regular paid jobs.

Soraya's judgement and description about the Iraqi Women's Union might be a bit harsh, given that the Union had been active throughout the 1940s and 1950s, not only in charity work, but also in women's education and networking between different women's organizations inside Iraq and across the Arab world. Most significantly, however, members of the Iraqi Women's Union had addressed previous taboo issues such as prostitution, divorce and child custody, women's working conditions and property rights (Efrati, 2004: 169). Yet, it is evident that members were largely affiliated with the political establishment under the monarchy and did not share the revolutionary spirit of the younger Rabitat women.

Iraqi Women's League March in 1962

When Salwa returned from her studies abroad, in 1959, Rabitat
had evolved from a clandestine underground organization to one that
was supported by the previous leader of the Free Officers' Movement
and post-1958 prime minister 'Abd al-Karim Qasim:

> After the revolution, we had over 40,000 members all over Iraq,
> including the south and Kurdistan. Qasim himself attended the first
> Congress in 1958. A year later he also came to the Second Congress.
> He asked us to change the name of the organization. He told us:
> 'Now you do not need to defend the rights of women anymore!'
> So we changed it to *Rabitat al-Mara' al-'Iraqiya* [Iraqi Women's League].

This willingness to change the name upon the leader's request might
be symptomatic of the level of co-optation by the new regime. Yet
Qasim's government was initially very supportive of Rabitat's aims
and demands. Despite objections from the *'ulama* and pressures from
conservative forces, the revolutionary changes brought about by the

new government extended to improving women's legal rights. Soraya, who had been in the midst of debates and campaigns revolving around changes in women's legal rights, feels proud of Rabitat's achievements at the time:

> The most important thing we did in the Rabita is the Qanun al-Ahwal al-Shakhsiya [Personal Status Laws]. We had a group of women lawyers working in the Rabitat. What we ended up achieving was not complete, but it was the best we could do. In the media and in the mosque, we were accused of not caring about religion. But our friends and family were happy and they appreciated the changes. Reactionary people and Ba'thists attacked it.

A unified code replaced the previously differential treatment of Sunni and Shi'i women and men with respect to legal rights in marriage, divorce, child custody and inheritance. Although still based on shar'ia (Islamic law), the Personal Status Code of 1959 was relatively progressive in interpretation and entailed some radical changes to previous laws: women were given equal inheritance rights; polygamy and unilateral divorce (i.e. on the part of the man) became severely restricted; women's consent to marriage became a requirement; and women's right to mahr (bride price) was stressed (Efrati, 2005). Although these legal changes would not have been possible without the support of the male political leadership, it was women activists' lobbying, campaigning and participation in the legislative processes that led to the relatively radical changes.

First Ba'th Coup d'État in 1963

Throughout his rule, 'Abd al-Karim Qasim maintained an ambiguous relationship with the ICP, needing its support but also fearing its influence. The appointment of Dr Naziha al-Dulaymi and two known communist sympathizers to ministerial posts had been an attempt to bind the party closer to the regime while keeping it in check (Tripp, 2000: 175). Yet, by the end of 1960, Dr al-Dulaymi, who was also the head of the Iraqi Women's League, was dismissed, as were the two other ministers. This was in the context of an increasing crackdown on the ICP, as Qasim feared its influence among the population. Most significantly, the government closed down the main associations linked with the ICP, including the Iraqi Women's League, which then had to operate underground once again.

Being increasingly under pressure from Arab nationalists and Islamists, both forces that were strongly anti-communist, Qasim faced a number of assassination and coup attempts. In 1961, relations with Mulla Mustafa Barzani, the head of the Kurdish Democratic Party (KDP), which had been officially licensed as a political party by the government in 1960, started to deteriorate. After having invited Barzani to return to Iraq from exile in the Soviet Union, and showing other signs of good will towards the Kurdish political leadership, Qasim tried to isolate him by favouring other Kurdish nationalists (Abdullah, 2003: 163). Barzani sought support for Kurdish autonomy from the USSR, which refused to help. After Barzani's memorandum proposing autonomy was rejected in 1961, he returned to the north, where fighting between rival Kurdish factions broke out (Tripp, 2000: 162). When the Iraqi army was attacked, a full-blown war broke out, involving two-thirds of the Iraq army in fighting in the north (Abdullah, 2003: 163). Soraya, a communist activist of Kurdish origin, feels that the war should have been prevented by both sides:

> I blame both the Kurds and 'Abd al-Karim Qasim. Mustafa Barzani came back from exile in Russia. He was treated as a hero. Everything was going well. But they wanted things too quickly. They did not have patience. I thought of myself not as a Kurdish activist but as a communist. I had relatives who were more involved in the Kurdish struggle. But there was discrimination against Kurds. They were treated as second-class citizens. There were only two Kurdish ministers. They always preferred Arabs in high positions. The Kurds had good reason to want their rights, but *shwaya, shwaya* [slowly] they would have reached their aims. The war in the 1960s made the Kurdish people more nationalistic. Before that the Communist Party was very strong. Irbil was mainly communist.

By 1962, some members of the KDP decided that the only way to end the conflict was regime change in Baghdad. They made a secret pact with Arab nationalists and the Arab Socialist Ba'th Party (Ba'th),[10] offering a ceasefire if Qasim were to be overthrown (Tripp, 2000: 168). In 1961, Qasim had threatened to annex Kuwait after it had become independent from Britain. Although no military operations took place, already tense relations with Egypt worsened after Iraq's failure to recognize Kuwait's sovereignty, and Iraq became more isolated from its neighbours (Abdullah, 2003: 163–4). Arab nationalist forces, especially members of the Ba'th Party, became convinced that the only way to bring Iraq back out of its isolation within the Arab world and to stop the influence of communists once and for all was to overthrow Qasim's government.

Despite his problematic foreign policies and the internal war with the Kurds, Qasim had remained relatively popular among the majority of the population. The coup was staged by Ba'thist and Arab nationalist officers, like 'Abd al-Salam 'Arif, who had been one of the Free Officers with Qasim in 1958. Unlike in 1958, though, the coup did not trigger support from significant numbers of the population. On the contrary: masses of people poured out onto the streets expressing their support for Qasim and fiercely resisting the coup, especially in the poorest neighbourhoods. The level of violence in the immediate aftermath of the coup is described by many women as a turning point in the modern history of Iraq. Within only one week of the coup, some 3–5,000 communists and sympathizers of the Qasim government were arrested, tortured and killed. Soraya, a known figure in both the communist movement and the Iraqi Women's League, managed to escape: 'I put on the *abaya* and hid in the house of relatives. I hid there with my children for about ten days. My husband was arrested and tortured. It was a terrible experience for all of us.'

Su'ad, with whom I spent an afternoon and a morning in her small apartment in Amman, listening to the ups and downs of her life and that of her family, had not been very happy with the revolution in

1958. However, she respected Qasim and, as many other women I talked to, felt that he was genuinely interested in improving people's living conditions. With great sadness, she remembers the day of the coup in 1963:

> I hated the way they arrested 'Abd al-Karim Qasim, killing him and showing his body on television. They made people more and more get used to killings and violence. Those days were horrible. The Ba'thists organized a militia called al-Haris al-Qawmi (the National Guard), who were responsible for much of the killing. They were thugs. They went into people's houses, beat people up, arrested them, and killed them. Lots of people were tortured. They were also responsible for raping hundreds of women.

Ibtesam, who had been living in Najaf, had told me that the gossip about her sister's unhappy predicament with an admirer and a failed marriage to a cousin had forced the family to move from Baghdad to Najaf. When talking about the coup in 1963, she adds that the fear related to the Ba'th National Guard was one more factor which convinced her father that it was time to move:

> In 1963, after the Ba'thist coup, al-Haris al-Qawmi [the National Guard] started raping women in Najaf. They looked for good-looking girls and took them from their families, not because of political reasons, but because they looked nice. There were lots of fathers who killed their daughters to prevent them being raped by al-Haris al-Qawmi. One of our distant relatives was interested in my sister and he joined al-Haris al-Qawmi. This was one more reason we left Najaf.

Schools and sports grounds were transformed into concentration and interrogation camps (Abdullah, 2003: 166). The scale of the violence and fear experienced in the immediate aftermath of the first Ba'th coup in 1963 is often referred to as a foretaste of what was to come during Ba'th rule from 1968 to 2003. At the time, however, widespread resentment against the thuggish and brutal National Guard linked to the Ba'th Party, as well as deep divisions within the party itself, eventually allowed the non-Ba'thist officer

'Abd al-Salam 'Arif to install a military government in November, dissolve the National Guard and arrest a number of leading Ba'thists (Abdullah, 2003: 166).

According to most women I talked to, the violence and repression receded dramatically once 'Arif had managed to contain the Ba'th and especially the National Guard. Lamia K., a writer and retired journalist, describes the brief period between the two Ba'th coups of 1963 and 1968:

> Although it was still a military regime, things started improving again after 'Arif took over. There was less violence and the rule of law started again. Many of us had great hopes of 'Abd al-Rahman al-Bazzaz,[11] who was a civilian and became prime minister in 1965.

Although dependent on the patronage and military support of President 'Arif, al-Bazzaz tried to ensure respect for civil liberties and introduce some democratic structures into the state (Farouk-Sluglett and Sluglett, 2001: 98).

The death of 'Abd al-Salam 'Arif in a helicopter crash in 1966 weakened the civilian government of al-Bazzaz. When 'Abd al-Salam's weaker and far less charismatic brother 'Abd al-Rahman 'Arif took over as president, military forces within the country became increasingly discontented with the policies of the civilian prime minister al-Bazzaz. One controversial policy related to his attempt to recognize the national rights of the Kurds. In June 1966, he offered a twelve-point programme to Barzani recognizing the bi-national character of the Iraqi state, the Kurds' particular linguistic and cultural identity, and full representation and self-government for the Kurdish area (Tripp, 2000: 187). A few months later, 'Abd al-Rahman 'Arif responded to increased pressures from the high military ranks and replaced the civilian al-Bazzaz with another former Free Officer, Naji Talib.

At the same time, the internal instability of the government increased in reaction to regional developments. The Arab–Israeli war of 1967 left the pro-Nasserist Arab nationalists in disarray and on the defensive, strengthening the Ba'th camp of Arab nationalism.

The party had reorganized itself after the crackdown following the coup of 1963, allowing a faction controlled largely by members from Tikrit to take control. In 1968, a second Ba'th coup paved the way for one of the longest-lasting and most violent post World War II fascistic regimes to emerge.

Social Lives

Throughout the various upheavals and political changes during the 1950s and 1960s, many of the women I interviewed appear to have been enjoying active and varied social and cultural lives. Despite widely documented class differences prior to the revolution, many of the upper-middle-class women who regretted the fall of the monarchy were quite keen to play down class differences. When I asked Leila K., whose life story indicates that she was from a well-to-do family, about socializing across social classes, she became slightly defensive and told me:

> Baghdad as a city was small in the 1950s. It had about half a million inhabitants. It is not a question of social level. You should not see it from a Western point of view. There were good families, but poor people lived with them. Socially there were some ranks and differences. But the ranks were not as definite as they are in Western countries. There was a house of rich people and beside it lived poorer people. But socially they always mixed, at weddings and at funerals, and because of the zakat.[12]

Despite Leila's insistence that social class was a fluid category and that women of different social class backgrounds would mix regularly, the accounts of many women point to the contrary. Most of the contacts across social classes took place in the context of hierarchical relationships and contexts of charity and employment.

Families socialized along social class lines rather than within ethnic or religious groupings. Nour H., having enjoyed a privileged childhood in an upper-middle-class family, acknowledges that she grew up in a world very much apart from the majority of the Iraqi population:

My father had been a surgeon during the monarchy. Politically, 1958 was bad, but socially we did not feel too much. My aunt was under house arrest, but she would still go to parties with foreigners. Her father had been an important politician during the monarchy. There was a huge gap between the rich and the poor before 1958. This is what started the revolution. But I do not think it affected our life styles much. We lived in a big house next to the Tigris. I went to an American high school. We had a big swimming pool. We had lots of mixed parties. I had lots of friends, and I was very sociable. Before I got married in 1967, I used to go out a lot in the 1960s. I had lots of fun. There was a period of engagement when I used to go out with my fiancé. I used to go to clubs. I went swimming a lot at al-Mansur club. Two or three times a year we went to Beirut.

Although numerous families directly associated with the monarchy left Iraq after the revolution, many of the wealthy landowners and professional classes remained behind without changing much of their lavish lifestyle. Despite the hardship that Nour and her family experienced at a later stage of her life, when her husband was arrested and tortured under Saddam Hussein, I could still get a flavour of her previous lifestyle, as her apartment in Amman was buzzing with women visitors stopping by, drinking tea and coffee, eating sweets. Nour's house was obviously one of the lively hubs frequented by members of old well-known Iraqi families, who descended on Amman from all over the world during the summer months to meet up with friends and relatives from inside and outside Iraq.

Socially, the post-revolutionary period has been associated with a liberalization of social relations, dress codes and gender relations as a result both of policies associated with the Qasim government and of the influence of the Communist Party, which continued to mobilize large segments of the population. One obvious sign of the many social changes taking place in the context of modernization, urbanization and political mobilization was the changing dress code of women. Traditionally, Iraqi women had worn the *abaya* – a head-to-toe black cloth similar to the Iranian *chador* – over their indoor clothes, which differed according to class, age, urban or rural background and level of religiosity. In the late 1940s and 1950s, more and more urban middle- and upper-class girls and women stopped wearing an *abaya* over their Western-style clothes. Salwa, who was active in the ICP, recalls that she would only wear the *abaya* in certain traditional quarters in Baghdad:

> We lived in Adhamiya. Maybe 5 per cent of our neighbours were wearing an *abaya*. Sometimes I would go secretly to Kadhimiya for political meetings. I would borrow an *abaya* from a friend. After 1958, most girls threw the *abaya* off. My mother used to wear *abaya*, and my father pressured her to stop wearing it. When we moved from Adhamiya, she finally agreed to stop wearing the *abaya*. Now, fifty-six years later, we are going back centuries.

At the time, educated husbands and fathers who embraced ideas of modernization, reform and progress, were instrumental in changing women's dress codes, as they perceived the *abaya* as a symbol of tradition and backwardness. Yet girls and women were surrounded by apparently contradictory forces, ranging from progressive to conservative, some promoting ideas related to modernization and reform, others stressing the need to remain true to one's tradition and culture. Ibtesam, who earlier related her rather traumatic experiences in primary school in Najaf, had been encouraged by her relatively progressive and open-minded parents to walk to school without the *abaya*. In Najaf, which was much more conservative than Baghdad at the time, this was perceived to be a severe digression, even though Ibtesam had not even reached puberty:

> I went to high school in 1964. My school was close to Al-Kalante, a religious school for men. I was taller than other girls and I did not wear an *abaya*. The men from the religious college started to hit me every day. I had two braids and they used to hit them. I went every day to my mother and asked for an *abaya*. My mother refused to give it to me. I told her that I was afraid of the men hitting me. I was crying out of fear. Then I finally got an *abaya*. I would put it on when I passed that religious school and then take it off right

away. I had lots of problems in Najaf because I did not wear the
abaya. In Najaf even small girls were wearing the *abaya*. One day I
visited my uncle. There was a shop selling ice. The owner said:
'Who is this girl not wearing the *abaya*?' He and my uncle started
fighting. I was only 7 or 8 years old. The ice shop owner said that
I was not too young to wear it. They started fighting physically. I
only wore the *abaya* for a few years.

Ibtesam and her family moved to Baghdad in 1966. A few months
after their arrival she and her sisters stopped wearing the *abaya*:

> We rented a house in al-Waziriya close to the *Kulliyat al-Tarbiya*
> [College of Education]. In Baghdad we first kept the *abaya* on. But
> after a few months, a friend of my father said: 'Look, 'Ali. It is
> better for you and your daughters to take off the *abaya*. Only people
> from outside Baghdad are wearing the *abaya*.' My father did not
> want to be perceived as traditional and out of touch with modern
> times. My mother agreed, so we all took it off. When our family in
> Najaf heard that we had removed our *abayas*, they sent a delegation
> to Baghdad to enquire whether it was really true. My mother told
> them: 'Yes, of course, they removed their *abayas*. And if you bother
> us any more, I will remove mine as well and wear trousers.'

As in similar situations all over the world, women in the capital
wore more daring and fashionable clothes than women in the rest
of the country, especially the countryside, where women continued
to wear more conservative dress. In the 1960s, it was not unusual
for younger women in Baghdad to wear miniskirts as it was the
fashion at the time in Western countries. Several women told me
about the Ba'th's attempt to restrict women's dress codes. Maysalun
K. had a bad experience:

> From 1963 we started to see the changes with the Ba'th, especially
> after it came to power. At the time women and girls were wearing
> miniskirts because it was the fashion. Saddam's uncle, Khayrallah
> Talfah, issued a law stating that women should not wear miniskirts
> and that those who did would have their legs painted. Skirts were
> supposed to be ankle-length to the ground. One day, after I went

to university, I went to McKenzie's bookshop in Rashid Street. I came out of the bookshop and, all of a sudden, two to three men approached me. I was wearing my skirt below my knee because I knew about this new law. But they still started painting my legs black. It was during that time that women started to worry about this. The mentality of the modern way of thinking was demolished.

Despite the Ba'th Party's commitment to modernization and development, which I explore in greater detail in the next chapter, many urban women associate the Ba'th Party with tribal and patriarchal ideologies and practices. Nour, who was also a big fan of miniskirts in the 1960s, argues though that the law did not work:

Miniskirts in the '60s were very short. Girls continued to wear miniskirts. Some got their legs painted, but it did not stop us. We were mixing with boys at university, but there was a hint of difference after the Ba'th came to power. There were some boys who were getting more conservative.

Among the upper classes in the urban areas, especially in Baghdad, girls and women had been able to move about relatively freely, and socialized frequently with boys or men. Hana F. remembers fondly her childhood and teenage years:

Families used to have *jurdagh* [summer huts; sing. *jaradigh*] on the river built from reeds. Families would go there. Boys and girls would go together and play. We used to weave *karab* [part of the palm tree] with ropes and put them around us so that we would not drown when swimming in the river. People sat by the river, talking, eating, having barbecues, singing and we were always mixed in terms of boys and girls and women and men.

Her memories correspond to those of Soraya, who was in her twenties when Hana was only a young child in the 1950s. Soraya, who had been a political activist since her high-school years, stresses that, as a young woman growing up in Baghdad, she never felt restricted or oppressed:

From the late 1940s, when we were students, we used to wear
sleeveless shirts and shorts. We would go to the club, swim and
play tennis or ping pong. Nobody would say 'Don't go out!' I
would just inform my parents that I was going out. We had lots of
freedom. I would be home by ten. And all activities were mixed.
We used to listen to classical music together, both Arabic and
Western. We read a lot. I would borrow books from my older
brothers and sisters. During the holidays I would read all day.
Sometimes we would go to the cinema.

Not all women of upper-class background had parents as liberal
and progressive as Soraya's. Several such women told me about
conservative fathers and mothers, restrictions on their movement and
on their socializing with boys and young men. And most parents of
women from more modest social backgrounds were more concerned
about traditions and their daughters' reputations. Mona stresses that
she grew up being acutely aware that she was supposed to behave
in certain ways different from boys and that staying away from boys
was part of growing up:

We used to play games on the roof with our neighbours or we
played in the garden. We were not allowed to play on the streets.
We mainly played with girls. We used to do a lot of picnics during
the weekend. There was not much mixing between boys and girls
after a certain age. Even later on when I got involved in politics,
I made sure that I did not ruin my reputation in terms of my
relationships with men.

The impression I gained from listening to the various women's
accounts is that most parents of the urban middle and upper classes
were quite happy for their daughters to mingle with boys or young
men in the context of their studies, their social activities and, as far
as was known and tolerated, their political activism. There were,
however, restrictions and limitations with respect to dating, having
boyfriends and choosing a marriage partner. Nour, who was studying architecture at Baghdad University in the mid-1960s, put it the
following way:

I was working on a final project with five or six boys at home. We worked on the boards in our salon and we worked day and night. But we were not allowed to go out for a date. We could study or work together. The normal way to get married was to meet your husband while studying at university, or at work after university, or through family arrangements. For me, I was introduced to my husband through friends. At least at this level of the upper and upper middle classes, Sunnis and Shi'is would intermarry, although it was more difficult between Christians and Muslims. Marriage arrangements varied from class to class. Often lower-class people would meet someone from the neighbourhood or marry a relative. But we were not allowed to go out with boyfriends.

Love Stories and Marriage Patterns

Nour, and many other women who shared their stories about lost loves, old boyfriends and husbands, talked about social conventions and restrictions but also about secret boyfriends, flirting in classrooms and on the university campus, failed relationships and the joys and tribulations of marriage, just as women would do anywhere in the world. Ibtesam's detailed description of the play and flirting among teenagers during the early 1960s in Najaf, a city generally described as having been particularly conservative because of its significance within Shi'i Islam, reflects a sense of universalism:

We went to school by bus with my father. We took a bus from Hayy al-Sa'ad to al-Walaya. Teenagers are the same wherever you are, whether with *abaya* or not. There were lots of games and flirting going on inside the bus. My problem was that I felt that I was not pretty. I felt ugly. I had a real complex. At the time people liked white skin, curly hair and a bit of flesh on the bones. I was the opposite: I had dark skin, straight hair and I was skinny and tall. When we got off the bus, we would pass a busy street with lots of shops and cafés. There was a boys' school close to our girls' high school. We would open the *abaya* a bit to show off our dresses and our hair. Girls in Najaf take very good care of themselves. When we left the school, the streets and sidewalks were watered with hoses. I still remember that nice smell of earth and water. We watched the boys who were hanging around. We showed off

the fringes of our hair. Sometimes my father took us home, but
sometimes we went by ourselves. The buses were green. The boys
would smile. Sometimes we would pass letters secretly. Some of the
boys would follow us when we left the bus to see where we lived.
The houses were raised, and the gardens were lower. If you were
tall enough and you stood on the balcony, you could be seen from
the street. Sometimes the boys would throw letters. Sometimes
they would sit behind a girl in the bus and would whisper something in her ear. Sometimes they would meet in the dark, but the
problem was that the girls were afraid since all the families knew
each other. Sometimes I was jealous of my sister, who had many
admirers following her while I had none.

Despite envying her sister's appeal to boys, Ibtesam soon pointed out
that her sister got trapped in an unfortunate situation that forced the
family to move from Najaf to Baghdad:

My sister Naziha fell in love with one admirer. He was very handsome. He seemed very rich. He met her often after school. Then she
found out that he was married and that he had four children. That
was a big shock! He wanted to marry my sister, but my parents
refused since they did not want my sister to be the second wife in a
polygamous marriage. Even my father, who was very open-minded,
got upset. Many people were gossiping about my sister, so he pressured her to get married to one of our cousins who was very ugly.
It was like a funeral day not a wedding in our house when she got
married to him. They went away on their honeymoon but came
back after only two days. They went to Baghdad and Kurdistan.
And then they broke up. Nothing happened between them. She told
him: 'If you touch me I will kill myself.' My father felt very bad
and he was very sad. He knew it was not good for my sister. The
cousin was not only ugly but he also had a bad character. So my
sister wanted a divorce. Because of this episode, my father felt that
we should leave Najaf and move to Baghdad. We moved in 1965. A
friend of my brother had also liked my sister and wanted to marry
her, but she got married to my awful cousin. My mother liked the
friend of my brother much more because he was handsome. When
the friend heard that my sister had come back and had asked for a
divorce, he came again and asked for her hand. They got married
and are still happily together.

Of course, not all stories had a happy ending like Naziha's successful marriage to her brother's friend. Some stories were sad, some bordered on the tragic. Often a love affair never actually started despite mutual attraction. Mona, who was quite shy and worried about her reputation, recalls with regret a missed opportunity:

> I loved university. I enjoyed classes, attending lectures, reading. We socialized a lot. I was in a circle of five girls. We were always together. We used to sit with the other students in the student union. We used to go on trips outside the university. Boys and girls were mingling all the time. A lot of love stories were developing. Two boys in my class fell in love with me. One was out of the question and I used to laugh at him. The other one was Jordanian. I liked him a lot but he was very close to a Christian friend of mine. We all thought that something would develop. Only after four years, shortly before returning back to Jordan, did he tell me that he was in love with me. How stupid: he stayed for four years without letting me know.

The university was a place where young people could mingle freely and possibly find a future spouse, although only a few of the women I talked to seem to have ended up marrying their boyfriend from university if they had one. Another important milieu in which to find a potential marriage partner was among the friends of brothers or family acquaintances. Salwa accepted the marriage proposal of a man who was a friend of her brother:

> He was not unknown to me. He was a doctor like my brother. I knew that he was a very good person. I was 26 at the time. I thought it was time for me to get married. But there was no pressure. My father left everything to me. He proposed and I accepted. I liked him so I did not mind. I thought he would be a good husband. I had a very good life with him. I published his memoirs after he died.

One other reason why Salwa accepted the marriage proposal was her husband's political orientation and activism. Like Salwa, he was an important member of the ICP. Her friend Soraya also ended up marrying a fellow political activist, although their marriage was preceded by a period of courtship and falling in love:

> I met my husband at the bank where we both worked. He was very handsome and always very well dressed. I was shocked when I found out that he was a communist. One would never have known by just looking at him. We courted for about two years before we got married. We used to go out for lunch, or spend time in a café. We would go for walks by the river. We married in 1957. My family knew about him and they liked him. His family objected because I was a communist. He was from an upper-class family, and they did not know that he was a communist as well.

Bubbly and rebellious Nour K., who did not have politics on her mind, was determined to have fun during the 1960s. Despite a conservative family background, she managed to go out frequently, meet young men and fall in love on numerous occasions:

> I broke up engagements twice before I met my husband. Both times I had been in love with the men I became engaged to. Both times I broke it off and ran away. I was not ready for marriage. My husband was a doctor in my father's private hospital in Baghdad. It was my father's decision to get me engaged to him. He had become fed up with my behaviour. I objected. I made a big fuss, but nobody listened to me. Both of my parents were old-fashioned. Not even my brother supported me. I was in my own world. I was the only rebel in the family. But my girl friends were supportive. We all wanted to go out and have boyfriends. But society was conservative, especially my father. My father said: 'This man wants to marry you.' I said: 'I have to go to Beirut.' I only saw him once. He was handsome, a doctor. He had a degree from the States. He and his sister came to the airport to say hello. I stayed in Beirut for two months digesting the idea. He had seen me and I was very pretty. I was in the second year of my archaeology studies. I was attractive and outgoing. In Beirut I was preparing myself. They sent my brother after me to bring me back to Baghdad. He said: 'You have to come back to Baghdad to get married.' I got the wedding dress made within two days.

Nour eventually did fall in love with her husband, whom she describes as handsome, generous, smart and charming. In her social circle, young women ended up marrying their sweethearts in some instances, but arranged marriages through family connections and friends appear to have been more frequent. Usually young women were not forced to marry someone they did not know or like, but, in Nour's case, her father exerted pressure after two broken engagements. Social class background, family reputation and looks seem to have been much more important criteria for the women themselves, as well as for their parents, rather than ethnic or religious background. According to Nour and other women I interviewed, inter-marriages between Sunnis and Shi'is − called 'Su–Shi' by Nour − and between Arabs and Kurds were relatively commonplace.

The marriage of an Iraqi woman to a non-Iraqi foreigner was extremely rare, even if the foreigner was a fellow Arab. This is obvious from the memoirs of the famous Palestinian writer Jabra Ibrahim Jabra, who was teaching English at the College of Arts and Sciences in Baghdad in the early 1950s. Despite his professional success and his considerable standing as a poet and painter, there was significant social opposition to his marriage to Lamia, a beautiful young Iraqi woman with a captivating laugh who was also teaching English at Baghdad University. When Lamia asked her maternal uncle, who, at some point, was the legal adviser to the Iraq Petroleum Company, what he thought about her plan to get married to Jabra, he replied: 'Lamia, it is better for you to ask for the moon…' And the conversation ended (Jabra, 2005: 150).

Much more common and socially acceptable was the marriage of Iraqi men to foreign wives. My German mother would often tell me about her big adventure. After having dated for almost five years secretly (to avoid confrontation with her conservative parents) while my father was a student in Germany, he proposed, but he also told my mother that he was intending to return to his home country. Before replying to his marriage proposal, my mother decided to see for herself. The following summer, of 1964, as my father returned to

My parents sitting at a restaurant by the Tigris in 1964

Baghdad for a family visit, she sold her bicycle, took her savings and without her parents' knowledge, booked herself a flight to Baghdad. Because of problems at the airport in Baghdad, my mother got stranded in Beirut for a few days until my father made the journey through the desert by bus, opting to travel back with her by taxi. So my mother arrived in Baghdad shivering and tired after a long and cold journey in a taxi with a broken window.

In Baghdad she was welcomed by the whole family. My grandmother and my Aunt Salima were especially warm and made my mother feel welcome despite the language barrier and the incredible summer heat. My grandfather had initially had reservations when hearing that my father was intending to marry a foreigner, but was persuaded by the persistence of my grandmother. By the time my mother arrived in Baghdad, he had not only accepted the idea of his son marrying a German woman but had bought a big sack of potatoes, a rarity at the time – in honour of my mother's origins!

Conclusion

Almost fifty years after the fall of the monarchy and the revolution, it is obvious that Iraqi women are re-evaluating their past in light of more recent events. Throughout this chapter, I have stressed that a particular range of social class backgrounds and the specific political orientation of the women very much shaped their attitudes towards the monarchy, the revolution of 1958 and the first Ba'th coup. Overall, I could detect a tendency to stress the relative freedom and rule of law of past governments, which were considered to be repressive at the time by large segments of the population. In light of the repression and suffering associated with the Ba'th regime, and particularly with the dictatorial rule of Saddam Hussein, as well as the present situation of lawlessness and chaos post-2003, I could detect a certain sense of nostalgia and a degree of romanticizing of the past. Even women who were at the forefront of struggle against the government and the establishment of the time valued the social and cultural dynamics and relative openness that characterized the 1950s and early 1960s among the educated urban classes.

Also evident in the accounts featured in this chapter is the fact that sectarian divisions did not significantly dominate Iraqi politics and social lives. Women of all ethnic and religious backgrounds were attracted to the two main political trends: communism or Arab nationalism. While the political establishment prior to the revolution of 1958 was largely dominated by Sunni Arabs, the government of 'Abd al-Karim Qasim was much more inclusive of the various ethnic and religious groups. Outside politics, women's social and cultural lives were not solely dictated by their ethnic or religious backgrounds; rather, social class and political and intellectual orientation shaped people's social circles.

Although all the women I interviewed for this chapter were from urban backgrounds, their narratives and their histories show evidence of the sharp disjuncture between urban and rural lives during this period. Women in the countryside, for their part, did not benefit from either the expanding education system or the innovative and dynamic cultural and intellectual movements and events that made the 1950s and 1960s such an exciting period for the participants. The other tremendous gulf, as I explained earlier, existed between social classes, with the majority of girls and women belonging to impoverished classes having no access to education and suffering inadequate health-care facilities. Tribal and traditional patriarchal values circumscribed the majority of women's lives. This stood in harsh contrast to the revolutionary changes and relatively liberal social values and norms experienced by educated young women activists. Despite widespread opposition and protest by conservative social forces, the revolutionary regime of 'Abd al-Karim Qasim did take seriously women's demands for increased legal rights and equality, passing one of the most progressive family laws in the region in 1959.

In the accounts of the women I talked to, the initial period after the first Ba'th coup is associated with increased political violence, growing sectarianism and a reversal of progressive laws and reforms. Yet many women viewed the period of the rule of the two 'Arif brothers as among the best years, when hopes for a return to a more civil and democratic government coincided with another period of relative social freedom and cultural vibrancy.

My parents got married in Germany in 1966, shortly before the death of 'Abd al-Salam 'Arif in a helicopter crash that year. They were planning to live in Iraq after my father had finished his studies. A few months later, my Aunt Salima visited Germany for medical treatment. She stayed for about three months and charmed everyone with her optimism, warmth and vivaciousness. During her six weeks in hospital, doctors operated on the cornea in both eyes. At first the operation appeared to have been successful, and for a few months, she was able to see more than just black-and-white shadows. Sadly, however, her condition deteriorated, and slowly she started to lose the vision in both eyes again. Back in Iraq, her darkening vision did not stop her from seeing that a period of hope, creativity and relative openness had come to an end with the second Ba'th coup in July 1968.

THREE

Living with the Ba'th

My earliest childhood memories of Iraq revolve around my grandmother, Omi Baghdad, sitting cross-legged on the patio leading from the kitchen to the garden. When I think about her, I see her surrounded by heaps of vegetables – onions, beans, okra and tomatoes – and her massive aluminium bowls, while cats eye her from a safe distance. I also recall her washing huge mounds of amber rice, timn, a staple food in Iraq. In the background my Aunt Salima would lend a helping hand, often instructed by my grandmother to fetch a particular knife or spice from the kitchen. It always amazed me to see how Salima would move confidently around the kitchen and the house, not only assisting my grandmother with cooking but also tidying up and cleaning despite her poor eyesight. Later when my grandmother became unwell and too sick to cook, Aunt Salima, by then blind, took over the kitchen and herself prepared all the delicious dishes, like bamiya, timn bagila, tashreeb, and even the more complicated ones like dolma, kubbet halab and kubbet mosul.

My brother and I would spent hours in the garden, sometimes on our own, sometimes with cousins, watching my grandmother and my aunt prepare the food, playing hide-and-seek and football, or just relaxing on the squeaky swing seat. One of our favourite activities

Aunt Salima cooking

was to look out for frogs, catch them and play 'frog circus' or chase after my girl cousins, who were frightened of the small animals. The mouthwatering cooking smells from the kitchen would mix with the wonderful scents of jasmine, orange blossom and *razqi* flowers¹ that filled the garden. On one occasion, in the late 1970s, we even had the company of a sheep to keep us entertained. Although 'Schnucki' was destined for slaughter, it soon became my companion and source of everyday laughter and affection. The sheep was supposed to be slaughtered as a sacrifice to express gratitude for my survival after an electrical accident with faulty garden lamps that left me unconscious and my hands burnt. Yet my parents begged my relatives to delay 'the feast' until after our departure, as I had grown attached to Schnucki and was in a rather fragile state after the shock of the accident.

If we were not in the garden or in our grandmother's house, we would visit our numerous aunts, uncles and cousins. There were always plenty of children to play with and many things to see and do. Language was not a problem during my childhood years although my father had not taught us to speak Arabic at home. During our visits, I would quickly pick up words and phrases and, as all children do, used hands and gestures to communicate. Food was plentiful and at the centre of our family visits. In fact, we seemed to eat much of the time, between lunch invitations in the early afternoon and dinner parties that would start late at night, taking long naps in between. Some evenings we would go to Abu Nuwas Boulevard overlooking the Tigris and eat the delicious grilled river fish called *masgoof*. Or we would stroll on the busy shopping streets in the evenings, enjoying the cool air after a hot day, and eat orange or pink *dondarma* (ice cream).

Everything seemed wonderful and fun, except that there was always a faint sense of danger lurking in the background. It might partly have to do with an unfortunate series of accidents and incidents I experienced, which involved food poisoning, a head injury and the near fatal electrical accident. I might also be reading significance back into those times, but I seem to remember that, even early on, I had some sort of awareness of the fact that people were mistrustful of, and even scared by, the government. Obviously I did not understand the ins and outs of politics and oppression at the time, but I seem to recall hushed voices and whispering every time the name Saddam Hussein or *al-hukuma* (the government) was mentioned.

Women's accounts of the period starting with the Ba'th coup in July 1968 up to the 1980s shift between experiences of the 'days of plenty' and the advancement of women's position in society, on the one hand, and painful memories of repression and suffering, on the other. In this chapter, I will attempt to show through personal narratives and testimonies the various forms of support the regime initially gave to women, especially in the realm of education and participation in the labour force. However, this was in the context of a dictatorship that systematically suppressed all forms of opposition or dissent and that arrested, tortured and killed hundreds of thousands of Iraqis.

Zeynab's story

The story of Zeynab J., a devout Shi'i woman in her mid-fifties, illustrates some of the problems and contradictions of the first decade of Ba'th rule. I will detail her specific experience before exploring some of the issues emerging out of her story by referring to other women's accounts and memories. Zeynab, who left Iraq in the late 1970s, is nowadays a sympathizer of the Islamist Dawa Party. She stresses, however, that she has never actually been a member of any political party. She expressed her hatred of and aversion to the Ba'th Party on numerous occasions. While Zeynab was telling me her story, the rather intimidating person I met a few months earlier was transformed into a sensitive and vulnerable woman. As we sat in her sister's living room in Dearborn, after having enjoyed a wonderful meal of traditional Iraq foods prepared by her sister Fatima, Zeynab made it clear to me that she, as many others who were more religiously inclined, initially preferred the Ba'this to the communists, whose secular ideology and policies she perceived to be anti-Islamic. However, she states that she became disillusioned in the aftermath of the Ba'thi coup in 1968:

> When the Ba'th took over, they started to take revenge by killing people just the same way as the communists did in 1958. They were executing people. They placed uneducated people in power. They were forcing people to become Ba'thi. They started to oppress people. Arab unity, Muslims and Islam were pushed aside. Their behaviour became worse than the communists.

Zeynab's equation of the Ba'this with communists is obviously much contested and challenged among the women more sympathetic to the Communist Party. Yet, among women who were politically active at the time, there seems to be a general agreement about the political violence and repression used by the Ba'th. In contrast, women who were not involved in politics often depict the first decade of Ba'th rule as the 'golden age': a period of economic boom, of rapid expansion of the middle classes, of the introduction of women-friendly state policies and a relatively liberal social climate in the main urban centres.

Despite Zeynab's condemnation of the Ba'th Party and its ideology, she differentiates between the early phase of Ba'th rule (1968–79) and the period following the resignation of Ahmad Hasan al-Bakr in 1979. In the first decade of Ba'th rule after 1968, al-Bakr, the general secretary of the Ba'th Party, was simultaneously president, prime minister, chairman of the Revolutionary Command Council (RCC) and commander-in-chief of the armed forces. Saddam Hussein was officially only the second man in power, holding deputy titles while being responsible for the establishment of an internal security apparatus (Abdullah, 2003: 169). Rather than stressing ideology, as the party did, the security apparatus was purely a tool for repression, control and enforced obedience. While many analysts argue that it was only in the late 1970s that the party and the army gradually yielded power to the security apparatus controlled by Saddam Hussein, Zeynab feels that al-Bakr was never more than a puppet:

> He did not really have power. The real power was with Saddam.
> He [Saddam Hussein] looked handsome. People liked him. He wore
> nice clothes. He was very charming. He was very eloquent. He
> could persuade people easily. He was using lots of Quranic verses
> in his speeches. He started to visit families and ask them what they
> needed, just as 'Abd al-Karim Qasim did before. Saddam would
> help people, bring them refrigerators, televisions and so on. Al-
> Bakr was just used by the Ba'th Party. I met him. He was nice and
> humble. He looked like my father. He lost his wife and had several
> kids. He wanted somebody to play with his kids. We lived close to
> his home. I went to his house several times to play with the kids. I
> never felt scared. He liked it that my family was very conservative.

Although Zeynab was clearly distancing herself from both the revolutionary secular ideology of the Ba'th and, more significantly, the regime's repressive policies, it becomes obvious from her account that both political leaders, al-Bakr and Saddam Hussein, were charismatic figures, who were attractive to the population in different ways: al-Bakr as a 'father figure' and Saddam Hussein as a 'charming man'. Although most women would not admit to it nowadays, many of the older and middle-aged women I talked to concurred in their description of al-Bakr as being less threatening and dictatorial than Saddam. Also they often depicted Saddam Hussein as charming, eloquent, well-dressed and even handsome, particularly when they spoke about the early years of the regime. In the general context of political authoritarianism and patriarchy, it is not surprising that the lure of the 'strong man' was evident in the memories of several women I talked to. The moustache so typical of the majority of Iraqi men during the Ba'th was not only a symbol of loyalty to, or the attempt to appear loyal to, the regime, but many Iraqi women started to associate masculinity, strength and good looks with a moustache.

Yet, even the faintest sense of admiration and attraction gives way to outright hatred and revulsion when women of various ethnic and religious backgrounds recall incidents involving fear, repression, arrests, torture and execution. Zeynab's ordeal started when she rebelled against the discriminatory practices at the college she was working in. Despite Ba'thi rhetoric and indeed positive policies aimed at encouraging women's education and labour force participation in the 1970s, many women still faced traditional conservative gender ideologies and norms at home and at the workplace. Zeynab recalls:

> I was working as a lab assistant. Most of the people in the college were men. People in the top positions were men. I worked there for fifteen years and they never allowed me to go to graduate school. They all focused on men, especially in my college. The male students looked at women as second-class citizens. They thought we were not capable. It always bothered me. When al-Bakr came to the university for a visit, I told him that I wanted to talk to him in private. He could see that my feelings were genuine. He was a bit like a father. He tapped me on the shoulder to comfort and encourage me. I told him: 'I want them to allow us [the female employees] to study here.' He said: 'Fine, how many

are you?' I said: 'Fifteen.' He said: 'Fine.' That turned everyone against me. They all started to speak very badly about me. But I nevertheless entered graduate school. They had to let us in. We were only four women in the end. It was a big revolution. They really disliked it. The dean, the professors, everyone was against me. I took a place that belonged to a man. They said: 'We are sure you will fail.' But we challenged them. We did very well. My supervisor said that he was very proud of me. We gave an example to other women.

When I heard Zeynab's story, I started to understand that her apparently strong and domineering personality had been partly shaped by the struggles she had fought as a young woman working in the lab at university. Given the circumstances, it was also a man, President al-Bakr, 'the patriarch of the nation' at the time, who enabled her to break existing prejudices and to enter a profession traditionally associated with men.

After finishing her M.A. in 1977, Zeynab increasingly became subject to harassment by Ba'th Party officials at the university as she refused to become a party member while obviously being an influential figure amongst her female colleagues:

The Ba'this started focusing on me. They did not like me. They tried to force me out. They wanted me to become a Ba'thi. They were always sending me their people to put pressure on me. I asked for study leave when I saw al-Bakr the last time. But after he resigned, I got very worried.[2] I was transferred to Sulamaniyya in the Kurdish area. There was a war going on between the Kurds and the Arabs. They sent people there whom they wanted to execute. Everyone was against me in my college. The head of the Ba'this in my college – he was my neighbour – respected me; he told me that there was a conspiracy against me. He advised me to leave. He told me that they would try to kill me in Sulamaniyya, that they would send someone after me to kill me. The same night, a police truck came and they tried to get me out of bed. They wanted to take me to the police station. I refused to go. Another neighbour, an officer in the army, ordered them to leave. Then they tried to capture me while I was walking on campus. The Ba'thi neighbour came again and told me: 'You really have to leave

now!' He took me and protected me. He helped me get my paper-
work to be able to leave the country. He helped me a lot. I heard
he was killed after I left. The dean was killed as well. He had also
been trying to help me as I had worked with him for twenty years.
He knew that I was conservative and that I had never been in any
political party before. When I got out, there was a big fuss. They
interrogated lots of people.

Zeynab's story does not end there: she continued to experience
harassment and actual threats by Ba'thi students and officials while
doing a Ph.D. in the USA. Her experiences, although not necessarily
all her views and interpretations of events, resonate with the accounts
of many other women I interviewed. However, other women had
much more positive memories of the 1970s. It became obvious that
women were differently affected, depending on their social class,
political orientation or lack thereof, place of residence as well as
ethnic and religious affiliation.

The Ba'th Coming to Power

Since the 1968 *coup d'état*, the Arab Ba'th Party, ideologically rooted in a
mixture of Arab nationalism, anti-imperialism and socialism, became
officially the ruling party in Iraq. Despite the inclusion of socialism in the party's ideology, it is important to stress that the Ba'thi
interpretation of socialism had less to do with the equal distribution
of wealth than the nationalization of the economy. In fact, Ba'this
were hostile to the communist notion of class struggle, as it was
perceived to be a 'foreign' ideology threatening to the unity of the
nation (Abdullah, 2000: 166). Later, with the rise of Saddam Hussein's
dictatorship, the original revolutionary Ba'thi ideology, rooted in the
writings of Michel 'Aflaq,[3] became less and less significant.

Rather than being controlled by a political party, the regime
became a dictatorship based on a tightly knit security apparatus and
the personality cult around Saddam Hussein, his clan and family-based
inner circle, as well as networks of patronage in which privileges

were exchanged for loyalty (Tripp, 2000). Instead of following a
clear-cut party line, Saddam Hussein's speeches and policies reveal
several rather radical shifts which relate to changing economic,
political and social conditions inside Iraq but also to regional and
international developments, such as the Islamic Revolution in Iran
(1979), the Iran–Iraq war (1980–88) and the rise of the 'New World
Order' in the early 1990s. This is particularly obvious with respect
to the regime's changing attitude and policies towards women.

Initially, throughout the 1970s, the Ba'th Party established political
hegemony in all parts of the country and throughout society in general (Farouk-Sluglett, 1993: 51). It did so in the early days by controlling the main opposition parties[4] and former ministers and officials
in campaigns of terror and persecution, but also with carrot-and-stick
tactics.[5] The latter strategy led to a temporary alliance of different
groups and parties, forming a Ba'thist-led National Progressive Front
in 1973. Al-Bakr and Saddam Hussein also tried to 'Ba'thize' the
armed forces by dismissing high-ranking officers and commanders
and replacing them with Ba'th Party members and sympathizers
(Farouk-Sluglett and Sluglett, 2001: 120).

The memories of the women who had been members or sympathizers of the Communist Party at the time of the Ba'thi coup differ
radically from Zeynab's in terms of the comparison between the rise
of the Communist Party after the revolution in 1958 and the rise of
the Ba'th Party after the *coup d'état* in 1968. Dalal P., a 'retired' member
of the Iraqi Communist Party, in which she had been politically
active since the mid-1950s, became quite agitated when I asked her
about the rise of the Ba'th, when sitting in a café in West London
on a cold winter's day:

> Yes, there had been violence during the revolution in '58 and
> afterwards, but this unfortunately happens when a mob is angry.
> But the violence was limited in comparison to the atrocities com-
> mitted by the Ba'this throughout their long rule. It was clear that
> the Ba'th did not have the popular support that we communists
> had. So they had to rely on force, on arresting people, on putting

on show trials, on killing thousands who did not agree with them. While the leaders in the Communist Party were very well-educated and encouraged cultural production and expression, the Ba'this felt threatened by highly educated people and tried to control what was being published. I was working as a journalist at the time and experienced lots of harassment from Ba'this. Many of my friends were arrested and some even killed. But at the same time the Ba'th tried to get us involved in the government. That we eventually accepted was a big mistake.

Under pressure from the Soviet Union (who supported the communists' alliance with the Ba'th Party), as well as being attracted by the prospect of being able to re-emerge finally from clandestine underground activities and even exile abroad, the ICP decided in 1973 to participate in the National Patriotic Front (Farouk-Sluglett and Sluglett, 2001). Several of the women who had been active in the Communist Party during this period describe the enthusiastic outburst of activities, the building up of cadres and the writings in newspapers, such as the daily *Tariq al-Sha'b* (The Path for People) and the cultural journal *al-Thaqafa al-Jadida* (The New Culture). Yet, the various narratives also reveal increased recognition that the alliance was not an equal partnership and that Ba'this were using the credentials of the communists to gain more popular support while trying to curb the party's influence wherever possible. One way of trying to co-opt the communists and limit their power was to demand the dissolution of communist-led mass organizations, such as the General Federation of Students (*Ittihad al-Taliba al-'Amm*) and the Iraqi Women's League (*Rabitat al-Mara' al-'Iraqiya*) in favour of joint associations. The Ba'th established numerous organizations and associations for youth, students, professionals, workers, peasants and women, trying to reach all elements of society. The General Federation of Iraqi Women (*Ittihad al-Nisa'i al-Iraqi al-'Am*) became the 'female face' of the Ba'th Party, although, as I show later on in this chapter, there were occasionally tensions between the demands and expectations of 'women revolutionaries' and their male counterparts.

In general, no independent grassroots organizations were allowed, and people trying to act outside of these Ba'thi-led associations were severely punished.

By the late 1970s, it was clear that relations between the communists and Ba'this had deteriorated beyond repair as the Ba'th had tightened its grip on power, and systematically arrested, tortured and even killed communists and other non-Ba'thi activists and dissidents. Dalal, who had also been an active member in the Iraqi Women's League since the mid-1950s, found herself under growing pressure at work:

> When I was in the teacher's union, I was approached by a colleague who said that all teachers are required to attend a speech directly coming from the Ba'th Party every Thursday. All teachers should deliver the content of the speech to all their students even if they are not members of the Ba'th Party. I refused and went to the head of the teachers' union. He said: 'I might be able to accept your refusal now, but within one year all teachers should be Ba'thi.'

Dalal and many of her comrades had to flee Iraq shortly after this incident in 1978, as the clampdown on communists and other political opponents of the Ba'th became increasingly brutal and dangerous. By 1979, most of the communist activists who had not been arrested or killed had fled the country.

The majority of women I talked to had not been directly involved in any form of party-political activism. Yet simply refusing to join the Ba'th Party became a political act in and of itself and was increasingly punished by the regime. Wafaa K. who has devoted most of her life to education, was visiting Amman for a couple of weeks in June 2005. She was accompanied by Zahra M., a former colleague and friend, who, prior to her recent retirement, had also worked in the education sector for decades. Both women were contemplating whether to stay in Amman or to risk the journey back to Baghdad, as the security situation was deteriorating by the day.

When I asked the women questions about the past, Wafaa stressed that she had never belonged to any political group or party, and had just wanted to get on with her work:

> I worked as a principal in a school and every day the Ba'this put an application to join the party in front of me. Every day I threw it in the waste basket. When they held a peace summit with Sadat in Baghdad in 1978, one Ba'thi colleague accused me of not speaking about this visit more positively in front of the pupils. They made it into a big problem. I had to see Saddam. Then I was transferred to another school, demoted from principal to teacher. I appealed and had to see Saddam again. I explained the situation to him and he ordered a re-investigation of my case. But I ended up resigning anyway.

One of the strategies of the Ba'th was to gain greater broad-based support by trying to indoctrinate large segments of the population. Iraqis of all ethnic, religious and social class background were first encouraged and later pressured to become party members. At some point, in the late 1970s, it became clear that certain career paths and professions were only available to people who had officially affirmed their loyalty to the party. Teachers and headmistresses were under particular pressure, as schools were seen as one of the main sites for indoctrination of future generations.

I remember one of my cousins telling me about the various things schoolchildren had to say and do first thing in the morning: salute the teacher, salute the picture of Saddam Hussein, citing Saddam's speeches and singing patriotic songs. I was surprised at the time that my cousin was mocking the whole ritual, and I wondered how many pupils in schools were actually practising wholeheartedly the daily affirmations of loyalty to the leader, the party and the country. And how many children were just putting their heads down, doing as they were told but secretly rolling their eyes and wishing themselves elsewhere?

While control of the education system was a particular focus of the regime, there was slightly more freedom within universities than schools, especially within disciplines that were not perceived to be that prestigious. Dr Sawsan K. was extremely upset and bitter when I met her in Amman in the summer of 2005. She was still teaching philosophy at the University of Baghdad, although conditions for academics had become increasingly difficult. Of Kurdish origin, she felt particularly compelled to stress her anti-war position and her dismay with the current situation. At some point during our conversation, she burst out angrily: 'I regret having dedicated my professional life to the study of Anglo-Saxon philosophy. See what they are doing to our country!' When I asked Dr Sawsan about her first years as a philosophy professor in the 1970s, she said:

> Nobody ever interfered with what I said or what I did, and I was never reprimanded. They knew me. I was never a Ba'thi. They invited me to join and I refused. That was it! Some of my students were Ba'thi. I am surprised how much I got away with. One day, we were looking at Babylonian theatre. I asked my students sarcastically whether they thought Babylonian theatre was Ba'thi. But nothing happened. Of course, if I had competed for a position with someone who was Ba'thi, I would have been disadvantaged. But I was allowed to do my job. The main problem was that we could not go to conferences. It was a big problem for the standard and quality of our work, but we were not allowed to leave the country. You had to go through so much paperwork and requests before you got permission to leave. Their fear and suspicion was their problem. This caused the standards at university to deteriorate.

The extremely efficient and far-reaching security apparatus was the main tool for controlling and repressing the population and eliminating all forms of dissent. Yet the regime did not merely rely on force. It also used more sophisticated means to obtain support and consensus among large parts of the population. The state systematically manipulated and controlled the production of knowledge and culture, especially with respect to the 'historical memories' of Iraqis. As Eric Davis (2005) so convincingly shows, the Ba'thi ideological approach to Iraq's history and contemporary political community was based on a complex balancing act between Iraqi-centred Arab nationalism, 'Mesopotanianism' and anti-imperialism.[6] The promotion of Arab nationalism as opposed to Iraqi nationalism was a clear strategy to weaken the ideological basis of the Communist Party, which historically had been associated with the promotion of a multicultural Iraqi nationalism. Yet, by emphasizing Iraq's glorious past associated with ancient Mesopotamia, the regime managed not only to satisfy the nationalist pride of Iraqis but also to legitimize its assumed leadership role among Arab countries.

At the same time as historians, intellectuals and writers were busy with the state-imposed 'Project for the Rewriting of History' (*Mashru' l'adat Kitabat al-Tarikh*), the regime also tapped into more popular culture and took an active role in promoting Iraqi folklore (Davis, 2005: 148–75). Suad M. was one of many Iraqi women I spoke to who started to become interested in Iraqi heritage and folklore in the 1970s:

> I heard about a big crafts exhibition at the Baghdad Fair in the early 1970s. It was an annual event. Every year they would pay craftsmen from north to south to come and display their work. The exhibitions were really beautiful. The government started to document *al-turath al-Iraqi* (Iraqi heritage). They would send people to all the villages throughout Iraq to document people's culture, their customs, crafts and traditions and to bring some crafts back. My interest in Iraqi culture and folklore started there. The government really started to take an interest in reviving our culture, reviving an interest in calligraphy, in weaving, basket-making and even creating furniture from palm trees.

The regime's focus on folklore was obvious during my own family visits to Iraq in the 1970s and 1980s, although I did not understand it as such at the time. I remember visiting the Museum of Popular Heritage[7] and the Museum of Costumes several times during my childhood. The museum was often filled with schoolchildren and their teachers, who eagerly pointed to the colourful traditional costumes and various crafts on display in the museum. During a later visit in the 1980s, we went to eat in the newly restored Khan

Murjan[8] restaurant, as my relatives proudly pointed out that the building dated from the fourteenth century.

National governments and local councils all over the world invest in folkloric museums, the renovation of ancient sights, the organization of cultural festivals and the publication of glossy magazines with beautiful young women wearing traditional costume. Yet, as in other multi-ethnic and multicultural places, the Iraqi regime's interest in culture and folklore was more than an expression of pride in national heritage. It was also used to create a sense of unity, loyalty and national identity beyond ethnic and religious affiliations. Shirin S., a Kurdish woman who grew up in Sulamaniyya, but studied at the University of Baghdad like thousands of so-called *banat al-muhafithat* (girls of the provinces), recalls how she and her Kurdish friends were regularly pressured to wear traditional Kurdish costume during national holidays and particularly on *munasabat al-Baʿth* (Baʿthi events):

> Every time there was an event, they wanted us to wear Kurdish clothes and hold Saddam's picture. I said: 'I can't do that! I would feel embarrassed. I could not even hold up a picture of my father.' My professor was very angry and shouted: 'How could you compare Saddam to your father? You will face the consequences!' I was so scared. At the same time, they were propagating all these myths and lies about Kurds. One of my classmates asked me about Sulamaniyya. I told him he should come and visit one day. He said: 'I am too young to die. I was told that the Kurds are like Red Indians. They shoot everyone who comes near, especially Arabs.'

Elements of folklore, and cultural expressions more generally, were systematically used to manipulate historical memory, either to create a sense of unity or to foster feelings of paranoia, xenophobia and distrust (Davis, 2005: 6). *Asala* – authenticity – became a core concern for the regime's project of rewriting history and defining who belonged to the Iraqi nation and of creating and policing cultural boundaries (Davis, 2005: 171). Depending on the specific political and economic conditions, 'the enemy within' – the 'non-authentic'

– were Iraqi Jews, the Shi'i, the Kurds, Christians and also non-Tikriti urban middle-class Sunnis.

The Kurdish Struggle

Worried about their inability to control the Kurdish national movement militarily, the new Ba'th regime under Hasan al-Bakr initially made overtures to the Kurdish leadership and appointed three Kurdish ministers to the new government in 1968. Two ministers were associated with Mulla Mustafa Barzani and his Kurdish Democratic Party (KDP), and one minister with Jalal Talabani, who established the rival Patriotic Union of Kurdistan (PUK) in 1975. While the new regime was trying to play the two Kurdish factions off against each other, Barzani started to step up military operations. In 1969 his forces launched a bold attack on oil installations at Kirkuk, severely reducing its oil pumping facilities for ten days (Farouk-Sluglett and Sluglett, 2001: 128–9; Tripp, 2000: 199).

A military retaliation by the regime was followed by secret negotiations. In 1970 the Kurdish national movement under the leadership of Barzani's KDP signed an agreement with the Ba'th regime that recognized Kurdish rights with respect to national identity, the use of Kurdish as a national language alongside Arabic, agrarian reforms and Kurdish political participation. The agreement also stated that autonomy would be granted to areas with a Kurdish majority population, which would be established after a census was carried out. The latter point proved to be particularly controversial as the Ba'th regime did not want to give up oil-rich Kirkuk. It started an Arabization campaign, forcibly removing thousands of Kurdish families and encouraging Arab families to move north. Not trusting the regime in Baghdad, especially in light of several assassination attempts on his life, Barzani opened channels of communication with Iran, preparing for possible joint military action.

On the ground, the situation had become increasingly tense and dangerous for the Kurdish population, as Iraqi security forces had stepped up their arrests and persecution of people linked to the Kurdish movement. Although Kurdish society continued to be very conservative and tribal in nature, many women were involved in the Kurdish struggle, supporting their male relatives who were fighting by taking over responsibilities traditionally associated with men, providing logistical support, cooking for *peshmergas* (fighters), passing on secret messages, working as couriers, transporting and distributing leaflets, but also providing political leadership. Taavga A. recalls the sense of anxiety and fear linked to her elder sister's involvement in politics:

> My sister had become one of the leaders of the Kurdish freedom movement. And even my mother had been very active for the Kurdish cause. We were living in the city of Kirkuk, in one of the poorest neighbourhoods. *Al-Amn* (the security apparatus of the Ba'th regime) started to find out about people involved in the Kurdish struggle. They went around with their big moustaches and sunglasses and arrested people. In 1974, Leila Qasim, a Kurdish student who was studying at Baghdad University, tried to assassinate Saddam Hussein. Her show trial was public and we watched it on television every day. They tortured her and finally executed her by hanging. We were all scared that this would happen to my sister as well. And then, one day, they came to our alley and apprehened a woman who was about my mother's age. They drugged her and shaved her hair. They took her from house to house and asked her to identify people involved in the Kurdish struggle. She identified my sister-in-law. We knew we had to leave immediately as we would be next in line.

Twelve-year-old Taavga fled her hometown of Kirkuk with her mother, a teenage sister, her politically active sister Nisreen and a nine-month-old nephew in the middle of the night in 1974. They spent two weeks walking, riding donkeys and wading through rivers while the military confrontation developed into a full blown war:

> We were constantly hiding from fighter planes and often could only walk at night. Many villages were emptied out and destroyed by napalm bombs. People had fled over the border to Iran. We

stopped at villages trying to find something to eat. My mother was very tough with us. We were not supposed to cry. She was even reluctant to hug us as she was afraid that this would spoil us. We were scratching everywhere from the bugs that had bitten us. My baby nephew was sick with diarrhoea. When we finally arrived at the headquarters of Barzani in Haji Omran at the border with Iran, we were the only family among fighters. I was made to wear traditional Kurdish clothes, which I had never worn when I was growing up in our city Kirkuk. After a few days Barzani ordered that we had to leave to a refugee camp in Iran as we were disturbing the camp.

As it became increasingly clear that the Ba'th regime was not ready to implement the 1970 agreement, Barzani, along with some of his rival factions, confronted the government and open war broke out in the summer of 1974. More than 100,000 Kurds fled to Iran during the first months of the war. The Kurdish *peshmerga* inflicted a heavy toll on the Iraqi army, increasingly relying on Iranian military support (Tripp, 2000: 212). Despite the Iranian government's repression of its own Kurdish population, the Shah was initially eager to help the Iraqi Kurds in order to destabilize what he perceived to be a hostile regime. Yet, in what proved to be devastating to Barzani and the Kurdish resistance, secret negotiations between Baghdad and Tehran led to the Algiers Agreement in 1975.

In the Agreement, Saddam Hussein and the Shah settled the long-standing border disputes between the two countries, particularly with respect to the Shatt al-Arab. Iraq gave up its claim to the entire waterway and accepted the *Thalweg* (mid-point) as the border line. In turn, the Shah agreed to stop supporting Barzani and the Kurdish resistance, closing the border to fighters and preventing the supply of new weapons (Abdullah, 2003: 173). Without Iranian support, the Kurdish resistance collapsed almost immediately. Thousands of Kurds fled, and *peshmerga* and civilians were killed in reprisals by the Iraqi army, who created a 'security zone' in the border areas of the Kurdish region, destroying about 1,500 villages (Yildiz, 2004: 23).

'Days of Plenty'[9]

Despite indisputable political repression in the 1970s, a relatively large segment of the Iraqi population enjoyed high living standards in the context of an economic boom and rapid development, which were a result of the rise in oil prices and the government's developmental policies. These were the years of a flourishing economy and the emergence and expansion of a broad middle class. State-induced policies worked to eradicate illiteracy, educate women, and incorporate them into the labour force. Most of the women who were neither themselves nor through family links involved in any sort of political activism generally spoke about the decade of the 1970s as 'the golden age'. The initial period after the nationalization of the Iraqi oil industry in 1972 was characterized by economic hardship and difficulties. But the oil embargo by member countries of the Organization of Petroleum Exporting Countries (OPEC) in 1973, known as the 'oil crisis', was followed by a period of boom and expansion. Oil prices shot up and oil-producing countries started to become aware of their bargaining power relative to Western countries' dependence on oil.[10] Iraq's oil revenues increased from $600 million in 1972 to $8.5 billion in 1976 and $26.5 billion in 1980 (Abullah, 2003: 169).

The significant growth in revenues enabled the regime to invest heavily in the country's infrastructure: expanding the electricity grid and the water and sewerage systems, constructing roads and highways, establishing mostly free and efficient health care, building schools and universities and investing in the education and training, not only of teachers and academics but also of other professionals. Unlike most of its oil-producing neighbours in the Gulf, the Iraqi state did not rely on imported foreign skilled labour, but tried to mobilize its own human resources. With an expanding economy and labour market, the state's mobilization of the Iraqi population included the participation of women, who were perceived to play a crucial role in the development and modernization of the country.

Fedwa K. was just one of many middle-class Baghdadi women of different ethnic and religious backgrounds who appreciated the Ba'th regime for its development and modernization projects:

> I was not a Ba'thi, and I hated the regime, but at that time there was something constructive happening in the country. The education system improved tremendously. We got excellent health care. Iraq started to establish economic relations with countries like China and Turkey. By the end of the 1970s, all of Baghdad was modernized. Although the mayor was cruel, and Baghdadis hated him, he managed to make Baghdad very clean. UNESCO gave us a prize for our achievements in education, especially women's education. In the beginning of the 1970s, there was reconstruction in the north and there was peace with the Kurds. Kurdish was taught even in schools in Baghdad. You can't have a perfect situation. You have to use force to bring some good.

During my interviews with middle-class women who had not directly suffered state repression during the 1970s, I started to realize that the state didn't just rely on its coercive and repressive control mechanisms to rule the country. The regime also managed to silence dissent and even obtain people's approval by providing a prospering socio-economic context in which many Iraqi families flourished. Siham A. recalls how her family moved from a relatively modest and small home in al-Kadhmiya, a pre-dominantly Shi'i area, to al-Mansur, an ethnically and religiously diverse upper-middle-class neighbourhood. Siham's father ran a family-based construction company that had expanded rapidly in the context of the economic boom and state-led development projects. Many small businesses, companies and small-scale industries benefited from the economic policies of the state, and experienced instant capital accumulation and wealth (Farouk-Sluglett and Sluglett, 2001: 232). Siham reminisced about the 'good old days:

> We moved to a nice big house in al-Mansur in 1978. It had many rooms and the garden was so nice. I got my own room with my own bed. Before we moved, I had to share a bed with two of my

sisters. We bought new furniture, a big new fridge and freezer and a television. My parents had lots of parties at home. In the summer, my parents' friends and relatives would come late in the evening and sat in the garden until the early hours of the morning, chatting, eating, and sometimes singing. My mother was a fantastic cook, but we all used to help her. And then there was Bahira, our maid, who would chop all the onions as none of us children wanted to do that job. At the weekend, my parents would take us to the club, where I spent most of the time swimming or playing with my friend Amina by the pool. In the summer, we sometimes travelled abroad. I went shopping to London twice, and I also visited Beirut. Life was good before the war with Iran started.

Siham acknowledges that her parents and her relatives were initially very sympathetic to the new regime. Her family was just one of thousands that experienced dramatic upward social mobility through rapid wealth and became part of an expanding middle class, made up of increasingly new social groups with 'new money'. (For me, one of the symbols of this expansion was the characteristically big chest freezers which were part of the living room décor of most Iraqi middle-class families.) As a secular Shi'i family they were also hopeful that the Ba'th would not pursue sectarian policies, but enforce the stability and calm needed for economic prosperity.

Yet even during the so-called 'golden era' of the Ba'th regime, there was a darker side to economic expansion and state-led development. The Iraqi state had become dependent on a single commodity, oil, and the Iraqi population had become more dependent on the Iraqi state for its welfare, fortune and security. The nationalization of the oil sector and the centralization of other aspects of the economy resulted in a situation where people had to queue for goods despite having more cash in their pockets. Claire M., a Baghdadi women who worked for decades in the antique business, recalls the difficulties of everyday life during the 1970s:

> The government started the Great Development Programme, al-Tanmiya al-Infijariya. All these companies from abroad came to build factories, companies, hotels and so on. More and more Iraqis

managed to find work and make money. Prices were controlled. If anyone raised prices by just 10 fils,[11] they would be punished. Some people were getting rich, and lots of people were imprisoned. The foreign companies and workers were happy inside Iraq. In 1980, there were about a thousand French families working with French companies. Each community had their own school – the Indians, the French. But for Iraqis, despite the Great Development Programme, you could not easily find things in the market. You had to queue for eggs, meat, milk, because the government controlled all the trade inside as well as into the country. This had a great impact on us. We felt so humiliated having to queue for hours to fulfil our basic needs. Friends of mine had a factory which produced sanitary towels. I used to fill my car with sanitary towels and distribute them among my friends. It was quite funny, thinking about it now. Then in the 1980s, there was a big conference for all the non-allied countries in Baghdad. The government imported lots of fruits and foods, which we hadn't had for a long time. During this period, we kept on buying and buying. I used to bring boxes of fruit to my Aunt and asked her to make jam.

Claire's account of the economic conditions in the 1970s expresses her generally nuanced and thoughtful reflections. I felt respect and admiration for Claire, who was conscientiously avoiding simple truths and black-and-white depictions of the past and present. Having left reluctantly in 2004, she emphasized that she did not directly experience discrimination being a Christian or a woman. Repeatedly, she expressed a strong sense of 'being Iraqi'. Since 1973, she had been working in her father's antique business and was the only female antique dealer working in the suq (market), dealing with carpets, art crafts and various antiques:

> Through my work I mixed with people of different class backgrounds, poor and rich, I got to know the daily problems poor people face. All these people knew my father very well and respected him, so I had the opportunity to work with them on an equal basis.

In Claire's case, her father's good reputation and professional credibility allowed her to transcend prevailing ideas about what a woman should or should not do without raising too many eyebrows. However, the beginning of Claire's own career as an antique dealer took place in a context where the state also took an active interest in promoting women's participation in the labour force.

'Women – One Half of Our Society'[12]

The complete emancipation of women from the ties which held them back in the past, during the ages of despotism and ignorance, is a basic aim of the Party and the Revolution. Women make up one half of society. Our society will remain backward and in chains unless its women are liberated, enlightened and educated.... We are all – in the Party and the Government, and in the social organization – expected to encourage the recruitment of more women to the schools, government departments, the organization of production, industry, agriculture, arts, culture, information and all other kinds of institutions and services. (Saddam Hussein, 1981)

It seems hard to believe, in the light of common perceptions of the regime of Saddam Hussein, and what is known about the backlash against women's rights in Iraq today, but words such as those above were quite common in speeches delivered by members of the Iraqi regime throughout the 1970s. In the early days when the revolutionary ideology of the Ba'th still played a significant role in influencing both rhetoric and policies, the emancipation of women was central in the attempt to transform society (Joseph, 1991; Rassam, 1992; al-Sharqi, 1982). Yet, even when the revolutionary spirit was still alive, women's liberation, emancipation and inclusion had less to do with principles of egalitarianism and women's oppression (let alone feminism!), and more with the state's paternalistic attempts to widen its basis of support. In addition to creating loyal Iraqi women who were dependent on the state for the benefits associated with its modernization and development policies, women were also seen as the main vehicle for ideologically influencing future generations. In a speech delivered by Saddam Hussein in 1971, long before the war with Iran, he said: 'An enlightened mother, who is educated and liberated, can give the country a generation of conscious and committed fighters' (Saddam Hussein, 1979: 16).

Yet there were also other, more pragmatic, reasons for the mobilization of Iraqi women. Arguably the most important aspect in the period after the oil boom in 1973 was the fact that women were needed badly in the labour market. The expanding economy had led to severe labour shortages. And while the other oil-producing countries in the region mainly relied on labour migration from poorer non-oil-producing Arab or South Asian countries, the Iraqi government tapped into its own human resources. Subsequently, working outside the home became for many Iraqi women not only acceptable, but the norm and even prestigious. Educational posters and banners produced by the state would read: 'He who does not produce, does not eat', or 'He who does not work is without honour' (Rassam, 1992: 88), with the 'he' referring to both men and women.

Suma A., who continues to live in her birthplace, Mosul, recalls how it never occurred to her and her friends not to work, even after having children:

> After I finished my degree in architecture in 1978, I managed to get a job in urban planning right away. I did not have the sense that certain jobs were for men only, or that a woman should stay at home. Quite the contrary: we all had great hopes and expectations for our working lives. Within the social circle I was in, most of the young men would not have wanted to get married to housewives. They all wanted someone who was educated, had a job and contributed with a salary. There was a general feeling that the country was getting more modern and advanced and that we all needed to play our role. I continued to work after my two children were born. I had a few months of maternity leave and then left my children either in the nursery or with my mother.

The Iraqi regime actively sought out women to incorporate them into the labour force. In 1974, a government decree stipulated that all university graduates – men and women – would be employed automatically. According to Amal al-Sharqi, whose analysis and

Students at Mustansariya University, Baghdad, in the 1970s

government statistics should probably not be taken at face value, women's labour-force participation in non-agricultural sectors rose from 7 per cent in 1968 to 19 per cent in 1980 (al-Sharqi, 1982: 83–5).[13] By the 1980s, women were not only working as government employees, teachers, university lecturers and professors, doctors, lawyers and engineers, but could also be seen working on construction sites, as truck drivers, street cleaners or petrol station attendants (Rassam, 1992: 182).

Several women I talked to gave accounts of the various ways the ideal of the 'working mother' was not only widely accepted but encouraged by the state and society at large. Dr Hala, a religious woman from Baghdad, was working in a pharmacy affiliated to an oil factory in the south, when she had her first child:

I have four children: two girls and two boys. We have to tell the truth. Not everything was bad under Saddam. We got maternity leave with full salary. But the manager had to agree and sign. When I had my first boy, my boss called and said that they had no

one to cover for me in the pharmacy. I asked my boss: 'So where
shall I put my child?' He said: 'I will solve that problem.' My boss
got one of the Bangladeshi workers at the oil refinery to look after
my baby. He got a small bed for my son. I told him: 'You must be
joking!' But he was serious and this is how we solved the problem.
The worker would make the bottle, feed my baby, look after him
while I was giving out medicine to the patients. I worked two
shifts and took the baby with me both times. After about four
months, there were other women with children, so they opened a
nursery in the factory.

Middle-class women generally benefited from the double support
networks of extended families and state provisions. However, as
everywhere else in the world, some women in Iraq clearly suffered
from the double burden of having to pursue a full-time job, or even
a career, and looking after young children and a husband. Dr Sawsan,
the philosophy professor at Baghdad University introduced earlier,
found juggling between the regime's expectations about her work
and her childcare and home responsibilities difficult:

Initially we earned very little, but in the late 1970s, the government issued the Law for the Service to the Republic (*Qanun al-Khidma
al-Jumhuriya*). This required us to stay at the university for longer
hours. We received a 120–150 per cent increase in salary. But
while our physical presence was required, there were no proper
research facilities and secretaries. I would come home at five in the
afternoon and would be so exhausted. And then I had to look after
my children. My husband did not really help around the house,
so I was left with having to do the homework with the children,
cooking and making sure that everyone in the family was happy
and provided for.

Despite the fact that several women experienced stress and strain
as working mothers, the majority of professional Iraqi women I
interviewed, who are now based in the UK or the USA, said that
they had found it much easier working while having children during
the 1970s and up to the mid-1980s inside Iraq than coping with
the conditions that working women living in Western societies face

nowadays. Aside from free and extensive childcare facilities and transportation, working mothers were also heavily reliant on their extended families for sharing childcare as well as with cooking, shopping and cleaning. Many middle-class families could afford to hire a maid on a regular basis to help with the daily household chores.

In my own family in Baghdad, it was my blind unmarried Aunt Salima who helped to raise several of my cousins, and even some of their children while the parents pursued full-time jobs. My late Uncle Majid dropped off his third child, Hamid, at my grandmother's house three days after he was born in November 1975. His wife, my Aunt Hamdiya, wanted to go back to the primary school where she was employed as a social worker. Within a couple of weeks both Omi Baghdad and Amme Salima were so attached to the little boy that they were reluctant to give him up. After the death of my grandmother in 1982, Hamid continued to be raised by Aunt Salima whom he considered to be his 'Mama Salima'. And so my Amme Salima became known as Umm Hamid (mother of Hamid) by family members, neighbours and friends.

'She made me', my cousin told me, still mourning the loss of his 'mother'. 'She was so loving and caring. She always made sure I did my homework, and asked me if I had studied. Before the exams for my B.A. in engineering at university, she made a vow to God that she would fast every year for ninety days so that I would pass. And she did. For all the years until her death in 2003, even when she was sick and had to take medicine, she never broke her vow.' Several other children and babies passed through the loving hands of my aunt. Yet some of my family members also resorted to childcare facilities provided for by the state. Almost every company, factory and school had a nursery attached to its premises, and children were looked after, fed and also received regular health check-ups.

Free childcare, generous maternity benefits, transportation to and from school and workplace were all part of the regime's attempt to bring women into the labour force and ultimately to modernize and develop Iraq's economy and human resources. The prominent

vehicle for women's inclusion and participation in the public sphere
was the General Federation of Iraqi Women (GFIW) founded in
1968 shortly after the Ba'th *coup d'état*. In 1975 the GFIW had been
merged with the communist-led Iraqi Women's League in the context
of the temporary alliance between communists and Ba'this in the
Progressive National Front. It had branches all over Iraq, with an
estimated 200,000 members in 1982 (Joseph, 1991: 182). It was
initially generously funded by the regime and organized in a strict
hierarchical structure, similar to the Ba'th Party: 18 branches, one
in each province; 265 sub-units based in most important towns; 755
centres based in villages or towns; and some 1,600 liaison committees (Helms, 1984: 99). Despite the fact that the Federation was a
branch of the ruling party that lacked political independence, the
government's initial policies of social inclusion and mobilization of
human capacity did facilitate a climate in which the Federation could
play a positive role in promoting women's education, labour-force
participation and health, as well as providing a presence in public
life. The GFIW collaborated with state-run industries to train women,
with trade unions in educational and service programmes, and
with peasant co-operatives (Joseph, 1991: 182). It also participated
in implementing the law that grew out of the literacy campaign in
1978, requiring all illiterate adults between the ages of 15 and 45
to participate for a two-year period in one of the numerous literacy
programmes established by the regime (Joseph, 1991: 181).

Even some of the women I interviewed who were extremely
critical of the Ba'th regime and had suffered themselves in various
ways stressed some positive policies vis-à-vis women. Dr Hala, for
example, who had been working for a Muslim charity organization
in Baghdad under very difficult circumstances and pressures during
the Ba'th, told me:

> We were always afraid of the government. But despite the fact that
> the *Ittihad* [GFIW] was a branch of the Ba'th, they did some good
> things. Everyone remembers the phrase *Rasheed yazra* [Rasheed is
> planting]. They taught peasant women how to read and write with

examples from their own society. It was obligatory for all women of all ages to attend literacy classes. There were branches all over Iraq, including the countryside. They also opened large sewing centres across the country. They taught women how to sew and they also bought them sewing machines so that they could make a bit of income. But in their ideas and ideology the Ittihad was Ba'thi. Women would have accepted them more if they hadn't tried to get them to join the party.

Dr Hala's account resonates with the observations and the nuanced analysis of the Iraqi-born anthropologist Amal Rassam, who visited some rural GFIW centres in the 1980s. During her visits some of the achievements were clearly evident: women were instructed in sewing and other domestic crafts (Rassam, 1992: 85), and most importantly, women were taught how to read and write. Rassam describes how many women would walk a long way after a day's work in the fields to reach one of the GFIW centres, where dedicated young teachers would eagerly wait for them (Rassam, 1992: 86). However, absenteeism was a problem. When Rassam asked the teachers about the reasons for women staying away, they replied:

> their men try to stop them (i.e. the women) from coming, they do not want them to take off the two or three hours it takes daily to come here, and they claim that the women are needed at home and that at their age (these are adult women) they can do without reading and writing. We suspect, however, that they are worried about the new ideas we are putting in their women's heads. But the women are thrilled to be learning to read and write and besides it gives them a chance to get away from house chores and to relax. So it is a continuous battle, and often we have to go out in the villages and settlements and argue with the men to allow the women to come here. (Rassam, 1992: 86)

Although penalties could be imposed on those women who failed to attend or on those who hindered them, there is no evidence that men who prevented women from going to the classes were actually penalized (Joseph: 1991: 181). It is obvious, however, that the literacy campaign of the Ba'th was not merely aimed at encouraging women's

labour-force participation; education was also perceived as a vehicle
for indoctrination. The creation of the 'new Iraqi woman' and 'new
Iraqi man' required re-socialization, which mainly took place in
school, at university, in the media and in various workplaces. Adult
education was one way to reach those men and women who moved
outside state institutions and the main channels of indoctrination.
Clearly it was much easier to reach out to and recruit women when
they were part of the so-called public sphere and visible outside the
confines of their homes.

Whatever the government's motivations, Iraqi women became
among the most educated and professional in the whole region.
How far this access to education and the labour market resulted
in an improved status for women is a more complex question. As
in many other places, conservative and patriarchal values did not
automatically change because women started working. The impact
of state discourse and policies on Iraqi women varied depending on
the class background of the woman, her place of residence (rural or
urban) and her family's attitudes towards religious and traditional
values and norms. Moreover, even at its most revolutionary the
regime remained ambiguous at best or even conservative where
changes in traditional gender ideologies and relations within the
family were concerned.

As for the role of the General Federation of Iraqi Women, an
in-depth analysis by Achim Rohde (2006) of speeches and articles
written by its leading members, particularly Manal Younis, compared
to the pronouncements of senior male Ba'thi politicians, including
Saddam Hussein, reveals an astonishing level of tension and diver-
gence between the GFIW and the Ba'thist leadership. In contrast
to the common perception of the GFIW as merely a mouthpiece
of the regime, Rohde documents numerous instances in which
GFIW women insisted on adherence to women's rights and gender
equality while the regime pointed to economic and pragmatic needs.
Obviously open criticism or dissent was out of the question, but in
this most recent and detailed analysis by Rohde a more nuanced

A literacy class in 1978

picture emerges in which there is a certain space of manoeuvrability and independence.[14]

Limits to the Revolution

Before the total repression of any form of pluralism in the late 1970s, the more radical women in the Ittihad (GFIW), many of whom had originally been members of the communist-led Iraqi Women's League, demanded radical changes in the Personal Status Code of 1959, which governed marriage, divorce, child custody and inheritance, based on a relatively progressive interpretation of shar'ia. Yet the regime was reluctant, and consciously avoided being 'revolutionary' in the context of patriarchal family structures and the role of religious authorities.[15] Many Federation women advocated the secularization of the personal status laws (Joseph, 1991: 184). More concretely, women activists, such as Nasrin Nuri, Budor Zaki and Su'ad Khayri, asked the government to make the following changes:

a ban on polygyny; eliminating ambiguity in the minimum age
of marriage (stated as 'sanity and puberty' in Article 7 of the 1959
Code); outlawing forced marriage and marriage by proxy; women's
right to divorce; prohibiting divorce outside of court; prolonged
custody rights for mothers; and women's equal right to inheritance.
(Efrati, 2005)[16]

While the new Personal Status Code of 1978 failed to enact radical
change in gender relations inside the family or to curb patriarchal
power, it did take on board some of the demands of the women
activists. It widened the conditions under which a woman could seek
divorce; outlawed forced marriage; curtailed the power of extended
family members, such as uncles and cousins; prolonged the period
of child custody to the age of 10 (previously 7 for boys and 9 for
girls), which, at the discretion of a judge, could be extended to 15;
required the permission of a judge for a man to marry a second
wife; and prescribed punishment for marriage contracted outside
the court (Efrati, 2005; Farouk-Sluglett, 1993: 69; Joseph, 1991: 184;
Rassam, 1992: 90–93).

However, many women activists were disappointed that their
demands for secularization and for more radical changes in the
laws were not met. Instead, the regime combined more progressive
aspects of Sunni and Shi'i interpretation of laws and modified them
(Joseph, 1991: 184). Being careful not to alienate the large part of the
male population that benefited from the prevailing power structure
within the family, or to offend conservative religious establishments,
the regime was far more ready to engage in land reform than in
the reform of gender relations. In a speech at the Seventh Congress
of the General Federation of Iraqi Women in 1976, Saddam Hussein
reacted to the criticism that the government's legal reforms with
respect to women were lagging behind other more radical reforms:
'But when the revolution tackles some legal matters related to women
without taking a balance of attitudes to the question of equality and
its historical perspective, it will certainly lose a large segment of the
people' (Hussein, 1981: 36–8). He carefully articulated a position that

expressed commitment to changes in gender relations and greater women's rights, but that also took into consideration prevailing conservative norms and values.

Saddam's strategy did not differ much from the modernist secular regimes in other Muslim countries, most notably the Egyptian regime under Nasser, which restricted their revolutionary policies and laws to the so-called public sphere and stopped short of revolution in the 'private sphere'. Nowadays, this lack of radicalism in the sphere of women's legal rights and patriarchal norms would probably not raise eyebrows among women themselves. For even women's rights activists in most Muslim societies tend to emphasize the need to avoid alienating large segments of society and to take cultural specificities into consideration.

Even within the Communist Party, the more radical feminist women had to struggle with male authoritarianism and a patriarchal culture inside the party, as well as conservative gender ideologies in the wider society. Sawsan B., one of the older communist women, who had been active since the 1950s, stressed that despite her political activism inside the Communist Party and within the public sphere, she was still struggling with conservative notions about women's roles and behaviour when she was politically active in the 1970s:

> When I was younger it was mainly my parents who were trying to restrict my movements. Mainly because they were afraid that I would be arrested. But there were also other social pressures on us and as communist girls we had to be particularly careful to show that we were honourable and not lose our reputation. Later on when I was married and was active in various organizations in the 1970s, I still encountered some backward ideas about women. Fortunately my husband was different. He really believed in equality and we were partners in our marriage and our political life. But many other men in the party preferred for their wives to make tea rather than be leaders.

The phenomenon of leftist progressive men not extending their struggle for social justice and equality to their homes and partners is not unique to Iraq or Muslim countries, of course. Women's rights activists all over the world have lamented this trend and continue to struggle with it. Also not unique to Iraq and Muslim societies was the fact that young women who were politically active had to be careful about their reputation. Even Zeynab, with whom I started this chapter, associated lack of morality and improper behaviour with communists.

Maysoon J., who has focused on women's issues over the past two decades, recalls with slight amusement her sense of disappointment when she realized that the male communist leaders were not 'prophets but just men':

> I had some shocks in my life. When working with political leaders,
> I discovered that at the end of the day, whether intellectual or
> not, we were still just a woman and man in front of each other.
> Especially if you are pretty, they end up looking at you as a
> woman. They always put me in front, when we had events, parties
> or talks. I hated being pretty, because I did not like being used as a
> pretty face to hand over flowers and smile.

Maysoon's experience reveals not only the instrumentalization of women's looks but also the power that might come along with it. And most women would also be able to relate to the sometimes uncomfortable feeling of being made conscious of their gender no matter what the context.

For the majority of Iraqi women who were not involved in any political party or organization, struggles with conservative patriarchal values and norms mainly took place within their immediate community, family, and in the context of their marriage. Sana al-Khayyat paints a very depressing and bleak picture in her ground-breaking study of Iraqi women's experiences within the family, marriage and wider society in 1982 published as *Honour and Shame: Women in Modern Iraq* (1990). Most of the fifty women interviewed by al-Khayyat had not known their husbands before marrying and were unsatisfied with their marital life for various reasons, ranging from a general sense of being oppressed, a lack of understanding and communication, not enjoying sexual relations, to their husband's bad temper, jealousy and sometimes even domestic violence.

Many of the views and experiences quoted by al-Khayyat could probably be applied to unhappy wives in any cultural context – complaining about husbands who come home late at night, who do not talk or listen, who fail to help around the house, who spend more time with their friends than their children, who cannot stand their in-laws and do not bother to hide it. However, others are linked to notions of honour and shame that are common in patriarchal Muslim and Mediterranean societies. A woman's proper conduct and behaviour, especially in terms of her body and sexuality, affirms not only her own honour but that of her family, especially her male relatives. In other words, if a woman deviates from socially and culturally acceptable behaviour or norms, it is not only her reputation but that of her father, husband, brother or son that are at stake. What constitutes proper behaviour and conduct has varied according to social class, family background, place of origin and residence, relationship to religion, as well as political orientation. While a member of a southern tribe in the marshlands might have found it improper for a girl to go to school or mix with boys, a middle-class urban father might have drawn the line at her having a boyfriend.

Most of the middle-class urban professional women I talked to recall mingling freely with young men during their university years, studying together, going out for ice creams and walks, enjoying trips in mixed groups of young men and women having picnics or visiting ancient sights. Some, like Sawsan H., who has recently moved to Amman, even shared secret love stories:

> I did not know my husband well before we got married. He had seen me at a family function and asked his mother to speak to my parents. He was from a good family, known to my parents. He was educated and handsome, so I agreed. I ended up falling in love with him, although it took some time. During the first years of my marriage, I was still thinking about Salem, my big love.

I met Salem when I was studying in the College of Medicine. I had noticed him a long time before we talked for the first time. He was so charming and, his eyes, oh, his eyes were so beautiful. He would pass me messages through a common friend. He could not call me at home, but we managed to see each other at university almost every day. We were hardly alone, but on the few occasions, he declared his love to me and we talked about our future together. But then, when I thought that he would ask me to marry him, he decided to leave for the United States to continue his studies. He did not ask me to go with him. I would even have waited as long as it needed. At the time I did not understand, but I think that he did not want to marry a woman who had lied to her parents to be able to see him.

Several women I talked to appeared to have come to similar conclusions about boyfriends and marriage patterns. Only a few couples that fell in love during their university years ended up actually getting married. Although there are numerous reasons why couples split, the women I talked to seemed to agree that most men were eager to have a girlfriend before marriage but preferred to marry someone who had refrained from any relationship or at least had managed to keep it secret. All of the women I talked to emphatically stressed that any premarital relation never went further than holding hands or maybe a fleeting kiss.

My own family in Baghdad exemplifies the differences in marriage patterns, even within a single generation. Among my uncles and aunts there are both stories of arranged marriages and love stories leading to marriage. My eldest Uncle Salem ended up marrying the elder sister of my Aunt Hamdiya so that his younger brother Majid could marry Hamdiya, the woman he loved. This was to satisfy a widely accepted social norm that older sisters should be married before younger sisters. One of my younger uncles met his wife at university, where they fell in love and eventually got married. My Aunt Widad, on the other hand, got married to a man considerably older than her after a relative brokered the arrangement. And then there was of course my father, who pushed his luck by not only marrying the woman he loved but a non-Iraqi to boot! While my family was extremely welcoming of my German mother and did not object to my father's wish to marry her, it is clear that their reaction would have been very different if one of my aunts had fallen in love with a foreigner.

A Time of Contradictions

Women's experiences of the early Ba'th period differed not only in terms of ethnic and religious affiliation, but also, and maybe more significantly, in terms of class and political orientation. Many secular and apolitical middle-class Shi'i, Kurdish and Christian women concur in their perceptions of the achievements of the Ba'th with many of the middle-class Sunni women I interviewed. Even women who were imprisoned or had to flee as political refugees during the early 1970s or early 1980s acknowledge the positive impact of developmental modernist policies on women during that period. Historically, Iraq is not the only country in which a repressive dictatorship did initially open up certain social, economic and professional spaces for women.

For others, especially those who voiced their resistance to the Ba'th, the initial period of the new regime is remembered as a series of systematic attempts to eradicate any opposition and stabilize the regime. Political repression, mass arrests, torture and executions fill the memories of those women who were politically active themselves or had family members that were involved in opposition politics. Towards the end of the 1970s, even women who had not been involved in any political activism started to feel the pressure in terms of Ba'th Party membership.

Yet, despite the far-reaching powers of the centralized state, some women benefited more than others. For women in the countryside or women of low-income background, Saddam Hussein's speeches about women's emancipation and the passing of new, more women-friendly laws and policies did not change prevailing gender norms, roles and expected behaviour. At the same time, although limited and driven by pragmatic considerations, the Ba'th regime's policies of pushing women into the public sphere, especially the education system and the labour force, started to impact positively on some of the traditional attitudes and roles between women and men. This was particularly the case within the expanding urban middle classes. For women of the old upper and upper middle classes, education and more liberal attitudes had been part of their parents' upbringing. However, for the newer middle classes that emerged in the context of economic boom and expansion, modernization policies leading to women's greater participation in education and the workforce clashed with traditional conservative ideas about women's and men's roles and forms of conduct.

What one might coin 'state feminism' – the state's active promotion of women's rights and attempt to change existing gender relations – might prove to be problematic when the state lacks credibility among the population. By providing women with certain legal rights, social services and access to education and the labour market, the Iraqi regime tried to shift patriarchal power away from fathers, husbands, brothers, sons and uncles. The state became the main patriarch and patron of the country. Many of the middle-class men and women went along with the relatively progressive social policies of the Iraqi state as long as the economic conditions were right. Yet, among the more religious and conservative forces in Iraqi society, such as tribal leaders and Islamists, there was a strong resentment against the state's attempt to interfere in people's traditions and sense of propriety. As so often when reforms and changes are imposed from above, they prove fickle and can easily be reverted. I show in the following chapter how the Iraqi regime changed both its tone and policies towards women as soon as the political and economic conditions changed.

FOUR

Living with Wars on Many Fronts

For the many Iraqis who lived relatively unscathed through the first decade of Ba'th rule after 1968, the wake-up call came after Saddam Hussein replaced al-Bakr in July 1979. My own family had its first proper taste of the cruelty of the regime in 1979 when my Uncle Majid was arrested shortly after Saddam Hussein assumed the presidency and systematically replaced existing army officers with those loyal to him. Uncle Majid was executed in 1980, following a mock trial during which, outraged, he removed a shoe and threw it at the judge. My Aunt Salima thanked God for not being able to see with her own eyes what was going on around her, a phrase she would use many times in the years before her death. Aunt Salima became the main support and point of stability in the lives of my uncle's children.

Saddam Hussein's assumption of absolute power was heralded by increased repression, arrests and executions. For thousands of Shi'i, the crackdown came in the form of deportations to Iran; for Kurds it took the form of Arabization programmes and brutal atrocities, such as the infamous Anfal campaign, during which thousands died and numerous villages were destroyed. Furthermore, regardless of ethnic, religious and class background, people's sense of stability was shaken by the eight-year war with Iran, which Saddam Hussein started in 1980. Although all Iraqis could and did become victims of the regime, depending on their political views and affiliations, I will pay particular attention to the atrocities committed against the Kurds and Shi'i during this time, as many became victims of collective punishments. The women's accounts of this period also reveal how the eight-year war with Iran impacted on Iraqi society, especially on women and gender relations.

The Iraq–Iran War (1980–88)

> The war has been dragging its heavy feet from the day the first
> military communiqué was issued. The ages of those called up for
> compulsory military services have been extended to both younger
> boys and older men. Calls have gone out for more voluntary
> contributions. Laws forbidding travel abroad have become more
> numerous and varied. Foreign magazines have disappeared from
> the shelves in bookshops. Imported goods have been replaced by
> local produce. Pharmacies have been banned from selling contra-
> ceptive pills in an effort to increase the population and replace
> the losses at the battlefield. The television natters with promotions
> encouraging marriage and early conception. In a new trend, called
> 'mass weddings', large halls are hired out, complete with all varie-
> ties of foods and sweets. Couples are married there *en masse*. Each
> couple takes their turn at cutting the gigantic white cake, using a
> knife decorated with coloured ribbons. (Khedairi, 2001: 140)

This passage from Betool Khedairi's novel *A Sky So Close* alludes to some of the social and economic changes triggered by the long war with Iran. Increased military spending, damage to oil installations and a decline in oil exports led to dwindling foreign currency reserves and a looming economic crisis. The state reduced imports and curtailed development programmes while borrowing heavily from the Gulf states. It asked its own population to endure austerity measures, refrain from taking out large amounts of foreign currency and, particularly significant for women, to donate their possessions of gold and jewellery, which traditionally represented women's main form of economic security in times of crisis. But, most importantly, Iraqi women were asked to be 'superwomen' during the prolonged war: initially they were put under pressure to replace men in the workforce and government institutions. Soon, however, their roles became redefined from producers to reproducers, as Saddam Hussein tried to increase the Iraqi population to guarantee future generations of soldiers in his 'Qadisiya army'[1] defending Iraq and the Arab nation from the perceived Iranian threat.

Tensions had been building up between the theocratic government of Ayatollah Ruhollah Khomeini, in the aftermath of the Iranian Revolution in Iran in 1979, and the secular regime of Saddam Hussein. The downfall of the Shah and the end of the monarchy in Iran were celebrated by many people in the region and sent shockwaves through neighbouring Arab states, including the Iraqi regime. Doubting the loyalty of the sizeable Shi'i population, Saddam Hussein hoped for a quick, successful military strike against a country that appeared chaotic, weak and isolated in the aftermath of the revolution.[2] A victory over Iran would not only have limited the risk of an Islamist uprising inside Iraq but would have asserted Saddam Hussein's leadership role among Arab nations, especially the neighbouring oil-rich Gulf countries. These, in turn, supported the war, fearing the spread of the Islamic revolution in Iran to their own countries. In September 1980, the Iraqi leader announced the abrogation of the Algiers Treaty of 1975 that had regulated border disputes between the two countries. Regaining control of the Shatt al-Arab, the strategically and economically significant waterway between Iran and Iraq, was a particularly burning issue for the Iraqi regime. A series of border clashes and pre-emptive air strikes were followed by the invasion of Iranian territory. Yet, instead of a quick military victory for Iraqi troops, the invasion increased the Iranian population's support for Khomeini and the resolve to defend the revolution (Abdullah, 2003: 184–5; Tripp, 2000: 230–34).

For many of the Iraqi women I talked to, the year 1980 marks a turning point in their own histories and the history of their country, the beginning of a series of bloody wars, violence and hardship. Widad M. was working as a *muwadhafa* (government employee) in the Ministry of Health in Baghdad during the 1980s. Widad, like many other urban middle-class women I talked to, had remained relatively unaffected by the repression and atrocities committed by the regime throughout the 1970s. It was only with the onset of the Iran–Iraq war that dreams and lives started to be shattered:

> The Iraq–Iran war was the first war we really felt. In the 1970s we were hopeful. Things seemed to be looking up. We had great expectations. In the 1970s, Baghdad became international. There were so many companies from all over the world working in Iraq. The designer of Baghdad University was American. The sports centre was built by the French. But then the war started. At first we felt it a lot because of the heavy bombing, but then gradually it stopped and the fighting only continued at the front. But many many families lost someone in the war. Almost all families had a son in the army. Fortunately my son was too young to be forced to fight. For the first time, we saw black banners appearing, indicating that someone had died. There were lots of widows and orphans and the economy suffered a lot. But people could still eat. There was an understanding among people that one should not have lavish wedding parties anymore, because there were so many people dying. For a time we almost got used to this life with black banners decorating most houses. But then the government started to recruit older men as well, and my husband Ali was forced to join the people's army in 1985. He left in July and never came back. I could not even bury him as there was no body. First I hoped that he had become a prisoner of war in Iran, but after years of waiting I realized that he was gone.

The regime was desperate to recruit more men to a war that was increasingly unpopular among the population. 'Human wave' attacks from Iran – a country of overwhelming numerical superiority – were resulting in high losses on both sides. Hundreds of thousands of Iraqi men were drafted into the army after conscription was introduced. Even the educated elites, who had hitherto been spared, began to be recruited to fight in what many people believed to be a senseless war. In one incident in 1983, as several women told me, Vice-President Taha Yasseen Ramadan gathered a group of male university professors, doctors, lawyers and engineers in Baghdad, and asked for volunteers to help with the war efforts in the *Jaysh al-Sha'abi* (the People's Army). Only two people raised their hands, provoking the anger not only of the vice-president but of Saddam Hussein himself. He appeared the following day, and furiously reprimanded everyone in a fiery speech. As a punishment, 'the traitors' lost not only their Ba'th Party membership (which was not a punishment but a reward for many) but also their jobs. Far worse, however, was Saddam Hussein's immediate order for everyone to fight in the war and to be sent to the most violent battle fronts.

Among the women I interviewed, experiences of the Iran–Iraq war varied greatly. Overall, women stressed that despite the hardship, life was still more bearable during this war than in the subsequent wars of 1991 and 2003. In particular, middle-class families in cities located far from the actual front in the south experienced relatively minor disruptions in their everyday lives in comparison to later suffering. Amal G., a 60-year-old art dealer in Amman, used to own an art gallery in Baghdad:

> Just a month after I started my own gallery, a missile destroyed it. All the windows came in, but no one stole anything, nobody touched anything. It was totally different from the last war in 2003. We just put pieces of wood to cover the window for the whole year, because I could not afford to replace the windows with new glass. People were depressed, but everyone rebuilt their own homes. At the time we were not allowed to withdraw more than 100 Iraqi dinar. Some friends brought some pieces of wood and glass so I could fix the windows. People were so helpful at the time and we were hopeful that things would get better once the war stopped.

Most Baghdadi women I talked to distinctly remember the first days of the war as being particularly traumatic, as many experienced air raids and missiles for the first time in the capital. Hana A. had

stopped working as an architect for a few years to look after her
two children when the war started:

> The first two days we had air raids on Baghdad. That was very
> difficult. Then we had missiles. I used to be with my kids all the
> time, because I did not want anything to happen to them. Once a
> missile landed close to their school. You can't imagine what I went
> through until I found them safe. I used to bring them to their
> teacher for French classes in the evening and I would wait outside
> her place for two hours reading a book. I just did not want to leave
> my kids. After a while, when the air raids and missiles stopped, I
> started to be more relaxed. Life went on, although we started to
> feel the impact on the economy after a few years. In the beginning
> of the war, there were no shortages where food was concerned.
> We concentrated more on our own agriculture. They asked every
> household, even those that had only a little garden, to plant a palm
> tree and an olive tree. They checked it when they were checking
> the electricity meter. They were so efficient.

Many women's experiences of the Iran–Iraq war were over-
shadowed by the loss of loved ones; all those I spoke to recalled
having lost someone dear to them. If it was not a son, brother, father
or husband, they remembered a cousin, a neighbour or a family
friend. The women who were living closer to the front in the south
had generally a much more difficult time during the war. Leila G.,
who grew up in Basra and was a student during some years of the
war, saw her family home nearly destroyed and witnessed the deaths
of neighbours across the street during the numerous bombing raids
on the city:

> Because we were so close to the battlefields, we were bombed
> many times during that war. We had to rebuild some walls and
> the roof of our house three times. But at least we were not hurt.
> One day, I saw our neighbours torn to pieces and lying dead after
> a bomb hit their house. Both of my brothers were fighting in the
> army, so we could never relax and always worried about them. My
> father was too old, so he was working. We had a really difficult
> time. I volunteered in a local hospital to help with the injured and
> I still cannot forget the images of all these terribly injured men,

some of them with missing limbs, some of them too shocked to say anything.

Leila, like many of her contemporaries, was helping with the war effort by volunteering in a hospital. Other women I talked to concurred with Leila's description of Iraqi women stretching themselves to respond to the conflicting needs of the Iraqi state – replacing the male workforce and simultaneously engaging in procreation to increase the population:

> The Iran–Iraq war had a big effect on society. It showed the efficiency of women in a very clear way. Most of the men were fighting at the front. There was a great dependence on women. And women proved their strength and their resourcefulness. You could even see women at petrol stations or women truck drivers. They took responsibility not only for work but also for the home and the children. There was a lot of pressure by the regime for women to have more babies and for young people to get married.

Despite the millions of 'superwomen', the state shifted from its previous rhetoric and gender ideology. It moved away from propagating images of men and women working side by side to develop a modern progressive nation to images of men protecting the land assaulted by the enemy.[3] And the land was invariably represented as a female whose honour might be taken away. In the coming-of-age novel A Sky So Close, one of the fellow students of the female protagonist sings a patriotic song while sewing cotton bandages for the soldiers in school:

> My homeland said to me
> I'm your mother
> And you are my son...
> You're the soldier, a bridegroom to be
> Your friends will celebrate
> And your wedding day will be my day of feasting.
> (Khedairi, 2001: 107)

Achim Rohde, who has analysed in great depth the changes in state rhetoric and discourses about the 'ideal' Iraqi woman and man, argues convincingly that the Iraqi regime traded its earlier commitment to gender equality for internal security in the context of increasing frustration and low morale among Iraqi troops:

> The Ba'th's gendered recruitment policies during the war and their gendered war propaganda can be expected to have reinforced images of male heroism and superiority, notions of gender difference, ideals of virility and practices of male bonding among the individuals affected by them and in Iraqi society in general. (Rohde, 2006)

In other words, as men were getting fed up fighting the war, the Iraqi regime tried to boost their morale by stressing male heroism and strength, and female honour and dependence on men. These changes became particularly obvious in the late stages of the war when the Iraqi leadership had clearly distanced itself from previous calls for women's rights, reforms and equality. Women's increased participation in the public sphere to replace male soldiers coincided with the further militarization of society and a glorification of certain types of masculinity: the fighter, the defender of his nation and the martyr.

The regime promoted literature, poetry and art generously during the war period in the 1980s. At the heart of this new genre was the image of a female symbolizing the nation and men depicted as lovers ready to sacrifice their needs and desires for the good of the nation. Sexualized images of women were also used for war propaganda: 'The Iraqi press sometimes published anti-Iranian caricatures which depicted Iranian women either as helpless victims of greedy Mullahs or as their docile sex objects' (Rohde, 2006: 364). However, open letters, short stories and poems written by Iraqi soldiers and artists published throughout the 1980s also included sexualized imagery related to romantic love stories about men and women (Rohde, 2006: 354).

With respect to poetry, Fatima Mohsen (1994) has documented how the Ministry of Culture generously sponsored poetry festivals and rewarded individual poets for paying lip service to the regime's war propaganda by reviving forms of popular tribal war poetry. The language of these poems was full of references to victory, blood and weapons and its metaphors evoked images of the female virginal land that needed protection from the enemy forces which threatened to rape it. In the visual arts, the state sponsored graphic works, poster designs and huge murals engaging visually with the themes of Iraq's glorious Mesopotamian and Islamic past in a trivialized fashion (Khamis, 2001; Rohde, 2006).

Although a small number of Iraqi women were recruited into female units of the Popular Army – which numbered some 40,000 troops in 1982 – most literary and visual representations depicted women's war efforts as subordinate to those of men, who were the soldiers and martyrs (Rohde, 2006: 374). The glorification of a militarized masculinity had its equivalent in the glorification of the Iraqi mother. Women were simultaneously encouraged by the state to replace male workers and civil servants who were fighting at the front, and to 'produce' more Iraqi citizens and future soldiers. During the last years of the war, the regime launched a fertility campaign, asking every woman to bear at least five children. Initially the state attempted to address the demographic imbalance with Iran, which mobilized an enormous army of child soldiers in the war. Later the state also changed its tone and policies towards women in order to appease an increasingly frustrated male population and prepare for the return of the troops to an economy and labour market in crisis.

Zamn al-Tasfirat (Time of Deportations)

During the eight years of war with Iran, it became obvious that Iraqi nationalism largely prevailed over sentiments of sectarian solidarity among the Iraqi Shi'i population. In fact, Iraqi Shi'i made up the majority of the rank and file of the infantry fighting the war and of men dying. Despite both a degree of discontent with the regime and a level of sectarianism as a result of discrimination before and under the Ba'th regime, there was no call for a merger with Iran or for self-rule of Shi'i in the south. Instead most Iraqi Shi'i continued to stress their Arab identity and allegiance to the Iraqi nation, although not necessarily to the regime. Saddam Hussein, on the other hand, continued to fear the lack of loyalty of the Shi'i population and collectively punished hundreds of thousands by forcibly deporting them to Iran. During the late 1970s, some 250,000 Iraqis of 'Persian descent' had been deported and their property confiscated. The deportations were stepped up with the beginning of the Iran–Iraq war. During the first year alone about 40,000 Iraqi Shi'i were forced to leave their homes, and in the course of the war an estimated 400,000 Iraqis ended up in Iran (Abdullah, 2003; Tripp 2000).

Many of the Iraqi Shi'i refugee women I talked to in Dearborn had vivid memories of *zamn al-tasfirat* (the time of deportations). Suad K., a lively and vivacious mother of three, followed her father and husband to Iran in the mid-1980s, fleeing the increasingly threatening security forces of the regime one night with two toddlers and an eight-month-old baby. She explained to me how a tactic of draft evasion during the Ottoman Empire[4] had been deployed by Saddam Hussein against many people:

> In Ottoman times, they [the Ottoman administration] established a system of who was Ottoman and who was not. Those who did not want to fight in the army, asked for a Persian identity certificate (*tabaiya*). Many Shi'i managed to avoid the draft at the time by not getting an Ottoman *tabaiya*. But Saddam said that all Iraqis of Persian origin were traitors and could not be trusted. They were pulling people from their beds and taking them to the border with Iran. These poor people could not even take spare clothes, or money or anything. My father was deported to Iran in 1979. My parents did not send me to school because they were afraid, because of the *tabaiya*.

After the collapse of the Ottoman Empire, Iraqis were given the choice to declare either an Ottoman or a Persian origin in a census taken in 1921. Those who declared themselves of Persian origin did not have to send their sons to the army. Many Shi'i families declared themselves of Persian origin in order to evade the army draft. As political tensions with Iran became more intense, Saddam Hussein started to turn against his own population and engaged in numerous waves of deportation of Iraqi Shi'i who did not have Ottoman nationality certificates.

Despite the regime's literacy programmes and push for girls' education, Suad's parents avoided sending her to school for fear that the family's 'Persian origins' would be discovered when formally registering in a school. Eventually, Suad's father was deported despite this precaution. Not having had any formal education, Suad got married in 1981 when she was only 16. Her story reveals that the regime's modernist and developmental policies of women's inclusion with respect to education and labour-force participation did not reach everyone.

Iraqi Shi'i with Persian *tabaiyas* were especially vulnerable to allegations of disloyalty and deception towards the Iraqi nation-state in the context of Saddam's Qadisiya campaign – a reappropriation of a historical battle in which Arab Muslims were victorious over Persians. History books, magazines, newspapers articles, poems and other cultural productions all stressed Iraqi and Arab cultural superiority, the evil intent of everyone Persian, and its corruptive influence on Arab Muslim civilization (Davis, 2005: 183–90). In 1982 a law was passed offering financial awards to men divorcing their Iranian wives (Abdullah, 2003: 189).

Among the innumerable heart-wrenching stories of deportation, many stood out for the hardships endured, the despair and humiliation suffered, feelings of homesickness, anger and sheer disbelief. The story of Khadija L., a retired dentist, is not the most upsetting in terms of hardships endured, but very moving in terms of a woman's resolve, enthusiasm for her work and resourcefulness. I met Khadija one afternoon in Fatima's home in Dearborn. Fatima had kindly offered to introduce me to some of her friends. Khadija had brought some old photos and mischievously asked me to identify her among a group of university students in the mid-1950s. Young, unveiled and in fashionable clothes, she looked rather different from the modestly dressed and veiled old lady in front of me. However, her smile was still as winning and youthful as in the old photo and I had no problem recognizing her. Pleased with this, Khadija told me the story of the photograph:

> I, my brother and two male cousins were forced to leave in 1980. When I left, I had no ID, no luggage, nothing. When I was kicked out of my house and deported to Iran, they [the government] locked up my house. My sister-in-law and one of my sisters climbed through one of the windows and recovered some of my personal belongings and brought them to a neighbour. The neighbour said that she would keep everything for a long time, even for ten years. Imagine, I went back last year, after twenty-four years, and she still had all my things in a bag. She cried when she saw me and said that she had been waiting for me all these years. My house had long been sold to someone else. I did not even dare to go and see the owners. When I looked inside the bag I found this photograph of me and my classmates. I did not even recognize myself at first. I was too shocked and moved by the whole situation, going back, seeing my neighbour and not being able to go to my old home.

Many of the women who visited Iraq after the fall of the regime in 2003 told me of their mixed feelings at finally seeing again the country they still called home, and the grief of not being able to return to their previous houses, as they had been confiscated and sold by the government. I wondered how any future government would deal with the issue of property if a reasonable level of security and stability were to be re-established; thousands of Iraqi Shi'i would start claiming back their property in which other families have been living for decades.

Dr Khadija's voice was trembling when she remembered her first night on Iranian soil:

> First the Iraqi soldiers took us to the border. We were very scared that the Iranians would shoot us. We felt that this was the end.

There was a big open space and we started to walk. After a little
while, we saw someone waving from the mountains. Many people
came. We could not communicate, because they did not speak
Arabic. But there were some other Iraqis who had been expelled
earlier on. They told us that there were tents nearby. At that time,
I could not say one word. None of us could say anything. We
were all in shock. It was April and it was already very hot during
the day. The area was open, like a desert. Yet at night, I shivered,
thinking that I must have a fever. None of us talked, so we did not
realize that we were all shivering because of the extreme cold. All
four of us lay on the floor. No one told the other what they were
feeling. We could not open our mouths. We could not accept what
was happening to us. The next night we got more blankets, but
whatever we did it was still very cold.

Khadija, unlike Suad, had not only received an excellent education
but had excelled at her job as a dentist. She radiated enthusiasm
and passion as she told me in great detail about her work. Having
to leave it and become an unemployed refugee in Iran was almost
unbearable for her:

We did not try to interfere with the government. I was never
involved in politics. I just enjoyed doing my job. I was one of the
first graduates in dentistry in 1958. I worked in a governmental
hospital and was employed by the Ministry of Health. I really liked
the work both in the governmental hospital and in the private
clinic where I worked later on. I liked dealing with the patients.
I was mainly doing fillings. The machines were not very good so
one really had to use physical strength at the time. I had to use
all my force. I did not complain, but I was working really hard.
In 1977, they selected me for a WHO [World Health Organization]
scholarship because I was so good at my work. This is despite my
being Shi'i. I went to England for one and a half years. I arrived
back in Iraq in 1978. I really enjoyed my studies and the stay in
England as well. But then we were forced to leave. When I went to
Iran, there was nothing in my hands to prove that I was a dentist.

Khadija's resolve, determination and professional skills enabled her
eventually to pick up her profession and practise dentistry in Iran,

before eventually moving to the USA via Lebanon. Other women had to endure ongoing poverty and hardship living as deportees in exile. But they were often better off than those who stayed behind in Iraq.

Thousands of apolitical Shi'i suffered because of their so-called 'Persian origins'. Yet the harshest treatment was saved for members or sympathizers of Islamist underground organizations, such as the Dawa Party, which are now part of the Shi'i alliance in government. In 1977, al-Dawa and other Shi'i Islamist organizations used the occasion of the demonstrations linked with the religious festival of Ashura to express their resentment against the secular government. Over 30,000 people took the security forces by surprise when their prolonged demonstrations against the repression of religious authorities and the government's networks of patronage ceased to be religious in nature (Tripp, 2002: 216). Troops were dispatched to Najaf and Karbala', and some 2,000 people were arrested (Farouk-Sluglett and Sluglett, 2001: 198). In the aftermath of the Islamic Revolution in Iran in 1979, al-Dawa organized numerous anti-government rallies and carried out a series of assassinations and assassination attempts of top Ba'thi officials. A severe crackdown followed, with hundreds of arrests, and a new law making membership of al-Dawa punishable by death, as the Iraqi regime feared the spill-over effect of the Islamic Revolution on its soil.

According to Hamdiya H., another Dearborn resident who fled Iraq in the mid-1980s, membership in the underground organization became increasingly difficult:

> I was a member of the Dawa Party and I was wearing a hijab. The culture was secular at the time. Wearing the hijab was a sign of resistance, a challenge to the regime. I was afraid of the regime, of neighbours, family, friends... If you were not a member of the Ba'th Party, you were in trouble. Back in the 1960s and 1970s, they accused you of being communist. Later on, in the 1980s, they accused people of being Islamists.

In June 1979, Ayatollah Muhammad Baqir al-Sadr, the spiritual leader of al-Dawa, was put under house arrest, provoking solidarity and anti-government demonstrations in Najaf, Karbala', Kufa and the Shi'i-dominated poor neighbourhood of Madinat al-Thawra in Baghdad. Nearly 5,000 people were arrested as the most violent security agents put down the protests (Tripp, 2000: 220–21). After an assassination attempt on Tariq Aziz in early April 1980 at Mustansariya University, allegedly by an Iranian, Ayatolla al-Sadr and his sister Bint al-Huda were executed in Baghdad (Farouk-Sluglett and Sluglett, 2001: 200). Sumayya R., an activist within the Shi'i community linked to the Kerbala Education Centre in Dearborn, had been a student of Bint al-Huda – the spiritual female leader of al-Dawa.

When I met Sumaya, she was surrounded by a number of young women who were all extremely respectful and admiring of her. It soon became obvious that the extent of Sumaya's suffering was unique even in the context of a community where most people had endured hardship in various forms. I asked the group of around six women about their views of de-Ba'thification and whether they thought it was right that people, amongst them doctors, engineers and various other technocrats, who had not held senior party positions, had been ordered to quit their jobs by the Coalition Provisional Authority, under the leadership of Paul Bremer. While the young women started to discuss this question, offering different views, Sumaya got quite agitated and insisted that all Ba'this were criminals. When one of the younger women questioned her view, stating that many people had only been nominally members and had not committed any crimes, Sumaya disagreed, offering her own experience as evidence.

Sumaya's husband, an Islamist political activist within al-Dawa, was killed by security forces at Baghdad University. When her husband was killed, Sumaya was one month pregnant with her second child. According to Sumaya, her husband's body was dissolved in a chemical solution in front of his colleagues, who were forced to watch. A few days later, she was arrested and tortured. To make sure

I believed her horrific story, Sumaya showed me some of her scars
on her head, her shoulders and arms:

> I had to have my shoulder blades replaced. They beat me, and hung
> me by the hair. They hit me with a cable that had iron inside. I
> thought people would die quickly when they are beaten, but we
> humans are strong. I was a student of Amina Sadr, also known as
> Huda Bint Sadr. I am the only one of her students who survived. I
> managed to get out of prison. Imagine, they used a woman's naked
> body as an ashtray and would put out their cigarettes on her body
> in front of religious prisoners. For all these reasons, I say that all
> members of the Ba'th Party are criminals. People did not have to
> join. They became complicit in these crimes by joining. In prison,
> we were 500 teachers from universities from all over Iraq. Do you
> think there was one Sunni among them?

Listening to Sumaya and seeing her scars in front of me, I could
not even imagine what she must have gone through. Yet she was
not a mere victim, but was full of life: she had re-married, had two
more children, continued her education and was working on another
postgraduate degree while being extremely active within the Shi'i
community in Dearborn.

It became clear to me during my encounter with Sumaya and
other members or sympathizers of Shi'i Islamist parties, like al-Dawa,
that their specific experiences and suffering were more related to
their political activism and membership of an underground organization rather than plainly being Shi'i. Most Shi'i women I talked to
were much less radical in terms of their views about Ba'th Party
membership, acknowledging that for a majority of Iraqis membership
had been more of a formality, and a necessity rather than a matter
of conviction. I was quite shocked by the extent of the sectarianism
expressed by Sumaya and other Islamist Shi'i women, directed
mainly at Sunnis but also at other religious and ethnic groups, such
as Iraqi Chaldeans and Kurds. The suffering of the Kurds was hardly
acknowledged in my interviews with members of Islamist parties,
while other non-Islamist Shi'i appeared to be much more ready to

acknowledge the plight of the Kurds and the atrocities committed against them by the former regime.

The Anfal[5] campaign

During the 1980s, the Iraqi government pursued its Arabization policies in the Kurdish region, forcefully moving Kurdish families and encouraging Egyptian and Iraqi Arab families to take their place. Another strategy by the regime to attack and infiltrate Kurdish society was to offer Iraqi Arab men an equivalent of £1,000 at the time to marry Kurdish women (Cobbett: 189: 132).

Veyan K., who left Iraq in the early 1990s, has been torn on the question of whether to return to Iraqi Kurdistan or not. With teenage children who are happily growing up in London, she finds it difficult to weigh her own homesickness and patriotism against the happiness of and opportunities for her children. Veyan herself was a teenager in the period following the collapse of the Kurdish resistance in 1975:

> We returned to our village close to Irbil after having spent some months in Iran as refugees. I remember how everyone was so depressed. My mother kept wailing, grieving because of the departure of Barzani, who had fled to the USA. People had put their hopes and lives in his hands. For me it was really difficult as we switched in school from Kurdish to Arabic. I failed some of my exams during that first year as my Arabic was not good enough. Our teacher was a Ba'thi and she was very strict with us. She did not want us to speak Kurdish in class although we all had been taught in Kurdish before. There were always Saddam's soldiers and security people threatening everyone and making us feel insecure. The only positive thing during that period was that we were less poor. The government built better roads, schools and hospitals and there were more jobs. More girls started to go to school and even to university. Our living standards improved but we were still living in fear.

The heavy investment in Kurdish infrastructure and economy was part of the regime's overall strategy to develop and modernize the

Kurdish women *peshmerga*

country and 'buy' people's loyalty. But it was also a means to divide
and rule, as the state's system of patronage benefited some Kurds
more than others. By the end of the 1970s, the KDP had managed
to regroup with Barzani's son Mas'ud taking over the leadership. Yet,
tensions with Talabani's rival Patriotic Union of Kurdistan, which was
more popular among urban Kurds, led to internal feuds and even
armed conflict. For years, this internal struggle continued, not only
weakening Kurdish resistance to the regime but causing death and
destruction among the Kurdish civilian population.

After initially focusing his attention on the war with Iran, Saddam
Hussein became more concerned about the north after the KDP and
PUK managed to end their feud and enter into an alliance in 1985,
enabling more effective military operations against the Iraqi army.
Saheena J., whom I met in El Cancun, a largely poor immigrant
community outside San Diego, recalls how she and other Kurdish
families moved to hide in the mountains after 1985. As mentioned

in Chapter 1, Saheena's brother had been fighting as a *peshmerga* and was wanted by the government. Saheena recalls:

Some years before, Saddam's soldiers had stormed Qushtapa, close to Irbil, and took all the men, even teenagers, with them. My father and my two elder brothers were in the mountains but two of my younger brothers were taken away. My mother tried to hide them in the house but the soldiers searched everywhere, breaking down doors, smashing up the furniture. Our house was destroyed three times. We fled to mountains. We lived there for four years. These mountains were controlled by Kurdish *peshmerga* from Turkey. We had no schools, no radio, no television. We had to cook, clean and wash all day. It was like old times. We washed clothes in the river. We had to move every single day to avoid being bombed. Moving became part of our lives for four years.

Despite the incredible hardship endured by Saheena, she and her family managed to escape the even more horrific fate experienced by thousands of Kurds who became victims of the regime's war of eradication from 1987 to 1989. As Kurdish insurgents had been receiving military and financial support from Iran, the Iraqi government retaliated brutally. The most notorious episode in this systematic killing of Kurds was the 1987–88 Anfal campaign, nominally a counter-insurgency operation but in reality a carefully planned and executed programme of ethnic cleansing in which between 50,000 and 200,000 people are estimated to have been killed, most of them men and adolescent boys.[6] Thousands of Kurdish villages were systematically destroyed, and more than a million and a half of their inhabitants deported to camps with no water, electricity or sewerage. Others were executed on their way out of the villages.

Under the leadership of Ali Hasan al-Majid, a cousin of Saddam Hussein, the Anfal campaign has been associated in particular with the use of chemical weapons, including mustard and nerve gases. One of the most notorious attacks took place in the city of Halabja on 16 March 1988. Approximately 5,000 civilians died on that day alone and thousands suffered horrendous injuries. Many people were covered with horrible skin eruptions, others went blind and suffered severe neurological damage. Long-term effects have included various forms of cancer, infertility, and congenital diseases. According to one woman I talked to, Kurdish men have been reluctant to marry women who originally came from Halabja, fearing infertility and genetic mutations.

Numerous images were circulated in the media at the time: civilians lying motionless on the street, dead and twisted bodies, mothers clutching their children and babies, trying to protect them from the deadly poison. Agiza, an 8-year-old survivor of a chemical attack in August 1988 (Anfal VIII) close to the picturesque mountainous region of Bahdinan, was looking after the family's livestock above her village when she saw planes dropping bombs, one of which exploded close to her house:

> It made smoke, yellowish-white smoke. It had a bad smell, like DDT, the powder they kill insects with. It had a bitter taste. After I smelled the gas, my nose began to run and my eyes became blurry and I could not see and my eyes started watering too.... I saw my parents fall down with my brother after the attack, and they told me they were dead. I looked at their skin and it was black and they weren't moving. And I was scared and crying and I did not know what to do. (McDowall, 2000: 359)

Although Kurdish men were the primary target in the Anfal campaign, many women and children also died as a result of the widespread and indiscriminate use of chemical weapons. In some regions, especially those in which Iraqi troops met armed resistance, large numbers of women and children were among those killed in mass executions. Tens of thousands of women, children and elderly people were deported to camps and forced to live in conditions of extreme deprivation. Children suffered from malnutrition and diarrhoea and many died as a result of the harsh conditions.

According to various human rights reports, rape was one of the weapons used against Kurdish women during the Anfal campaign.

Sexually abused women suffered not only through the actual crimes committed by Iraqi soldiers and security forces but also had to endure being the source of of the family's and the Iraqi nation's 'shame'. Some women who survived the atrocities committed by the regime became the victims of honour killings by family members and fellow Kurds (Mojab, 2000: 93).

In accounts of the hardship and struggles endured by Kurdish women, I was struck by the apparent contradiction between, on the one hand, the extreme conditions endured by families, forcing women and men to challenge traditional gender roles and relations, and, on the other, the survival of strong tribal and patriarchal norms and structures. I discussed this issue with a group of Kurdish women in El Cajun. Runak M., who has been working for a Kurdish Human Rights Centre, shared the following experience:

> For us Kurds, a girl's or a woman's freedom very much depended on social class and particular family background. I was 11 when we fled to Turkey. My family never told me to cover up and wear the headscarf. If I had wanted to go to school, my family would have been OK with that. But because my brother was a *peshmerga*, we had to move to the mountains, so I did not get much formal education. But I knew many women who were very much restricted. Society was very conservative. Some women had to eat after their husbands ate. Some parents did not allow their daughters to go to school. Some parents forced their daughters to marry someone they did not even know. I heard several stories of young women committing suicide by burning themselves. And we also had problems with honour killings.

Although the two major political parties, the KDP and the PUK, recruited women into their military and political ranks and established their own women's organizations, their measures were mainly cosmetic and did not actually help the case of Kurdish women, according to Kurdish academic Shahrzad Mojab (1996: 72–3; 2000: 90). In contrast, the independent Women's Union of Kurdistan, established after the Anfal campaign (not to be confused with the KDP-related Kurdistan Women's Union established in 1957), did help vulnerable women deal with their trauma and also promoted women's rights (Mojab, 2003: 24). It is been obvious that in Kurdistan, just as in many other nationalist and separatist struggles, women's rights and women's equality have been sidelined in favour of the fight for independence.

Militarization and Gender Roles

During the eight-year period of the war with Iran, there was a shift in state rhetoric and government policies vis-à-vis women and gender relations. Perhaps more than before, women were needed by the state to keep the country running as endless thousands of Iraqi men fought and died in the war. Women carried the conflicting double burden of being the main motors of the state bureaucracy and the public sector, the main breadwinners and heads of households but also the 'mothers of future soldiers'. At some point the regime's ambivalent position towards women – as educated workers and mothers of future citizens – tipped towards the latter role as both the ideological climate and pragmatic needs changed.

Women were increasingly used to demarcate boundaries between communities and carry the heavy burden of honour in a society that became more and more militarized. Women's patriotic duty shifted to being the producers of loyal Iraqi citizens and future fighters. Their bodies became progressively the site of nationalist policies and battles. During the war, a series of legal decrees were introduced to control women's marital and reproductive freedoms. In December 1982, the Revolutionary Command Council (RCC) issued a decree forbidding Iraqi women to marry non-Iraqis; another prohibited Iraqi women married to non-Iraqis transferring money or property to their husbands as inheritance (Omar 1994: 63). At the same time, Iraqi men were encouraged to divorce their Iranian wives, while Iraqi Arab men were encouraged to marry Kurdish women as part of the regime's Arabization policy in the north. During this period, Islamist and Kurdish women were again tortured and sexually abused, not only humiliating the women but also 'dishonouring' their male relatives.

Having listened to the numerous heart-wrenching stories, I was painfully reminded about the complacency that existed in the 1980s with respect to the atrocities of the regime. When the horrific pictures of Halabja circulated in the media, for example, there was at the time very little reaction, not even condemnation, by the international community, particularly on the part of world leaders. Saddam Hussein was still perceived to be on the right side of the equation, containing the Islamic Revolution that started in Iran in 1979.

Many Iraqis, especially those living in central and southern Iraq, felt very hopeful when the war with Iran ended on 20 August 1988. Celebrations on the streets of major cities and towns lasted for days. My Aunt Salima was overjoyed to be able finally to have all 'her boys' safely back at home, as two of my older cousins had been part of the million-strong army. I remember noticing that my cousin Huby, who had always been great fun during my childhood visits, returned home looking aged, serious and depressed after years of fighting in the war. It soon became obvious that things would not just go back to the 'good old days' of economic boom and generous state provision. Iraq's foreign debts were reckoned at between $100 and $120 billion. The estimated cost of reconstruction stood at over $452.6 billion (Abdullah, 2003: 190). Meanwhile oil prices had declined, and the bill for imports, especially food, had increased. The demobilization of thousands of troops pushed up the unemployment rate, and a general sense of frustration and unrest among the population grew by the day.

Women were often at the receiving end of the frustration felt by the returning Iraqi troops. Many came back depressed, injured and without jobs, seeing that their wives were not only competently running the family home but also working and earning a salary. There were incidents of jealous husbands accusing their wives of having taken advantage of their prolonged absence to have affairs with Egyptian migrant workers. During the Iran–Iraq war, many Egyptians worked in the public sector, helping to fill the gaps left by civil servants, farmers, and other Iraqi workers who were fighting at the front. After demobilization, there were a number of incidents of violence by Iraqi men against Egyptian migrant workers, but also increased incidence of domestic violence. However, the majority of women and men just wanted to settle back into a more peaceful life, making ends meet, bringing up their children, visiting their friends and relatives, enjoying big meals and trying to forget the years of hardship. Little did they know that worse was to come...

FIVE

Living with War and Sanctions

Trying to combine an increasing inquisitiveness about my Iraqi family, their lives and my own roots with a newly found enthusiasm for women and gender studies, I decided to write my M.A. thesis on the impact of the Iran–Iraq war on women's status in Iraq. In July 1990, I flew to Baghdad, accompanied by my supportive father who was not too sure what to think about my planned research project. It took no more than three days for me to realize that I had been naive. Discussions with friends and family and sympathetic professors at Baghdad University convinced me that no serious research was possible under a regime that controlled not only the media but also the wider production of knowledge and culture. I might have got away with doing informal interviews with close friends and relatives, enough to gather material for my dissertation, but I was worried about the possible consequences for my relatives in Iraq. Whatever my findings, they would have diverged from the official government rhetoric on the war with Iran, gender relations and wider social issues. So instead I spent my time visiting relatives in Baghdad and seeing the ancient sights in Babylon, Samarra, Najaf and Karbala'.

Little did I know that the course of events would in any case render my project impossible. On 2 August 1990, my father and I were back at Baghdad airport, as planned. We watched planes taking off to Amsterdam and Amman, but our own plane to Frankfurt never made it. Some 15 minutes before it was scheduled to depart, a menacing voice announced over the loudspeakers that the airport was closed and that Iraq's borders were sealed. 'Dicke Luft!' or 'thick air': my father used the German expression for trouble ahead without realizing that in the small hours of that day, the Iraqi army had invaded Kuwait. Neither did we know that during the night two of my cousins had been pulled out of their beds by military police, and sent to Kuwait, where over 100,000 Iraqi soldiers backed by some 700 tanks formed the invasion force.[1]

The ensuing period, when my father and I were stuck in Iraq, constituted the longest ten days of my life. Yet we were extremely lucky: we managed to get out by bus via Jordan during a 48-hour period when the border was open, one of only a handful of buses and taxis that managed to leave the country. Many others who had been visiting during that summer ended up staying for much longer, being used as hostages by Saddam Hussein in his negotiations and bargaining attempts with the United States and other international governments in the run-up to the Gulf War in 1991. And how infinitely more lucky we were in comparison to my relatives, who had to stay put, once more living through the horrors of war; only this time 'the front' was not far away, and nightly bombing affected civilians throughout the country.

The experience of those ten days evokes for me two distinct images of my Aunt Salima. The first image is my blind aunt moving her head backwards and laughing despairingly as one of my cousins and I describe to her what we were continually seeing on television: Saddam Hussein riding a white horse, waving to the masses in slow motion, as he used to do, with the caption stating 'Iraq and Kuwait – one family and one history.' There were times when Aunt Salima felt sad at not being able to watch the television, especially when Egyptian movie stars and famous singers were on. But this was certainly not one of those moments. In early August 1990, just a few days after the invasion of Kuwait, Iraqi television was, once again, given over to military marches and music, as well as various depictions of Saddam the warrior. My Aunt, as everyone else I talked to at the time, was very upset about the invasion, fearing that the tenuous peace following the ceasefire with Iran was over. And she was particularly worried about the lives of all the young male members of the family, especially the two cousins who had been forced out of their beds during the night of the invasion.

The second image that comes to mind relates to a later visit in 1997: Aunt Salima is sitting on a sofa, surrounded by children and other aunts and uncles of mine. Everyone's gaze is focused on several boxes and their contents, which are spread out on the carpet in the middle of the living room. Two boxes contain medicines: no specific medicines, anything that well-meaning pharmacists in a small town called St Tönis in Germany could spare. Watching my relatives look at the various pills, potions and creams as if they were candy and chocolates left a strong and disturbing impression. Only my Aunt Salima seemed to keep her cool; this despite the fact that she had been diagnosed with breast cancer a couple of years earlier, followed by a mastectomy but not much in terms of chemotherapy as the drugs she needed were in high demand. She was caressing and calming one of the new babies in the family, while everyone else hoarded away as many medicines as possible without provoking the anger of the others. Painkillers, sleeping pills and anti-depressants were particularly popular, but in this situation of scarcity, after seven years of sanctions, any medicine would do for any condition that might arise at some point.

The other boxes were full of second-hand clothes donated by our neighbours and friends in Germany. Over the years, I would often see my trousers, skirts and blouses being worn by one of my numerous younger girl cousins. It always left me with mixed feelings: a sense of satisfaction that my clothes had ended up with relatives who appreciated them, and a sense of shame that I was able to buy and wear stylish new clothes while my relatives had to struggle to make ends meet. Over the sanctions period, as my father collected and sent numerous boxes of second-hand clothes and medicines, as well as cash, to my relatives in Baghdad, Aunt Salima took responsibility for making sure that everything was distributed fairly. A pecking order of family members was in place determining who had the first choice, but often my aunt made sure that her friend, the impoverished widow next door, or someone in need living in the neighbourhood, would also benefit from the boxes and money sent by the 'lucky brother' who had made it to Germany.

Financial or material support by relatives in the diaspora often made the difference between merely surviving on the monthly food rations handed out by the government during the sanctions period and living a life without having to sell all one's belongings, including furniture and books. In a way, a division became apparent between those Iraqis with relatives abroad – even the poorest of them would try to help with whatever means available – and those without support from the outside world. Yet, more crucially, Iraqi society became divided between the majority – comprising all ethnic, religious and class backgrounds – who suffered to various extents from the combined effects of dictatorship and the most comprehensive sanctions regime ever inflicted on a country, and a small group, either part of or close to the regime, who not only managed to continue to live well but even succeeded in enriching themselves. Walking through the streets of Baghdad in the 1990s, I was shocked by the level of poverty – men, women and young children begging on the rubbish-filled streets and many others living in obviously destitute circumstances. At the same time, one could see villas and palaces being built in neighbourhoods like al-Mansur, which, according to my relatives, belonged to a new class of nouveau-riche war and sanctions profiteers.

The accounts and memories of the Gulf War in 1991 and the sanctions period (6 August 1990–22 May 2003) by the Iraqi women I talked to reveal some of the suffering and hardship endured by the majority of Iraqis during that period. In addition to portraying the widespread poverty, destroyed infrastructure and withdrawal of state services, the stories told by women also give insight into the profound social and cultural changes that accompanied shifting economic and political conditions. Women not only suffered in gender-specific ways; women and gender ideologies and relations were in fact at the centre of social and cultural change during this period of extreme economic hardship.

The 1991 Gulf War

At the time of the invasion in August 1990, my Aunt Salima was not alone in strongly condemning this act of aggression, albeit only in furtive whispers out of fear from the Mukhabarat (secret service). Yet, it was also clear that there was not much love lost between Iraqis and the neighbouring Kuwaitis, who allegedly kept oil prices low by exceeding their OPEC export quotas and who were accused by Saddam Hussein of illegally pumping oil from Iraqi wells close to the border. There also seemed to be a more general deeply felt resentment against the rich oil-producing Gulf countries, which were keen for Iraq to fight against Iran in the aftermath of the Islamic Revolution in 1979 but which did themselves not suffer the human losses or cope with the consequent economic crisis. Years later, in the aftermath of the 1991 Gulf War and the economic hardship brought about by economic sanctions, I often heard Kuwait and Kuwaitis being blamed in part for the suffering of Iraqis, even among those who sharply criticized the regime of Saddam Hussein. Stories of Kuwaitis or Americans being the instigators of the looting in 2003 form part of a widespread conspiracy theory that sees all bad and evil as rooted outside of Iraq.

However, several of the women I interviewed made a point of mentioning their linked shame and embarrassment regarding the invasion of Kuwait and the looting carried out by Iraqi soldiers. Although sensationalist media stories about Iraqis throwing hundreds of premature babies out of incubators in Kuwaiti hospitals proved to be propaganda eagerly picked up by US politicians and the media

selling the Gulf War to the American and international public,[2] there
is no doubt that Iraqi soldiers and officers engaged in the systematic
vandalizing of public buildings and spaces, as well as the looting
of shopping malls, factories, museums and hospitals. Dr Hala, a
middle-class Baghdadi pharmacist, was working for the Ministry of
Health in 1990. She recalls:

> The problems really started after the invasion of Kuwait. I was
> working in one of the biggest storage places for drugs in Al-
> Karrada [a quarter in Baghdad]. I remember when they brought
> the drugs from Kuwait in big lorries. They brought them from
> different medical centres. I felt very ashamed. They shuffled the
> medicine out of the lorries. I felt it was *haram* [forbidden, morally
> wrong]. Medicine is for all people not just for Iraqis. But we had to
> arrange the drugs in our storage rooms. Much of it was new drugs
> and we did not even know what to do with them.

Sitting with Dr Hala during a hot afternoon in July 2005 on the
terrace of a modest hotel in Amman, I was moved by the integrity
and honesty of this woman who must have been about the same
age as me. There were worlds between us: Dr Hala was spending
a few days of respite from the daily struggles and fears linked to
the occupation, having attended a workshop on the constitution in
the Jordanian capital. Her long coat and white, tightly worn hijab
revealed a rather strict interpretation of Islamic dress code. Yet
we connected, following a degree of initial mutual cautiousness.
One of the points that struck me most about Dr Hala was that
she genuinely tried to translate into her daily life and political
convictions the beliefs and ideals she saw rooted in Islam, such as
charity, generosity, justice and equality. Being of Sunni background,
she stressed on numerous occasions the importance of Iraqi unity
while also acknowledging that Iraqi Kurds and Shi'is had been
singled out as groups by the previous regime. Dr Hala quit her work
for the Ministry of Health a couple of years after the invasion and
took employment in a small pharmacy, juggling work and raising
four young children.

The looting and storing of drugs and other goods took place in the context of the imposition of economic sanctions, based on Security Council Resolution 661,[3] four days after the invasion, with the aim of forcing Saddam Hussein into unconditional withdrawal of troops from Kuwait. While some women I talked to claim that the looting only started as a reaction against the sanctions, it is clear that the Iraqi government perceived Kuwait as a rightful possession that would be retained either through a puppet government or through annexation (Tripp 2000: 252). When Saddam Hussein annexed Kuwait as the nineteenth province of Iraq on 8 August 1990, and appointed Ali Hasan al-Majid, one of Saddam's closest advisers, as governor of occupied Kuwait, the US reacted by forming a military coalition of thirty-four countries with the stated aim of liberating the country.

Diplomacy and negotiations failed, or – and not only in the view of some Iraqi women – was never given its proper chance, and a six-week-long bombing campaign codenamed Operation Desert Storm started just before midnight on 16 January 1991. It involved cruise missiles, cluster bombs and daisy-cutters. Around 10 per cent of the 85,000 tons of bombs dropped in the air campaign were so-called smart bombs. Yet they were not smart enough to avoid killing thousands of innocent Iraqi civilians. Nobody knows how many civilians died in the war, but estimates for civilian deaths as a direct result of the war range from 100,000 to 200,000. Estimates for the number of Iraqi soldiers killed range from 60,000 to 200,000 soldiers – some 25,000 to 30,000 in the ground war alone.[4]

The air campaign destroyed almost the entire infrastructure of the country, including water supplies, electricity grids, factories, storage facilities, and so on. After one month of relentless bombings comprising about 116,000 sorties (Abdullah, 2003: 195), the ground war started. Rana B., a retired teacher from Mosul, lived in Baghdad during the Gulf War. As we were drinking tea in the sparsely furnished flat she and her bedridden husband had been renting in Amman since they left Iraq in 2004, she shared with me her memories of the war:

The Gulf War in 1991 was a terrible experience. Before the war, we expected that they would bomb us with chemical weapons. Each household prepared themselves for chemical attacks. We bought gas masks, food, and water. We stored as much food as possible. Many Baghdadis left the city, because they thought it would be hit. The bombing was really frightening. The shelling was so heavy. I am lucky I did not have children, because children became traumatized. We did not sleep close to a window, and not on the second floor. There was little water, no fuel. It was winter. It was so cold. We used up the fuel that we had saved. We had to bake our own bread. You could not get in touch with people in other parts of town or across the country. Young people used bicycles for transportation.

Rana became agitated when telling me about Mahmoud, a small boy in the neighbourhood who stopped speaking for months after he was traumatized by the nightly bombing. His mother was injured when the impact of a missile shattered all the windows. Rana took care of the boy for a few days but remembered feeling quite helpless, as nothing she did − jokes, toys, hugs − made him talk. Eventually little Mahmoud found his voice again, but continued to be withdrawn and constantly frightened.

Women like Rana, who experienced both the 1991 Gulf War and the invasion in 2003, would often compare the two wars, describing the horrors of each but stressing that people pulled together much more in 1991:

Baghdad was really safe: there were no robberies, there was no theft. On each street, the neighbours got together and helped each other. We had friends in al-Mansur [an upper-class neighbour-hood]. They lived next to the Mukhabarat building. The bombing was very severe, so they left for Mosul. The house was not bombed, but because of the nearby explosion all the windows and doors were shattered. The furniture was in the garden. When they came back nothing was missing from their house. No one took anything. But after the sanctions, during the embargo, things changed completely.

Several women of differing ethnic, religious and class backgrounds echoed Rana's conviction that looting was not part of the earlier war. Fedwa K., a lively, agile and outspoken woman in her early seventies who, like Rana, only left Iraq in 2004 due to increasing security concerns. A close friend of the late sculptor and painter Nuha al-Radi, whose *Baghdad Diaries* (1998) provides insightful and original perspective on the Gulf War and the sanctions period, Fedwa spent most of the Gulf War with Nuha and a group of close friends:

> We tried to help ourselves. Nuha came to me and suggested that we meet twice a week with friends to take painting lessons. It really helped us. This is also how Nuha turned from ceramics to paintings. She had problems with her hands.... Nuha's house was so beautiful. It was in an orchard with palm trees. She loved palm trees. When the war started we all moved to her house. We used to carry water to her, because she did not have access to water there. We had a good time despite everything. We were like a community living together, trying to re-create old ways of life. Nuha had vegetables in the garden.... One day I said: 'Let's have a picnic.' We put the coal on the barbecue and started cooking in the garden. Airplanes flew over our heads, but they never touched her orchard. Everyone would take turns in making dinner. One day when I was preparing dinner, I fell down and broke my nose. Nuha always laughed at me, because I never used my glasses. She had such a great spirit. We all tried to sleep on the ground floor, but Nuha never left her room on the first floor. To save petrol, we would walk everywhere. During the day, we would go to our houses. I left my house without windows, but no one took any-thing. Nobody touched the house. The morale and the people were wonderful at the time. Nuha and her friend would cycle in what was a very conservative area. Nobody touched them. They would tease them, but no one protested at seeing women for the first time cycling on the streets.

The relative safety in terms of robbery existed in the context of a repressive dictatorship that used a wide-ranging network of secret police and agents, as well as harsh punishment for those who engaged in crime, in order to keep control of the population. All

the women I talked to agreed that widespread theft and robberies
started in the 1990s due to the combination of economic hardship
and widespread poverty and the weakening of the state's iron grip
after the Gulf War.

Fedwa's eyes filled with tears when she remembered the fun spirit
of her friend Nuha, who died of cancer in Beirut in September 2004.
According to Fedwa, Nuha's cancer was the result of a combination
of depleted uranium (DU) and paint fumes. Nuha herself worried
about the effects of DU and chemical pollution on the environment.
She noted the strange plants and creatures, such as malformed
cockroaches, in her garden, and the dramatic increase in cancer
deaths (Al-Radi, 1998). As I listen to Fedwa, my eyes scan the dark
basement apartment in Amman, the third place she has lived in since
leaving Iraq. It is decorated with books, artefacts, colourfully woven
shawls, and bits and pieces of jewellery. She had left behind only a
few remnants of her belongings in her house in Baghdad, and her
passion, al-Bayt al-Iraqi, the Iraqi Cultural House. Fedwa established
the Iraqi Cultural House, a centre for Iraqi culture, artefacts and
folklore, in the 1980s and managed to expand and nurture it despite
a series of setbacks and obstacles. Remembering the days of the
war in 1991, Fedwa is quick to point out that most people had far
harsher experiences of the Gulf War than the community of artists
and intellectuals hidden away in Nuha's house.

One of the passages in Nuha al-Radi's *Baghdad Diaries* that has stuck
in my mind is her description of having to eat more food than
usual during the first days of the war in order to avoid having to
throw away large quantities. Knowing that every middle-class family
in Iraq had at least one huge chest freezer in their house, often
prominently placed in the living room, stuffed with whole chickens,
lamb, minced meat and various kinds of *kubbah* and vegetables, I could
readily imagine the feasts and huge meals being cooked in middle-
class neighbourhoods in the second part of January 1991. It was, of
course, an entirely different story for the large group of families of
low-income background, who had already been badly affected by

over five months of sanctions and did not have the means to buy and store large quantities of food.

The accounts of women of low-income background reflect the huge gaps that existed between social classes, although Iraq had a relatively large middle class in comparison to other countries in the region. The stories revolve around the hardships related to a destroyed infrastructure, a crumbling economy and the killing of thousands of innocent civilians. Yet several of the women I met stated that their fear was mixed with hope, as many Iraqis thought that the Gulf War marked the end of the brutal regime. This hope, followed by a sense of betrayal, was a continuous thread in the stories of the Shiʻi refugee women I talked to in Dearborn. Ibtesam A., for example, who was a teenager in Basra at the time of the Gulf War, expressed with bitterness her feeling of being let down by the USA:

> We hardly had anything to eat and drink during the Gulf War. It was so scary, especially at night. Everything was so dark because there was no electricity. We could hear the airplanes and bombs flying just over our heads. I would cuddle up with my mother and sisters and could never sleep during the night. But we were all hopeful and in good spirits. My mother thanked God that our prayers were finally heard and we were going to get rid of this monster [Saddam Hussein]. But then when the war finished and our people started to fight against Saddam's troops, the Americans betrayed us. They watched our men being slaughtered by Saddam's soldiers. They watched our houses being demolished. One of my cousins died and my older brother disappeared.

Ibtesam grew up in a low-income family with two sisters and four brothers. She told me that she had never seen her mother as happy and hopeful as during the weeks of the Gulf War: 'We were hungry all the time, but our mother would tell us stories and sing us songs, which made us forget our hunger for a few hours.' However, happiness and hope soon turned into grief and anger. Ibtesam's modest family home was destroyed during the regime's violent counter-attack against the *intifada* in March 1991. Iraqis had been encouraged by President George Bush Sr to rise up against the regime. After the defeat of Iraqi troops and their expulsion from Kuwait, withdrawing troops in the south triggered the uprising by Shi'i in the south. The intifada, which spread to the north, where Kurdish troops managed to take control of the entire region of Iraqi Kurdistan, lasted for about two weeks. At one point, most parts of the country, except for Baghdad and its northern surroundings, were out of government control.

The brutal suppression of the intifada by Republican Guard divisions not only resulted in a sense of betrayal by the international coalition, particularly the USA, as well as increased resentment towards the regime in Baghdad. It also heightened sectarian divisions and senti-ments. Saddam Hussein used the counter-attack against the Shi'i in the south and the Kurds in the north to fuel sectarian sentiments. One example of this was anti-Shi'i slogans painted on army tanks attacking the rebels (Abdullah, 2003: 195).

Ibtesam's experience resonates with that of several Iraqi Shi'i refu-gee women in Dearborn. Most of the women were either members or sympathizers of Hizb al-Dawa, Munadhamat Amal or the Supreme Council for the Islamic Revolution in Iraq (SCIRI). These Islamist organizations – underground at the time – got involved in the local leadership of the uprising. Ibtesam and three of her siblings escaped to Saudi Arabia a few weeks after the brutal suppression of the intifada and arrived in the USA after having spent a year in extremely harsh conditions in the infamous Rafha refugee camp set up in the desert in northern Saudi Arabia. While a mass exodus of Shi'i refugees to Saudi Arabia and Iran was under way, hundreds of thousands of Kurds, remembering the chemical attacks of the Anfal campaign in the 1980s, fled to neighbouring Turkey and Iran. Within a short period of time more than two million Iraqis were on the move in search of relative safety. Many others were not as lucky to escape and ended up in one of the many mass graves discovered after the downfall of the Ba'th regime in 2003.

The mass exodus of Iraqis and particularly the plight of Kurdish refugees pouring into Turkey paved the way for the creation of a 'safe haven' north of the 36th parallel in Iraq.[5] A no-fly zone was also established in the south, but, as no UN troops were introduced, the Iraqi government remained free to act and to kill many people involved in the *intifada*. It was after the uprising in the south that Saddam Hussein started to drain the marshes, where insurgents had been hiding (Abdullah, 2003: 195–196). Once again, Saddam Hussein had managed to survive, and during the next twelve years he continued to inflict further suffering and hardship on the Iraqi population, helped by the international community's regime of economic sanctions, which proved to be devastating.

'Destroying Our Morale'

After our lucky escape in August 1990, it took me seven years to return to Iraq. As air travel was banned during the embargo, my parents and I flew to Amman, where we spent a few days with Palestinian friends, shopping for a list of foodstuffs and household goods my relatives needed badly and that we had not been able to find in German supermarkets and stores. We were all nervous when the driver pulled up in the middle of the night. We had heard so many stories of people being robbed or even killed on that long desert road between R'weisheid, the Jordanian border crossing with Iraq, and Baghdad. We loaded our bursting bags and suitcases into the four-wheel drive, packed mainly with useful things, which in my father's view meant medicines, clothes and staple food. He refused to pack chocolates, though one of our distant relatives in London had asked him to do so: 'People are starving and don't have medicines so we can't take candy!' Retrospectively, I feel that I should have made a case for bringing a huge bag full of chocolates. My cousin Hamid admitted only recently that he and all the other kids had been desperate for sweets and chocolates during the sanctions period, and that they were always hoping that the boxes sent by my father or the luggage accompanying us would carry some: 'I always dreamt of becoming the director of a chocolate factory when I grew up', Hamid told me.

We arrived in R'weisheid just as the sun was rising. That day
there was not much traffic, just a few cars and trucks. The border
crossing comprised a couple of sheds, run-down military buildings
and an empty duty-free shop. Like everyone else we had to undergo
a compulsory HIV test at the border. Being worried about the risks
of reused needles, as all medical equipment was in short supply,
we had brought our own disposable syringes. We all knew that
Iraqi authorities did not have the means actually to test the blood
samples for HIV. The cost of the test, $50, was merely a source of
hard currency.[6] The threat of the test might have also prompted many
travellers to check their HIV status before taking the journey to Iraq.
A little baksheesh (tip) convinced the male nurse administering the test
that only my father, as the male head of household, actually needed
to give blood. My mother was considered 'safe', being a married
woman whose husband's blood was taken. And with me the nurse
settled for a compromise: sticking the needle in my arm and leaving
a big bruise but not actually taking any blood.

Fortunately our journey to Baghdad was uneventful. I kept looking
out for street robbers but only saw burned-out and crashed cars and
trucks littering the sides of the road. I wondered whether these were
the result of recent accidents or, in some cases, remnants of the
Gulf War. As we entered the outskirts of Baghdad I started to look
out for destroyed buildings, but could not detect any. I am not sure
whether it was my imagination or a reflection of the changes that
had actually happened, but I felt that the whole city was covered in
a haze of dust, poverty, despair and oppression. The last I had sensed
on previous visits, but this time I was visiting not just a dictatorship,
but a poverty-stricken dictatorship.

In the early evening, after we had arrived, amidst a greeting of
laughter and tears by several aunts, uncles and cousins, I expressed
my surprise at the lack of visible destruction in Baghdad. My Aunt
Salima said: 'You know, bridges and houses can easily be rebuilt. It
will take time, but it is possible. But what they have really destroyed
is our morale, our values.' Throughout my three-week stay I heard

different variations on my aunt's statement over and over again as family members told tales of crime, corruption and the loss of values related to generosity, honesty and kindness.

At the time of my visit, Iraqis had already endured seven out of thirteen years of the severest multilateral sanctions regime in contemporary history. Sanctions froze Iraqi financial assets abroad and banned all imports and exports, except for medical supplies and, 'in humanitarian circumstances, foodstuffs' (Graham-Brown, 1999: 57).[7] According to Kamil Mahdi, the term 'blockade' more adequately describes the stringent siege imposed on Iraq: air travel was banned; sea lanes were blocked; no goods were allowed to be send in or out of Iraq, including books, magazines and journals; international banking ceased to operate; and personal and private business transfers were forbidden, and could only take place illegally (Mahdi, 1999).

Sanctions were upheld after the liberation of Kuwait through the Security Council's Cease-fire Resolution SCR 687 (3 April 1991), which linked the lifting of sanctions to various conditions: recognizing the sovereignty and territorial boundaries of Kuwait; agreeing to the payment of war reparations (estimated at over $100 billion); ending the regime's repression of its own citizens; elimination of weapons of mass destruction, monitored by a UN Special Committee (UNSCOM); and the release of Kuwaiti prisoners (Abdullah, 2003: 196; Tripp, 2000: 259). Although sanctions were officially intended to contain Saddam Hussein's power and to control his regional and domestic abuses of human rights, it was not the Iraqi regime but the majority of the Iraqi population that had to pay the heavy price. 'We think the price is worth it' were the words of former US Secretary of State Madeleine Albright, when asked on national television in May 1996 what she thought about the fact that 500,000 Iraqi children had died as a result of sanctions.[8]

In 1997, the Oil-for-Food Programme based on Security Council Resolution 986, of December 1995, had been in place for several months. The Programme was intended as a temporary measure to alleviate the humanitarian crisis in Iraq but did not substitute for normal economic activity. It allowed Iraq to export a restricted amount of oil and use part of the money raised, which was kept in a UN bank account, to buy basic goods.[9] While the Programme prevented a worsening of the humanitarian crisis and alleviated malnutrition, it did not have the capacity to solve the severe humanitarian problems of the country, which were related not only to a shortage of food and medicines but also to a destroyed infrastructure. A number of key sectors, including oil, energy, agriculture and sanitation, were in urgent need of investment, and repair. Yet the politicization and the flawed mechanisms of the Oil-for-Food Programme led to severe delays in the approval of badly needed goods, and to the inadequate funding of the Programme. Dennis Halliday and Hans von Sponnek, UN Humanitarian Coordinators for the Oil-for-Food Programme, resigned, in 1998 and 2000 respectively, to protest its shortcomings.[10]

These thirteen years of embargo had a particularly detrimental impact on women and gender relations in Iraq. Aside from the most obvious and devastating effects of economic sanctions, related to dramatically increased child mortality rates, widespread malnutrition,[11] deteriorating health care and general infrastructure, as well as widespread poverty and economic crisis, women were particularly hit by the changing social climate. State discourse and policies, along with social attitudes and gender ideologies, shifted dramatically during this period. The breakdown of the welfare state had a disproportionate effect on women, who had been its main beneficiaries.

Women's Employment

In southern and central Iraq, professional women were clearly pushed back into their homes and into the traditional roles of mother and housewife. The UNDP report of 2000 shows that from being the highest in the region, estimated to be above 23 per cent prior to 1991, women's employment rate fell to only 10 per cent in 1997.[12] Monthly salaries in the public sector, which, since the Iran–Iraq war, had increasingly been staffed by women, dropped dramatically and did not keep pace with high inflation rates and the cost of living. However, it is important to stress that while their employment in formal work decreased dramatically, women continued to be active economically and played a very important role in the increasingly significant informal sector. Whether sewing clothes, cooking food, baking cakes and pastries, cleaning houses, raising chickens, 'reading' coffee cups and concocting potions and love spells, or even getting involved in prostitution, Iraqi women had to be very creative and resourceful in order to supplement the monthly food rations and meagre salaries of those employed.

Stories of survival and coping found their way into literature. Dalal, the protagonist in Betool Khedairi's gripping novel *Absent* (2005), for example, lives in a crowded apartment building in Baghdad in the 1990s, and contemplates which 'career path' to take and how to make money in the dire circumstances. The aunt who raised her is sewing dresses to make a living. Her uncle recruits Dalal in his new business venture: beekeeping. One of the occupants of the building, Saad, employs her in his hairdressing salon to wash the hair of the dwindling numbers of customers. Her friend, the nurse Ilham, who daily watches children dying of cancer in hospital, is suffering from the disease herself. She encourages Dalal to study French and work as a translator for the UN weapons inspectors. Uncle Sami, the blind photographer, 'hires' Dalal as his scribe to continue the diary of his late wife in exchange for his old camera. And upstairs, the fortune teller Umm Mazin seems to make most money, as her services of coffee-cup reading and mixing of potions for a series of marital and family problems seem to be in great demand. Khedairi skilfully manages to imbue her writing with dark humour as her characters struggle in these difficult times, providing a window onto the everyday lives of ordinary Iraqis under sanctions.

The women I talked to either during or after the sanctions period all concurred that the sanctions have been detrimental for women's participation in public life. As with other countries undergoing economic crises coupled with high unemployment rates, the state discourse on gender ideologies and relations shifted in favour of more conservative and traditionalist norms, values and policies. Dr Hala, whose sense of embarrassment about the medicines looted by Iraqi soldiers in Kuwait I mentioned earlier, recalled how women were encouraged by the government to resign from their posts:

> In the early 1990s, I started to have serious health problems. I had hypertension. And I was constantly tired. Our salaries were just not sufficient to cover basics. It was very difficult with three children. During the sanctions period, all the ministries encouraged women to resign or retire early. If someone was sick, they could easily ask for early retirement. That is what I did: I went to a consultant and got a medical certificate, so I left the public sector and stopped working for the government, but I continued working in the pharmacy. I had my fourth child. I had to work in the morning and evening because my husband's salary was not sufficient to pay all the bills. I would take the baby in a carriage with me to the pharmacy to help my husband. Our living standard was not very high, but not low. It was in the middle, relative to the general standard of living at the time.

Dr Hala acknowledges that she and her family were relatively lucky, as the family's pharmacy allowed her to continue working and to live above the poverty level. Other women stated that they stopped working altogether in the early 1990s because their salaries were too low to cover extra costs, which emerged as the state withdrew its previous services of free childcare and transportation. Sawsan, an Assyrian woman in her later forties from the north of Iraq, had worked as a teacher in a high school until 1995. She told me when I interviewed her in London in 1999s:

> We did not feel it so much during the first years of the sanctions, but by 1994 it had really hit us. Social conditions had deteriorated. The currency had been devalued while salaries were fixed. Many women started to quit work. Some of my friends could not even afford transportation to the school. Before the sanctions, the school made sure that we were picked up by bus, but all this was cut. For me, the most important reason was my children. I did not want them to come home and be alone in the house. It became too

unsafe. And I know from my own work that schools deteriorated badly, because teachers had to quit work and there was no money for anything. So I felt that I had to teach them at home.

Working women like Sawsan suffered from the collapse of their support systems. One previous support system had been funded by the state and consisted of numerous nurseries and kindergartens, free public transportation to and from school as well as to women's places of work. The other support system was based on extended family ties and neighbourly relations, which also helped with childcare. During the sanctions period and in the context of the current occupation, women have been reluctant to leave their children with neighbours or other relatives because of the general sense of insecurity. In the 1990s, crime was on the increase. Many women reported that while they used to keep their doors open and felt secure, at least where ordinary crime was concerned, accounts of burglaries became numerous, and often involved violence.

However, economic conditions, increased crime rates and a sense of insecurity, as well as the wish to look after the welfare and education of children, were not the only factors that pushed women back into their homes. Social attitudes toward women's work had obviously changed in the 1990s. Unlike the modernist image of the 'good Iraqi woman' working side by side with men that was prevalent in the 1970s and up to the mid-1980s, the ideal and idealized woman became the housewife and mother, who should stay away from degrading work and mixing with the opposite sex. Umm bait muhtarama, the respectable housewife, replaced the educated working woman as the proper Iraqi female. Certain types of profession, such as pharmacist, doctor and teacher, remained socially acceptable, yet became less and less attainable for women in the context of competition by both men and women over scarce jobs.

Yasmin Husein shows in her in-depth research on the impact of economic sanctions on women and gender relations that alongside the changing constructions of femininity, masculinities also shifted: the ideal man was no longer merely the educated but also the provider

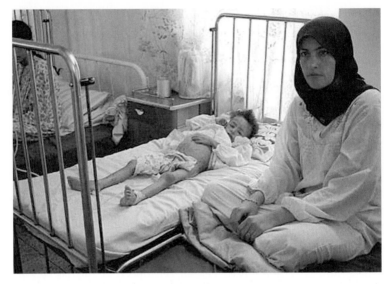

Medical care under sanctions

who could ensure that his wife did not have to leave the house to work (Husein, 2005: 107). Yet some women, especially younger ones, tried to resist social pressures to stay at home and continued to work despite the low salaries. Surah, a 39-year-old library assistant was unmarried and living with her family in al-'Adhamiya, one of the oldest residential areas in the east of Baghdad:

> For my family, my work at the university has no value now. It is better for them that I leave my job. I have to be careful to avoid a confrontation with them about this issue. The ultimate response to any problem is always that I have to give up my job. I really don't blame them. My family knows well that I go to work just to keep myself busy and communicate with other people outside the house. There is nothing more to it than this. All my female colleagues face the same problem, but there is a worse problem than that. We are witnessing a new 'culture' that tends to impose more restrictions on women, everywhere and for everything, so women are going to become totally dependent, economically and emotionally, on men. (Husein, 2005: 106)

While some women of middle-class background managed to continue work either to supplement the salary of their husband or to get out of the house and mix with people, for many women marriage was seen as the only way out of dire conditions at home. Instead of dreaming of becoming a doctor or a lawyer, more and more young women started to dream of finding a rich husband, preferably someone who would take them to live abroad.

Education

When Yasmin Husein interviewed young women in 2000 and 2001 in Baghdad for a study we jointly carried out on the everyday lives of Iraqi teenagers, few girls she talked to were still holding on to the idea of upward social mobility and opportunities linked to education – an ideal that had been prevalent when their mothers were growing up. The 16-year-old Leila, for example, was clearly aware of the depressing future prospects with respect to jobs, career paths and salaries. Nevertheless, she stressed the importance of education:

> I know the salaries are so low and would probably not be sufficient to cover the basic food needs of a small family for a week. But it is my ambition in life to become a civil engineer. In my family we have been taught to respect education. It is almost a sacred thing for us. My father and my mother are educators and, although they had to give up their jobs as teachers due to the low salaries, I still believe that their attitude towards education has not changed. My father has worked so many extra hours as a taxi driver in order to pay for my private lessons. And my brother, who is only two years older than me, is now studying economics, and at the same time helping my father driving the taxi. He has the same support by my parents even though as an economist he would receive less salary than a civil engineer. I mean, the salary is not an issue here. But I also believe and hope that the situation in Iraq will change in the near future and that life will be back to normal. (Al-Ali and Husein, 2003: 41)

Notwithstanding Leila's optimism where education and the future are concerned, many others we interviewed were clearly in doubt that, given the circumstances, education would help. Moreover, the education system itself has been the subject of much anxiety. During the 1990s, there was a sharp reduction across the board in numbers of girls and young women in education due to the fact that many families were unable to afford to send all of their children to school. Umm Majeed, a widow from al-Thawra, a poor Shi'i neighbourhood in Baghdad, known nowadays as Sadr City, told me that she had to choose which of her four children she would send to school: 'I could not afford to send all of them, since clothes and shoes were too expensive. I also needed some extra hands at home, so I sent the two boys and let the girls stay at home. Girls will be provided for, inshi'allah, once they get married.' Many girls had to engage in earning income in the informal economy in addition to taking on more household responsibilities. Some were forced to join the growing numbers of the hitherto unknown phenomenon of street children, surviving through begging and petty theft, and in some cases through prostitution.

Illiteracy, drastically reduced in the 1970s and 1980s, rose steadily after the Iran–Iraq war and grew between 1985 and 1995 from 8 per cent to 45 per cent. In the late 1990s, 55 per cent of women aged 15–49 years were illiterate,[13] and the drop-out rate for girls in primary education reached 35 per cent according to the United Nations Development Fund for Women Report of 2004.[14] UNICEF estimates that more than 50 per cent of schools in the south and centre of Iraq were unfit for teaching and learning: 'Schools are not being maintained and repaired and experience severe shortages of basic school supplies, classroom furniture, textbooks and teaching aids' (UNICEF, Iraq Donor Update, 11 July 2001). Several of the teenagers Husein talked to in 2000 and 2001 endured very difficult conditions in school, with walls crumbling and desks falling apart. Frequently, cardboard covered broken glass in the windows, library shelves were mostly bare, and children sat on cracked floors to read. Paper and pencils were often unavailable and textbooks were generally outdated.

The lack of adequate investment in teacher training, and in teaching and learning materials, seriously affected the overall quality of education. Teachers' salaries were grossly inadequate. This grim situation prompted increasing numbers of qualified teachers to leave the sector in search of better-paid jobs (UNICEF, Iraq Donor Update, 11 July 2001). Many teachers dropped out of the education sector altogether, especially in poor neighbourhoods, where teachers were unable to supplement their incomes with private lessons. Samira, 14 years of age at the time Husein interviewed her, was clearly distressed about the situation:

> This year, I had to take many private lessons because some teachers at our school so suddenly left the school. And we were stuck at school without receiving many classes this year. So it was absolutely necessary to have private teachers in order to complete the curriculum of many subjects, such as physics, mathematics, and chemistry. We had to study other subjects, such as geography or English, on our own (Al-Ali and Husein, 2003: 43).

Private lessons became an essential part of a pupil's education, and those who could not afford them tended to fail their exams. Some teenagers who were interviewed reported that their parents took over the role of teaching them, as many educated Iraqis no longer trusted the school system to provide an adequate education for their children. Yet, despite the poor secondary education available to Iraqi teenagers, end-of-year exams continued to be extremely demanding and nerve-racking. Leila, who failed her final exams in high school, complained:

> I think every year the state exams are becoming harder and harder, because the university has a limited capacity for new admissions. On the other hand, there are increasing numbers of new students who would like to continue their education in university. This is why I think that the examinations are made intentionally hard. Admission to university is so difficult that a big number of young people, especially boys, are pressured to go for the military service. You know, when the boys are not at university, they have to do

their military service and many of these men stay in the military for the rest of their lives. (Al-Ali and Husein, 2003: 44)

For girls, failing the exams could also be detrimental, as Leila explains:

> If I am not able to complete my university degree, it means that I am going to sit at home all the time doing housework, and I will be isolated from the rest of the world. But, the worst of all is that the only option left is to get married. I would have no other things to do with my life except being a housewife. Imagine, what a future would I have then? I know some cases where the girls could not finish their education because of the same problem and they have been pressured to marry anybody, even without their consent. I also knew a girl who committed suicide after a long time of depression, sitting at home without any hope for a better future other than a marriage without love. (Al-Ali and Husein, 2003: 44)

The fear of failure in their education increased the stress levels of a generation of young Iraqi women for whom trauma, worry and anxiety were already part of the immediate experience of growing up. Despite the ongoing deterioration of the education system, Iraqis in general still value education greatly, and the sense of confidence and self of a young person is often bound up with his or her achievements in school and university. Middle-class parents, in particular, may sell all their belongings to be able to help their children through school, thereby emphasizing the continuing significance of learning and obtaining a degree.

The deterioration of the education system affected not only primary and secondary schools but also universities. Thousands of university teachers left the country seeking employment, or at least refuge, abroad. Those academic staff who stayed behind struggled with extreme conditions inside the universities as well as students who had to focus on supplementing family income rather than concentrating on their studies. I met Dr Fatima, a professor of philosophy at Baghdad University, as she spent a few weeks in the summer holidays of 2005 in Amman with her husband. She was clearly worried about returning to the university that fall, as academics have been a particular target of assassination and kidnapping since 2003. When I asked her about the sanctions period, she recalled with bitterness how her job was made increasingly impossible:

> There were no new books or journals available. Before the sanctions, we would ask for books, and as long as they were not politically sensitive we would get them. But all of a sudden, we had to smuggle books and journals into the country. Salaries dropped. There was a time when we were earning about ten dollars a month. Things started to deteriorate rapidly. People's standards became very low. My colleagues started to take bribes. Many of our students had to work. Most of them were buying and selling things and they became part-time students. Students stopped coming from the provinces as they used to. At that time prostitution really became a problem. Psychologically, the whole situation affected people's morality: 'Why do I have to starve?' Everything is permissible if it means I do not have to starve. Some of my students used to faint or fall sick because they had not eaten all day. At the end, just before the war, salaries started to rise. I do not know why they did not pay people more before.

Despite the deteriorating conditions at university, and the economic and social pressures on students, female enrolment continued to be relatively high. Not all students were as idealistic about education as Leila, who wanted to become a civil engineer. For many, it was the only alternative to sitting at home or being married off.

Family and Gender Relations

While some women were putting a great effort into their university studies to avoid being 'married off', for others marriage became the only way out of desperate economic and personal conditions at home. In the context of the ongoing economic crisis, high rates of unemployment, and the demographic imbalance between men and women, marriage patterns were affected in various ways. For a large number of women, marriage actually became an unattainable dream. Hamdiya H. was visiting her sister Fawziya in Amman when I talked to her one afternoon amidst the laughter and noises of her 3-year-old niece and 5-year-old nephew:

> It used to be considered very shameful not to get married or to be in a polygamous marriage. But among my generation, there are many women who either did not get married at all or became the second wife of someone. I know several women, my sister included, who got married to much older men who were living abroad. I have given up hope myself. I was engaged once and was very much in love. But we couldn't afford love anymore. Ahmed's family was as poor as mine and could not afford the *mahr* [obligatory gift given to the bride by the groom]. I wanted to marry him anyway, but my family refused. 'A husband has to be able to provide for his wife', my father said. I thought my life would stop. In a way it did. The only thing I am living for now is seeing my sister and her children once in a while in Amman.

Hamdiya is among the growing number of Iraqi women who, despite the increasing social pressure to get married, remain without a husband. In Iraqi society, sexual relations between unmarried men and women have been socially unacceptable, although as anywhere in the world they happen in secret. The older urban middle-class women I interviewed told me on numerous occasions that they had been able to mingle relatively freely with boys and young men at university and in social clubs, often subsequently marrying their sweethearts. Yet for their daughters, as for Hamdiya, the situation had changed drastically. Increased social conservatism and economic pressures contributed to the abandonment of previous ideals and values, including the terms of securing a 'good husband'. Instead of embodying the virtues of family reputation, love and education, the ideal husband became the man who could provide for his wife and her family (Husein, 2005: 186–9). In practice, this also meant that old notions of social class, which had been very important in terms of marriage choices, started to be blurred. Impoverished middle-class families with reputable family names and histories increasingly agreed to have their daughters marry the sons of the nouveau riche war and sanctions profiteers.

Later that afternoon, Fawziya joined us. Hamdiya was obviously distressed and had been crying. She had shared with me some of her bittersweet memories related to Ahmed, with whom she was still in love. Fawziya tried to console Hamdiya, hugging her and saying: 'My dear sister, at least you know the meaning of love.' It was Fawziya's turn to cry, and she hesitated for a while, making sure that the children were busy watching television, before telling me, almost in a whisper, about her loveless marriage: 'I had never set an eye on Hasan before we got married. My Aunt showed him my picture when he was visiting Iraq. He had been married for over twenty-five years, had three children and was living between Amman and London. His wife was sick and he wanted a young wife.' 'A pretty wife!' Hamdiya interrupted her.

Arranged marriages, often polygamous, to much older men, some-times expatriates, became a common phenomenon during the 1990s. Prior to the Iran–Iraq war, polygamy was extremely rare, largely limited to some tribal communities and childless marriages, and very much frowned upon.[15] I remember the jokes and the teasing that one of my father's cousins had to endure for being the only one in my own family and circle of neighbours and friends who was married to two wives. My late Uncle Ali had met his second wife, a Lebanese woman, while vacationing in Beirut during a summer in the late 1960s. What made Uncle Ali a particular cause of amusement was the fact that his two wives lived in two houses, separated only by a garden with a garden shed in the middle. Uncle Ali took refuge in the shed every time he had a fight with both wives. Most of the time, however, the situation was relatively calm, not least because he diligently followed the prescription of equally dividing his time, affection and attention between the two wives and families. My mother never got over the sight of the two wives playing beachball together during one of our visits.

Sanctions also seem to have taken their toll in terms of the relationship between husband and wife. Even though there are no concrete figures, it appears that the divorce rate increased substantially during the 1990s. A caseworker involved with Iraqi refugees in London reported that there was a very high divorce rate among couples who had come over from Iraq. Some 25 per cent of Iraqi refugees in the UK are either separated or divorced. A few women stated that their husbands became more violent and abusive after Iraq began to experience an economic crisis and high unemployment. Widespread despair and frustration, as well as the perceived shame of not being able to provide for the family, provokes not only depression but also anger. Women have often been at the receiving end of men's frustrations. Domestic violence, as well as street violence targeting women increased particularly during the embargo, adding new risks and dangers to the continuous threat of state violence.

Family planning became one of the many sources of tension and conflict between married couples. As stated in the previous chapter, before the Iran–Iraq war all kinds of contraception were available and legal. During the war, though, contraception was made illegal as the government tried to encourage Iraqi women to 'produce' a large number of future citizens to make up for the loss of life during the war. During the sanctions period, contraceptives were still not legally available, but many women's attitudes towards children changed because of their material circumstances, the fear of congenital diseases due to environmental pollution, especially depleted uranium, and the deteriorated moral climate. Unlike in previous times, Iraqi women started to become reluctant to bear many children, although some women aimed to have more than three children to entitle them to the early retirement packages intended to encourage mothers to return to the home and allow men to take over their jobs. Because abortion was banned, many women risked their health, and indeed their lives, to have illegal back-street abortions. The director of an orphanage in Baghdad told me in 1997 that they were facing a new phenomenon in Iraq: women were abandoning newborn babies and leaving them in the street. These babies might have been the product of so-called illicit relationships, but according to the director, they were often left by married women who just could not face being unable to feed their children.

Despite the overall strain on marital relationships, some women state that their rapport with their husbands improved. Niveen, a housewife in her late thirties says:

> My husband never did anything in the house before the sanctions. He used to work in a factory outside of Najaf. Now that he has stopped working, he helps me to bake bread and to take care of the children. We get along much better than before, because he has started to realize that I work very hard in the house.

At the same time as marriage patterns started to change, wider family relations and dynamics were also affected. Traditionally, the extended family had played a very important role in Iraqi society, representing a social, economic and emotional support network. During the sanctions period, the nuclear family became more significant in an environment where people had to fend for themselves to ensure their everyday survival, carefully guarding the limited resources available. While the shift from extended to nuclear family is often associated with a shift related to industrialization and modernization in Western societies, in the specific context of Iraq under sanctions it has often meant a loss of security and an increased vulnerability for women. 'Nuclear patriarchy' has increased women's dependency on one male provider, especially in light of the fact that the state had withdrawn its previous support (Husein, 2005: 196).

Yet for many women economic dependency on a male provider was not really the issue. The demographic cost of wars, political repression and the forced economic migration of men triggered by the imposition of international sanctions account for the high number of widows and female-headed households in Iraq. In Basra, up to 60 per cent of all households were female-headed according to the October 2003 UNICEF report.[16] The Human Relief Foundation estimates that there are approximately 250,000 widows in Iraq, although estimates in 2006 go up to 1 million.[17] But it is not only widows who found themselves without husbands, as married men went abroad to escape the bleak conditions and find ways to support their families. Other men just abandoned their wives and children, after failing to live up to the social expectations of being the provider. Whilst those whose husbands were killed in battle received a small government pension, those whose husbands died at the hands of the former regime for political reasons received no benefits and were left to fend for themselves. During the 1990s, female-headed households, rural areas and poor households experienced the highest rates of infant and child mortality.

Nidal M. is a mother of three whom I met in Dearborn. She had joined her brother and his family a few years after they left Basra in the aftermath of the *intifada* in 1991. She described the poverty and despair among people she knew in Basra, a city that was suffering not only from economic sanctions but also from the continuous wrath of Saddam Hussein:

> I remember one day when I was shopping with my mother, there was one woman who needed to buy flour. She was a widow. We had known her husband, who was killed by Saddam's soldiers during the *intifada*. No one wanted to lend her money. She was so desperate because she had several children to feed. She started shouting: 'Do you want to have sex with me so that I can buy flour?' People told her never to say that again, and they gave her money to buy flour.

Economic hardship pushed an increasing number of women into prostitution – a trend that caused much anguish in a society where a 'woman's honour' is perceived as a reflection of the family's honour. Prostitution was initially supported by the regime, which, alongside an emerging class of nouveau riche war and sanctions profiteers, made up the main clientele. However, Saddam Hussein opportunistically engaged in a national faith campaign (al-*hamla* al-*wataniyya* al-*imaniyya*), responding to a changing domestic social climate – a population increasingly drawn towards religion and social conservatism alongside an attempt to increase regional and international support among the Islamic *umma*. The government condemned prostitution and engaged in violent campaigns to stop it. In a widely reported incident in Iraq in October 2000, a group of young men linked to Saddam Hussein's son Uday singled out some 300 female prostitutes and 'pimps' and beheaded them (Amnesty International Report 2001).

The increase in female prostitution did not stop at the Iraqi border: some impoverished Iraqi women travelled to neighbouring Jordan in order to make money, often in order to feed their children. And the imposition by the government of the *mahram* escort for females leaving Iraq failed to stop this trend. This law denied Iraqi women the right to leave the country without being accompanied by a male next of kin, unless they were over 45 years old. It was introduced after the Jordanian government complained to the Iraqi government about widespread prostitution by Iraqi women in Amman.

Increased Social Conservatism

On the level of government discourse as well as within society, Iraqi women became the bearers of the honour of the whole country. They became 'potential prostitutes'. Vulnerable to temptation, gossip and a tarnished reputation, they needed to be protected and shielded. Teenage girls and young women in their twenties and thirties frequently referred to changes in patterns of socializing, family ties, and relations between neighbours and friends. Often a parent or older relative was quoted as stating how things were different from the past when socializing played a much bigger role in people's lives. Zeinab, a 15-year-old girl from Baghdad, spoke about the lack of trust between people. On the change in dress code for women and the social restrictions she and her peers experience constantly, she said:

People have changed now because of the increasing economic and various other difficulties of life in Iraq. They have become very afraid of each other. I think because so many people have lost their jobs and businesses, they have a great deal of time to speak about other people's lives, and they often interfere in each other's affairs. I also think that because so many families are so poor now that they cannot afford buying more than the daily basic food, it becomes difficult for them to buy nice clothes and things, and therefore it is better to wear the hijab. Most people are somewhat pressured to change their lives in order to protect themselves from the gossip of other people – especially talk about family honour. (Al-Ali and Husein, 2003: 46)

The fears relating to a woman's reputation may have been aggravated by the occurrence of so-called 'honour killings' during and after the sanctions period. Saddam Hussein, in an attempt to maintain legitimacy after the Gulf War by appeasing conservative patriarchal constituencies, brought in anti-woman legislation, such as the 1990 presidential decree granting immunity to men who had committed honour crimes.[18] Fathers and brothers of women who were known to have, or often merely suspected of having, 'violated' the accepted codes of behaviour, especially with respect to keeping their virginity before marriage, could kill them in order to restore the honour of the family. Despite the fact that the law was abrogated after only two months without specific reasons being given (Rohde, 2006: 236), knowledge of the existence of honour killings worked as a deterrent for many Iraqi women and teenagers. Others might have been less worried about the most dramatic consequences of 'losing one's reputation'. For educated middle-class women from urban areas, it was not so much honour crimes they feared as diminished marriage prospects.

The most obvious change that took place during the sanctions period was in the dress code of young women. Aliya, a teenager from Baghdad, was clearly unhappy about the changes:

I do think that our life was much easier and happier in the past than it is now. My father used to be so open and believe in

women's freedom. He would let my mother go out without covering her hair when they visited our relatives in Baghdad. We only
had to wear the abaya[19] in Najaf[20] because it is a holy city. A few
years ago, he started to change his attitude to many things. And
lately he has become so conservative that he thinks the covering of
the hair is not enough and demanded that my mother wears abaya
everywhere outside the home. He said that I also should keep the
covering on my hair when I go to Baghdad. I am now not even
allowed to go out in trousers outside our home. My mother and I
have to wear long skirts with a long wide shirt covering the hips
when we go outside our home.

Yet, as much as Aliya detests the imposed dress codes and her
father's new conservatism, she understands the underlying reasons.
She explains:

I know why my father is doing this and I am not angry with him.
I discussed this issue with him many times, and I really do not
blame him for this change in attitude. I think it is not only my
father who is doing this, but that it may be all fathers in Iraq. They
are doing the same in order to protect their daughters from the
risk of becoming the victims of bad rumours. (Al-Ali and Husein,
2003: 47)

Girls, especially, suffer in a climate where patriarchal values were
strengthened and where the state abandoned its previous policies of
social inclusion vis-à-vis women. In the midst of the inversion of
moral values and cultural codes, economic hardships and political
repression, more and more women and men turned to religion for
comfort. The apparent increase in religiosity became very obvious
to me during my trip to Baghdad in 1997. None of my aunts or
cousins had ever worn the hijab, and religion had never been a big
issue within the family. But during the period of embargo all of my
aunts started to pray regularly, wear the hijab and frequently mention
religion and God when talking. I personally do not put any value
judgement on increased religiosity, in and of itself. Yet, in the Iraqi
context, as with Islamization processes in other countries in the
Middle East, the turn towards religion is coupled with an increased

conservatism and social restrictions that target women specifically. And it has to be stressed that this trend was not only apparent among Muslims but also Christians in Iraq. In other words, not only has there been a growing trend towards religiosity by women, but women have also been subjected to increasing social pressures that expect and demand the expression of religious adherence. For women this often culminates in the question of whether to wear the hijab or not – the hijab being the most visible and obvious sign of religious adherence and supposedly good moral conduct.

However, two refugee women in London added another dimension to the complex phenomenon of apparent increase in religiosity when they told me that in the late 1990s they only put on the hijab to cover up their hair. Khadija, a middle-aged widow from Mosul said: 'I did not have the money anymore to dye my hair. Even henna was too expensive. And it was also difficult to afford a haircut. My sister cut my hair, and she did a lousy job. I put on the hijab to cover up my awful hair.' According to Khadija, many women were motivated more by embarrassment and the sense of shame regarding their looks than by religious considerations. This is not to play down the societal pressures and restrictions that women have been confronted with, but to show that appearances can be misleading and that there are numerous motivations behind the the hijab.

Aside from increased religiosity, one could also detect a growing tolerance of superstition and the turn to spiritual realms. Belief in spirit possession and exorcism, called zar, existed previously in certain rural areas among people of low-income background without access to higher education. But during the sanctions period, more and more women rekindled old traditions and beliefs and turned to healers, exorcists and witchcraft to deal with their physical and emotional problems. Najah R., an Iraqi social worker in West London who has cared for refugee women throughout the 1990s, expressed her shock and disbelief to me:

> It was incredible. Many of the refugee women seriously believed that someone had put a spell on them when they experienced

problems with their husbands or family or when they fell sick. One woman was convinced that she was obsessed by a spirit who caused her to have headaches and heart palpitations. Once I had to take a young woman to the doctor because her mother had given her some herbal potion that some older woman healer had given her in order that she would become more beautiful.

Prior to the sanctions, Najah had never heard stories and beliefs related to spirits and witchcraft among the women she was working with. Yet from the early 1990s onwards, spirit possession, witchcraft and a whole array of superstitious beliefs became part of many women's everyday lives, as depicted skilfully by Betool Khedairi in her novel *Absent*. Her character Umm Mazin provides solutions for everything, ranging from a lack of sexual interest on the part of husbands or their falling in love with other women, to the treatment of psoriasis, hair loss and lost virginity. It doesn't take great psychological insight to understand that stress, anxiety, depression and various neuroses become pervasive in the context of war and sanctions. Coupled with the lack of adequate health care and therapy, many women have turned in on themselves and become silent; others have turned to religion to find solace; but an increasing number have also sought help through women like Umm Mazin.

Women in the Kurdish Safe Haven

At the same time as women in central and southern Iraq were losing state support in terms of socio-economic rights, semi-autonomy in Iraqi Kurdistan allowed women to establish civil society associations and become involved in party politics. The economy started to flourish in the north and women increasingly gained employment. This is despite the fact that the Kurdish region suffered from a 'double embargo': that imposed by the United Nations on Iraq and the Iraqi government's own embargo on the Kurdish region. In the first years of the sanctions regime, poverty, malnutrition and hunger were widespread among the population. However, a combination of factors, including the distinctly different impact of the economic sanctions regime in the north, the higher per capita allocation of funds under the Oil-for-Food Programme, more efficient distribution of food and medicine through UN agencies compared to that organized by the Iraqi government, and the fact that the northern border was more permeable to embargoed commodities than the rest of the country, led to an improvement in living conditions.

Another important factor was the heavy presence of humanitarian agencies: in 1999 there were thirty-four non-governmental organizations (NGOs) in the north while in the whole rest of the country there were only eleven. Significantly, in northern Iraq the Oil-for-Food money included a cash component, while the centre and south under the control of the Iraqi regime did not receive any cash. Richard Garfield, leading epidemiologist at Columbia University, stated in 1999: 'Food, medicine, and water pumps are now helping reduce mortality throughout Iraq, but the pumps do less for sanitation where authorities cannot buy sand, hire day labourers, or find many other minor inputs to make filtration plants work.'[21] He added:

> [The northern region] receives 22.5 more per capita from the Oil for Food program, and gets about 105 of all UN-controlled assistance in currency, while the rest of the country receives only commodities. Goods have been approved by the UN and distributed to the North far faster than in the Center or South. The UN Security Council treats people in that part of the country like innocents. Close to 20 million civilians in the Center and South of the country deserve the same treatment.

In a report by the United Nations Food and Agriculture Organization (FAO) in September 2000, the different impact of sanctions on the north and the south/centre is related to 'greater resources in the North, the North has 9% of the land area of Iraq but nearly 50% of the productive arable land, and receives higher levels of assistance per person'.[22] Finally, the Kurdish region's geographical position bordering Turkey, Iran and Syria allowed for lucrative smuggling on both small and large scales.

Within this context, women became increasingly active in the expanding economy and newly emerging civil society. At the same time, women's initiatives and political participation were regarded suspiciously and were even opposed by conservative Kurdish male political actors. Kurdish women activists campaigning against widespread honour killings in the north have been subject to harassment, and a newly established women's shelter for victims of domestic violence had to close down due to political opposition. Zouzan H., a Kurdish woman's rights activist based in London, told me in an interview in the spring of 2005:

> I was one of the founding members of a new women's organization in 1991. We were campaigning against honour killings, which became very widespread in 1992 with the PUK coming to power. We were a mass organization and were very active. We had branches all over Kurdistan. In 1993, we founded the Independent Women's Organization, which was supported by the Workers' Communist Party. But both political parties, the PUK and the KDP, gave us a hard time. They really harassed us. There was even a small bomb attack on our office. Some of us decided to leave Kurdistan and to set up branches abroad.

In March 1998, the Independent Women's Organization (IWO) set up a shelter in Sulamaniyya, in response to the growth in violence against women, so-called 'honour killings' and women's self-immolations. According to reports provided by several human rights organizations, hundreds if not thousands of women became victims of honour killings, cumulating in what Sharazad Mojab (2003) calls 'gendercide'.[23] Yet, pressured by male political leaders who continually harassed and threatened women working for the shelter, it had to close down in 2000.

Paradoxically, domestic violence against women had increased since the establishment of the 'safe haven' in 1991 and the creation of an autonomous government, the Regional Government of Kurdistan, in 1992. Both factions used women and gender relations in their nationalist movements, claiming that women's oppression, including honour killings, were part of Kurdish tribal and Islamic culture (Mojab, 2004: 122). During the elections in 1992 women and men were forced to line up separately to cast their votes, although Kurdish men and women used to socialize freely in rural areas. Only 5 of the 105 elected members of parliament were women (Mojab, 2004: 119).

Peaceful relation between the two rival Kurdish parties faltered in May 1994, followed by a period of tension and internecine struggle, destabilizing the Kurdish region and leading to the deaths of thousands. In a parallel development, Kurdish Islamic groups gained influence and, sponsored by Iran, attempted to Islamize Kurdish society 'promoting gender segregation, intimidating feminists and women activists, and advocating violence against women' (Mojab, 2004: 129). The political leadership of both factions tried to incorporate patriarchal tribal leaders, using women as a bargaining chip, similar to the way Saddam Hussein tried to co-opt tribal leaders in central and southern Iraq during the 1990s.

As if sanctions were not enough…

Throughout the embargo, Iraqi women, men and children continued to be subjected to ongoing bombing campaigns by British and American forces and to political repression by the regime of Saddam Hussein. Rather than weakening the regime, the sanctions strengthened the government's hold on power as it directed the scarce resources available towards its most loyal supporters (Abdullah, 2003: 198) while using the money generated through smuggling and black-market profits to build palaces and bestow favours. It is true that monthly food rations, upon which the majority of the population depended for their survival, averted an even greater humanitarian catastrophe. However, they were also used as a political tool to control the population and punish lack of loyalty or suspected sympathy with the opposition. The state's suspicions and acts of punishment were often based on people's ethnic or religious backgrounds, with the

Shi'i and Kurdish populations constituting a particularly vulnerable target. Coupled with the regime's favouritism, this behaviour resulted in an increased sectarianism, which in the aftermath of the invasion in 2003 has flared up to levels dangerously close to civil war.

Another strategy to maintain power was to encourage tribalism and revive the power of loyal tribal leaders. This was a radical shift from Saddam Hussein's previous policies of centralization and suppression of tribal powers in the 1970s and 1980s. After the intifada of 1991, Saddam Hussein tried to co-opt tribal structures and powers to fill the gaps that were emerging in the deteriorating state structures. Patrimonial ties and patronage systems were established to ensure the loyalty of tribal leaders (Abdul Jaber and Dawod, 2003; Tripp, 2000). Women and restrictions on women's rights were used as a bargaining chip with the tribal leaders as the regime accepted tribal practices and customs, such as so-called 'honour killings', in return for loyalty. Indeed, men murdering their female relatives for reasons of 'protecting the family honour' ('ird) were routinely acquitted in the state courts, and sometimes were not even brought to justice.

Iraqis were also suffering from the chemical and radioactive pollution that had been damaging the environment since the Gulf War in 1991 (and for the Kurds in the north since the Anfal campaign in the 1980s). By the mid-1990s, it started to become obvious that the use of more than 1 million rounds of ammunition carrying depleted uranium (Ammash, 2000: 169–78) by the coalition forces during the Gulf War was having devastating long-term health effects, contributing to elevated rates of cancer, congenital abnormalities, genetic defects, infertility and various other medical conditions and symptoms. Further evidence of the dangerous levels of atmospheric pollution may lie in the 'Gulf War syndrome' experienced by US and British soldiers.[24] Women were particularly affected, not only as mothers seeing their children suffer and even die but also because women's reproductive health has been negatively affected. Several young women I talked to expressed great fear about pregnancy-related complications, ranging from multiple miscarriages and stillbirths to children born with severe impairments.

Dr Hala, who had quit her job at the Ministry of Health in the early 1990s and joined her husband in the family pharmacy, tried to help her best friend, a paediatrician in a hospital in Baghdad:

> Every time I went to hospital, I saw children with birth defects. There were many children without limbs. And lots of children suffering from cancer. We had never seen so many young children with leukaemia before. It was heart-breaking, seeing their little emaciated bodies wither away. We did not have the right medicines for chemotherapy. It was very expensive, so it was only distributed in special hospitals. Sometimes we brought it from Amman but we could not afford much of that. Even educated people were living in poverty.

It is not only depleted uranium that has had a detrimental impact on public health in Iraq. The bombing campaign of the Gulf War in 1991 resulted in the destruction of oil installations, pipelines, refineries, storage facilities, factories and so on, leading to the release of thousands of tonnes of toxic chemicals into the air, water and soil (Ammash, 2000: 172). Throughout the entire period of sanctions, Iraqis continued to be exposed to bombing campaigns, which in turn increased both the civilian death rate and environmental degradation and pollution.

Between 1991 and 1998, the weapons inspectors of the United Nations Special Commission (UNSCOM) and the International Atomic Energy Agency (IAEA) revealed the existence of nuclear, chemical and biological weapons programmes inside Iraq and destroyed tonnes of chemical agents and munitions. Yet throughout their later reports UNSCOM inspectors stated that an extensive programme of disarmament had taken place. Inspectors were repeatedly prevented from entering sites, especially those linked to presidential palaces. Meanwhile, the Iraqi government accused UNSCOM inspectors of spying, an accusation that was later confirmed by the UN as UNSCOM had been infiltrated by US agents, who passed confidential information to the US government.[25] In August 1998, the Iraqi government declared that it would cease all cooperation with UNSCOM and threatened to end all monitoring by the IAEA. This was the same month that President Clinton finally admitted in taped grand jury testimony to an 'improper physical relationship' with Monika Lewinsky. The coming months, as Clinton was struggling with a Judiciary Committee investigating whether sufficient grounds existed for his impeachment, the threat of another intensive bombing campaign was evident as UNMOVIC repeatedly tested Iraq's compliance and cooperation.

Despite the loud sabre-rattling, my parents travelled to Iraq in December 1998, a few days before the beginning of Ramadan – the Islamic month of fasting – and a couple of weeks before Christmas. With the two important seasons approaching, my parents had felt confident that they would be safe during their visit. However, only a few days after their arrival, Operation Desert Fox, the military codename for a major three-day bombing campaign, started during the night of 16 December. A day earlier, the head of UNSCOM, Richard Butler, had declared that the weapons inspectors were unable to do their job because of the regime's ongoing non-compliance and obstructionism. Although my father had half-jokingly told me before the journey to Iraq that in the worst scenario he and my mother would leave the moment the weapons inspectors were evacuated, the speed of events took my parents by surprise.

Weeks later, my mother told me how when they were driving back from a visit to one of my uncles, she saw 'all these crazy drivers racing along'. She complained to my father about the chaotic way and speed of people's driving. I can imagine her facial expression and tone while she was complaining, and my father was probably shrugging his shoulders, replying defensively. My Uncle Jaffar, on the other hand, who was behind the steering wheel, had to drive very slowly as his car was in the process of slowly falling apart like so many other cars during the embargo. Only when they arrived home did my parents realize that the drivers racing through the streets of Baghdad that night were trying to reach their houses before the bombing started. My parents spent the following nights with other relatives, including several children, in the basement of the home of one of my father's cousins. I spent sleepless nights in London, following the news on BBC and CNN, trying to phone my parents. During the first night, after I had tried for over three hours to get through to my parents, with the phone lines either busy or dead, I finally reached my father. As I cried on the phone, fearing for my parents' lives, feeling quite helpless sitting in London, my father tried to calm me down: 'It is nothing. We are fine. Don't worry! We hardly feel anything.' Meanwhile I could hear the sounds of missiles and bombs over the phone line as my father had to shout louder and louder to make himself heard and calm his panicking daughter.

My mother, who was born in Germany in 1940, had flashbacks during and after Operation Desert Fox of memories related to World War II. She described to me how scared and disturbed the children of the family were when cowering next to their mothers in the dark basement during the bombing raids in 1998. If my mother remembers more than fifty years later the bombing she experienced as a 4-year-old girl in Germany, one can only guess at the extent of the psychological damage and trauma of the children caused by the continuous bombing campaigns in Iraq. Once again, my parents were infinitely luckier than my relatives, being able to leave the country safely while everyone else had to face growing economic hardship, more oppression and further bombing over the coming years.

It was shortly after my parents' departure from Iraq at the end of December 1998 that the health of my Aunt Salima started to deteriorate seriously. We did not know if the cancer that had been diagnosed years before had spread to her lungs, or whether she was suffering from a severe and prolonged lung infection. By 2001, my father started trying to obtain a visa for her so that she could receive medical treatment in Germany. But despite assuming financial responsibility for my aunt and vouching for her return to Iraq, my father's application was rejected by the German authorities in 2002.

He stepped up his efforts when it became clear that in the aftermath of the attacks of 11 September 2001, the so-called 'war on terror' would not be restricted to Afghanistan. While I fail to understand why my 65-year-old blind and cancer-ridden aunt was refused a visa, it is clear that she was one of thousands of Iraqis who tried to leave the country in search of medical treatment and safety.

Talk of so-called smart sanctions[26] was in vogue in the later years of the sanctions regime as the international community gradually realized that it was the Iraqi population that was suffering and not the Iraqi political leadership. Women were particularly affected in a situation where economic deprivation, widespread poverty, a deteriorated infrastructure, and high unemployment rates went alongside the state's withdrawal of free services, which had been key to women's participation in public life, accompanied by a shift towards more conservative gender ideologies and the strengthening of patriarchal power at the level of tribes and families. Yet Iraqi women were not mere victims during these extremely difficult times. The life stories and accounts of women who have lived through all or some of this period also give evidence to the fact that many women were extremely resourceful in trying to survive and cope with the new economic realities and social conditions, engaging in the expanding informal sector, providing education for their children in a collapsing education system, and preserving their dignity as the world around them became ever more corrupt and dismal. This dignity and the strong will to live and hope find expression in the character of Dalal, the protagonist of *Absent*. Her world is falling apart as she not only struggles to make ends meet but also is betrayed by a lover who turns out to be an informant for the *Mukhabarat*. Nevertheless, in the last scene of the novel, we see Dalal teaching the alphabet to the young illiterate newspaper boy Hamid.

SIX

Living with the Occupation

One hot afternoon on 11 September 2001, I was sitting in the living room in the house of my Egyptian–German friend Mona in a middle-class neighbourhood of Cairo. We were trying to catch up while looking after her 1-year-old daughter, who was crawling around the room, trying desperately to get our attention. I had not seen Mona for years but we had been very close during the years I had been a graduate student at the American University in Cairo. We were talking about our work, our respective relationships and common friends when Mona's husband stormed in breathlessly asking us to switch on the television. Mona went directly to CNN. The images unfolding in front of our eyes were unbelievable. All of a sudden everything we had talked about seemed insignificant. Aside from the shock and horror of what was happening in New York, we were both immediately aware that there would be consequences from 9/11 that would affect all of us, especially those of Middle Eastern origin. Yet, little did we know how the terrible events of that day, which led to the deaths of over 3,000 human beings, would be used to legitimize a long series of human rights abuses, atrocities and wars that would lead to the death of tens of thousands of innocent civilians and would create even greater numbers of extremists ready to blow themselves up in the name of Islam and the fight against imperialism.

As the so-called 'war on terror' started to sweep around the world, most obviously in Afghanistan and Guantánamo Bay, but also inside the USA and the UK, it became clear that Iraq would be the next target. According to notes of aides of Donald Rumsfeld, publicized on CBS news, the defense secretary immediately wanted to go for Saddam Hussein, not just Osama Bin Laden, saying 'Go massive', and 'Sweep it all up. Things related and not.'[1] Throughout 2002, the US government made it clear that removing Saddam Hussein from power was a major goal, accusing the Iraqi regime of continuing the production and use of weapons of mass destruction, and of having links with terrorist organizations, particularly al-Qaeda. The official position of the USA was that Iraq illegally possessed weapons of mass destruction in violation of UN Security Council 1441, and if necessary had to be disarmed by force.[2] France, Russia and later China signalled that they would use their Security Council veto power against any resolution that included an ultimatum allowing the use of force against Iraq.

On 18 November 2002, a team of about thirty experts, led by the chief weapons inspector, Hans Blix, and the director of the International Atomic Energy Agency (IAEA), Mohammed ElBaradei, returned to Baghdad to begin UNMOVIC's[3] work. Their findings were to determine whether or not Iraq would face another US military onslaught. The inspection teams searched Iraq for the weapons for nearly four months prior to the invasion and were willing to continue, but were forced out by the onset of war in spite of their requests for more time.[4] On 20 March 2003, the invasion of Iraq began.

The Iraqi women I talked to had different views about the reasons the USA and the UK took the decision to invade Iraq. Many were sceptical and even cynical of American and British motivations, mentioning, for example, oil and business interests or the support of Israel and Zionism. Other women – usually those who were in favour of military intervention by American and British forces – spoke of democracy, human rights and liberation. About a year after the invasion, I was sitting with Mona N., a fervent supporter of President Bush, and several other Iraqi women of similar political persuasion, in an Italian restaurant in Detroit. Mona told me:

> I have been waiting for this moment for years. We have been lobbying this government so hard, trying to get them to recognize the crimes of Saddam Hussein. Finally, they started to understand that he is a big danger because he works with terrorists. The brave soldiers of this country will make sure that we finally have democracy and human rights in Iraq.

Mona has been involved in a US based women's organization whose activities have been promoted and funded by the US government. The plight of Iraqi women did become a substantial element of the pro-war lobby even if not as significant as in the case of Afghanistan. I came across a number of women who had been actively involved, in both the USA and the UK, in promoting the recent war. They varied in terms of ethnic and religious background; some were secular and some were religious, but they were united in their hatred for the previous regime and their faith in the Bush doctrine packaged as democracy, human rights and freedom.

However, overall only a few of the women I talked to actively promoted the invasion, while a greater number expressed mixed feelings. Despite not being convinced by the rhetoric coming from the White House, several women felt that a US-led invasion was the only way to get rid of Saddam Hussein. This was the case with Widad G., for example, a housewife and mother of three teenage children, who had divorced her husband about ten years ago after they had settled in London. Unlike her husband, who had been an opposition political activist since his youth, Widad had not been involved in politics. Yet, during the sanctions period, she collected money, clothes and medicine to send back to her family and friends in Iraq. Sitting in her modest but impeccably clean and lovingly decorated council flat in North London, I asked her at the beginning of 2004 what she thought about the recent war. She smiled sadly, lit herself another cigarette and said:

I am under no illusion that the Americans did this for us, for Iraqis. They want our oil and they want to control the region. I don't trust them. But at the time I felt we had no other choice. I reluctantly supported the war because I saw no way out of the horrible situation: people being caught between Saddam and sanctions. This could not go on any more. No one wants to be occupied, but this is our chance. Things have been bad but now people have hope. It will take a bit of time, but, but, *inshi'allah*, the situation will improve in a little while.

Her scepticism regarding US and UK motivations, and her mixed feelings of resignation tempered by a sense of hope, pervaded many of the exchanges I had with Iraqi women in 2003 and 2004. By 2005, when the security situation had deteriorated beyond imagination and violence escalated continuously, any sense of hope and cautious optimism had turned to despair, anger and a great sense of helplessness. Yet, already during the early days after the invasion, I had spoken to many Iraqi women who had adamantly opposed the war and predicted a gloomy future. I met Suad G., in her late forties, and her daughter Amal, in her twenties, from Baghdad while they were visiting London at the beginning of 2004. Their family had suffered significantly under the previous regime, having lost a couple of male relatives to Saddam's notorious prisons and torture chambers. Yet both women felt that the invasion was not related to the welfare of the Iraqi people, and had more to do with US economic and geopolitical interests:

> *Suad G.* (mother): Of course, we all hated Saddam. But what do we have now? It is chaos on the streets. If they wanted to get rid of Saddam, they could have assassinated him. They did that in other countries. But it was clearly not about that, nor about weapons of mass destruction, but about the USA becoming richer and controlling the entire region.

> *Amal G.* (daughter): What kind of liberation is this? I am afraid to go to university now. I had to start wearing *hijab*. What they are doing to our country makes the past look good.

It is important to stress that I came across a great range of views and opinions – some clear-cut and others more nuanced or ambivalent – among both women who live in the diaspora and women who live inside Iraq. Rather than addressing ethnic and religious affiliation, differences of opinion had more to do with political affiliation and specific experiences with the previous regime. Overall, the Kurdish women I talked to were more positive and supportive of the invasion, thinking of it as a liberation, although I also spoke to several Kurdish women activists who opposed the invasion and were lobbying against the occupation. Members or sympathizers of previous opposition parties, such as the Shi'i Islamist Dawa Party and the Supreme Council of the Islamic Revolution in Iraq (SCIRI), or the Chalabi-led Iraqi National Congress (INC) and Allawi's Iraqi National Accord (INA), were supportive of the war and occupation, yet their attitudes towards US and UK motivations were also wide-ranging.

In this final chapter, I aim to show how different women have experienced the invasion of 2003, its aftermath, the ongoing occupation and political developments inside Iraq. I aim to shed light on the everyday realities of women's lives as well as discuss how gender relations and ideologies are being affected by developments since 2003. I focus particularly on different forms of violence that women experience in the present situation, and also discuss women's political participation, legal rights, and changing social and cultural norms and values.

Living through the Invasion

Saying goodbye to everyone outside college was the saddest moment of my life. Diary, I want to describe to you the meaning of 'goodbye'. It hurts. Whenever I try to stop the tears, I can't prevent them from falling. It makes my throat dry. There is an emptiness inside my chest. It makes my face pale. It makes me ask myself, *Will I see them again… in a new life?* The phone here at home does not stop ringing. Everyone's calling everyone else to say goodbye – my friends, my family's friends, relatives – and every

call ends with saying, 'We hope to see you again. Go in peace.'
A lot of people have already left Baghdad.... I don't know, I'm
nervous... I feel tense... I can't breathe because I have been crying
so much. I've always hated goodbyes. I'll write more another day.
I have a feeling the war is going to start soon. If the air-raid sirens
go off I'll know it has really begun. (Al-Windawi, 2004: 4–5)

Nineteen-year-old Thura al-Windawi kept a diary throughout the
invasion in 2003, recording not only newsworthy events and explosions but the everyday feelings, fears and hopes of a teenage girl.
Her description of the mood prior to the invasion resonates with
the accounts of various women I have interviewed over the past
years who lived through the war. While several families left Iraq for
neighbouring Jordan, Syria, Iran or Turkey, the majority prepared
themselves by stocking up on staple foods and medicines as much as
was possible, given the dire economic situation and debilitated health
system. Some women from urban areas, especially Baghdad, took
their children to the countryside to stay with relatives and friends,
hoping that the impact of the war would be more bearable there.
Thura and her family stayed in the capital, like the majority of its
civilian population, but moved twice within the city before leaving
for the countryside only when life in Baghdad became unbearable.

Thura's diary entries give evidence to the deteriorating living
conditions as electricity, water and telephone lines became unavailable and the stress of continuous bombardment affected all members
of the family. On 3 April, two weeks after the beginning of the
invasion, Thura recorded the following into her diary:

The bombardment is really freaking us out. The sound is so loud
you know the explosions are very near. It's like when you are
inside an elevator and it shoots to the top floor – you get a weird
sickly feeling in your stomach. When each bomb drops, you get
that feeling and you try to swallow it so you can listen for the
next one. It's too loud and too scary. You don't know what to do.
You see people in their windows. Everyone is inside their houses,
being together. We are always together. We cannot leave each other
because it is too scary. Your heart beats so fast. Your eyes are wide

open. We are all staring at each other. Dad does not know what to
do and neither does Mum. Mum is looking for something to do.
Then they start to discuss their plans with each other, in very low
voices so we can not hear. Just that we have to leave. It is so sad.
This is the third time. How many more times? Why do we have to
go from place to place just for safety? Where is a place that we can
stay at and not be harmed? A place that is quiet? It has to be the
countryside. We have no choice. (al-Windawi, 2004: 49)

Only six days after Thura recorded her fears and the impact of the
continuous bombing, the symbolic toppling of the statue of Saddam
Hussein on Firdaws Square in Baghdad was widely seen to mark the
end of the old regime. Leila H. was still overjoyed as she told me in
the summer of 2005 in a small café in Shmeisani in Amman about
the way she and her family experienced the toppling of the statue
on 9 April in the predominantly Shi'i Baghdadi neighbourhood of
Kadhmiyya:

We could not believe it. Once the statue came down, we forgot
about all our fears and the horrors of the bombing. It was all
worth it. We were finally free from that horrible dictator Saddam
Hussein. When the news reached my neighbourhood, there were
celebrations on the street. The first time we saw American soldiers
on the streets we greeted them happily. Of course, things changed
after some time and people started to feel more resentful of the
soldiers. But I will never forget the joy of that day.

When, a year later, the US-appointed Governing Council named 9
April as 'National Day', Riverbend, the famous female blogger from
Baghdad, wrote down her own memories of that day:

The day began with heavy bombing. I remember waking up at
5 a.m. to a huge explosion. The hair almost stood on my head.
We were all sleeping in the living room because the drapes were
heavy and offered some small security against shattering glass. E.
instantly jumped up and ran to make sure that the Kalashnikov was
loaded properly and I tried to cover my cousin's children better
with the heavy blankets. The weather was already warm, but the
blankets would protect the kids against glass. Their older daughter

was, luckily, still sound asleep – lost in a dream or nightmare. The younger one lay in the semi-dark, with eyes wide open. I sensed her trying to read my face for some small reassurance … I smiled tightly, 'Go back to sleep…' … My cousin's wife was awake by then. She sat in the middle of her two children and held them closer to either side. She had not spoken to her parents in almost a week now … there were no telephones to contact them and there was no way to get to their area. She was beyond terrified at this crucial point … she was certain that they were all dead or dying and the only thing that seemed to be keeping her functioning was the presence of her two younger daughters. At that point my mind was numb. All I could do was react to the explosions – flinch when one was particularly powerful, and automatically say a brief prayer of thanks when another was further away. (Riverbend, 2004: 246–8)

Unlike Leila, Riverbend's memories of what happened that day have not been erased by the toppling of the statue. Leila was obviously much more welcoming of the US troops and put much greater hopes on the toppling of Saddam Hussein than Riverbend did. But even Leila states that most people's attitude towards the presence of US and UK troops has changed with time.

Dr Hala, the pharmacist who had told me earlier how appalled she was by the looting of medicines by Iraqi troops during the invasion of Kuwait in 1990, provided the following account of the day:

The fall of Baghdad, the 9th of April, was a horrible day. We had no television, no phone. Only al-Hurra [Freedom] station from America. Most of the women and children had left Baghdad. I was very scared that day. It was the first day we saw the American army on the streets in Baghdad. We did not see any of our army. We did not know where they went. They evaporated. I started cooking for my family and for my neighbours, because all the other women had left. In the evening there was a knock on the door. There was a man shouting: 'I need help.' We did not have electricity. There were four men, who had been in hospital. They were injured. They had been lying in bed when thieves came and took the beds. They were bleeding. I did not know how to treat their wounds. We let them enter into the garage. We cleaned them with antiseptics and gave them antibiotics. After five days, one of them came back laughing and he thanked me. That moment when I saw the four men bleeding, I felt the only thing that is important is to help people live.

Three days after President Bush declared the end of major combat operations on 1 May 2003, my Aunt Salima died at our family home in al-Mansur. Her lung condition had worsened during the last days of the invasion. Lack of proper medication and adequate health care during the sanctions period had allowed the cancer to spread throughout her whole body including her lungs. Never wanting to draw too much attention to herself, she had hardly complained about the pain during these last months of the official war. She had so much wanted to get out of the country one last time to see my cousin Hamid and his sister Iba', who were living in Germany, but was refused a visa. When her lungs started to fail her on 3 May, a curfew prevented my relatives from bringing Aunt Salima to the nearest hospital. My Uncle Jaffar risked his life and went out in the neighbourhood in search of oxygen. He found a half-empty bottle at a neighbour's who had been sick. The bottle lasted until 4 a.m. Fifteen minutes later Aunt Salima passed away.

Chaos and Lawlessness

In the immediate aftermath of the invasion, chaos and lawlessness prevailed in the streets of many Iraqi cities, especially Baghdad. Images and accounts of the looting of shops, factories, homes, ministries, the National Museum, and even hospitals circulated widely in the Western media at the time. Several women I talked to described men armed with AK-47 assault rifles engaging in the looting and walking away with everything from furniture, industrial equipment and household appliances to pillows, mattresses and food. In addition to more organized armed thieves, ordinary impoverished Iraqi men, women and even children also participated in the looting, albeit on a smaller scale. Zeena D., who had left Iraq for Amman by the end of 2004, remembers the following:

> My husband was working with UNICEF. I have seen the last days
> of the Saddam regime and how they left suddenly, and then how
> the Americans came in. I had hopes, but my husband had not.
> He thought that there was no future for the country. We saw the
> looting of UNICEF and other places, including UNDP. First they
> took the big things and at the end they even took the windows.
> They were armed men, but later on, as they had carried away
> all the big things, they were joined by other, unarmed, people. I
> even saw women. And the Americans used to watch as if it was a
> movie. My husband used to cry every night. He felt that it was the
> end of our country.

There exists a range of views about where to place responsibility for the looting, with some women expressing a deep disappointment in their fellow Iraqis and others blaming Saddam Hussein and Ba'thi remnants; others speak of outside instigators. Yet, most of the women I talked to felt very angry about the lack of intervention by US troops. The US military stood by and permitted the looting and ransacking of hospitals, universities, libraries, social service institutions and the National Museum. According to some women, they even encouraged the looting. Salwa H., a medical doctor I met in Amman in June of 2006, was in tears as she recalled the following incident:

> I saw soldiers laughing and encouraging a group of young men
> who looted a hospital. They were just standing there and grinning,
> making their jokes about Ali Baba. It was so humiliating. I shouted
> at the soldiers asking them to help. I told them that under inter-
> national law they must keep things under control.[5] But they said
> they had orders not to intervene. I was so angry and cried when
> I saw the thieves going off with hospital beds. That afternoon,
> two US soldiers could have easily prevented this happening. But
> they did not care. They only protected the Ministry of Oil and the
> Ministry of the Interior.

Soon after the invasion the International Committee of the Red Cross (ICRC) issued a statement in Geneva declaring that the relief agency was 'profoundly alarmed by the chaos currently prevailing in Baghdad and other parts of Iraq'. The medical system in Baghdad 'has virtually collapsed', the ICRC warned, and it reminded the USA and Britain that they were obliged under international law to guarantee the basic security of the Iraqi population.[6] General Tommy Franks, however, the overall commander of all US and British forces in Iraq, issued an order to unit commanders that specifically prohibited the use of force to prevent looting. According to several Iraqi women who witnessed the chaos during the first days after the fall of the previous regime, the role of the US military went beyond simply standing by. Fedwa, who had run a venue for cultural events in the 1980s, was totally shocked by the destruction caused by the bombings and the subsequent looting in 2003:

> I could not have imagined anything like that. It was totally differ-
> ent in 1991 after that war. I did not think they would destroy the
> main resources of culture and heritage. I saw it with my own eyes.
> How terrible it was. The guard came to tell me. He was wounded.
> He helped me in picking up some pieces. By the time, I got
> there it was destroyed, bombed and the looting had started. After
> cleaning it, we locked it. A week later, they had stolen the door.
> It was of no material value. But it had a huge map of Iraq with
> archaeological sites on it. I found it torn with a knife. It is this
> vicious type. It is a type of mafia, directed by vicious people. I saw
> what happened to the museum. Tanks were watching and protected
> the looters.

Fedwa was not alone in suggesting that US troops, as well as people from outside, provoked the looting. Remnants of the previous regime, Kuwaitis and Israelis were often mentioned in the narratives of women who interpreted events as the outcome of well-orchestrated and planned conspiracy. Several women emphasized how different the situation was after the Gulf War in 1991, when no looting followed the bombing campaigns, and even half-destroyed shops and houses were not touched by anyone except for people helping to clear up the rubble. Although the role of US and UK troops in not preventing and even actively encouraging the looting is beyond doubt, it is important to point out that during the thirteen years of economic sanctions, petty crimes involving theft and burglary had increased dramatically, and many women spoke about the changes in people's morality and values during this period. As I showed in the previous chapter, poverty was widespread and deeply felt by the time the invasion took place.

The Climate of Fear[7]

I'll never forget the day my daughter, Rifqa, was born; she was born in 2004. The whole time I was pregnant I prayed to God that the birth would happen in daytime and not at night, because at night there were curfews and the streets were full of gangs hijacking cars and killing people. And that's aside from the random firing of US soldiers – they shoot whenever they see a car coming anywhere near them. And the streets are completely dark because there's no electricity. But in fact I went into labour at 11:30 at night and I was really in a quandary: do I wake my husband to take me to hospital or do I try to put up with the pain and wait till morning? I prayed and prayed to God to help the time pass quickly, but time played tricks me on. My pain got worse and worse, my contractions faster and faster and yet time seemed to slow down – the hours just crawled by. I started to cry in silence so my husband wouldn't hear. I was terrified for my child – thinking she might die or she would be damaged in some way. It went on like this, hour after hour, until 6 in the morning, when I finally screamed at the top of my voice for my husband to wake up: 'Wake up, wake up, I'm dying.' He sprang out of bed, without saying anything, gathered everyone in the family together and they all took me to hospital. There they found the baby was drowning in fluid and they began to blame me for delaying for so long – but who was really responsible? Was I?

Reem R. was lucky in many ways: her daughter Sumaya was in fact fine after she was born. Other young women have had even worse experiences, trying to postpone birth out of fear that something might happen on the way to the hospital in the particularly insecure hours of darkness. Reem, for whom Sumaya is her second child, is trying to study languages at college, but escalating violence and general lack of security make it more and more difficult for her and other women even to leave their homes.

During the initial period of lawlessness after the invasion in 2003, women started to experience the insecurity, threats, fear and violence that have circumscribed their lives over the past years. Just a few months after the invasion, Human Rights Watch published a revealing report about the climate of fear among Iraqi women and girls. At the time of publishing, incidents of kidnapping, abduction and sexual violence were not widely reported and possibly not that widespread. However, the knowledge about these acts of violence targeting women and girls prevented many from leaving their homes, from going to work, school and university. Neither the occupation forces nor the debilitated Iraqi police force was preventing or properly investigating these crimes.

The fear was clearly written in the faces of Huda M. and her teenage daughter Fatin when they were visiting their relatives in London a few months after the invasion. Huda's sister Mariam was living in a comfortable and spacious house in Wimbledon, an area home to a number of well-to-do Iraqi families. As I was arriving at Mariam's house, I was wondering how Fatin was experiencing London after everything she and her family must have been through. I was initially surprised to see that Fatin, just like all teenage girls everywhere in the world, was interested in shopping, was fussing about her weight, and spoke excitedly about the upcoming wedding of one of her cousins. When I asked her about her life in Baghdad, her facial expression, her composure and even the tone of her voice changed completely. Before my eyes, this fun-loving teenager metamorphosed into someone much more serious, older and full of fear. Fatin said:

> My life changed completely after the war. I am too scared to go anywhere, even with my friends. And my parents would not let me anyway. We heard many stories of girls being kidnapped and sold to other Arab countries. I am even too scared to go back to uni-

versity. But I get so bored just sitting at home. There is nothing to do. My mother and my aunts all stay at home as well. My smaller girl cousins are not even going to school anymore. Only my dad goes out, and when he leaves the house he kisses us goodbye as if he would never return. And we always worry about him.

Huda shook her head while her daughter was talking, repeating: 'This never happened before...' When pressed, Huda acknowledged that the fear of rape and abduction was present before the invasion, but was mainly linked to Uday, Sadam Hussein's son: 'Yes, everyone worried about their daughters, especially when they were pretty. But it was more a matter of avoiding certain areas or clubs. In general, women were not targeted by gangs as they are now. Now, the danger comes from all sides.'

Despite the general stigma attached to sexual violence, Human Rights Watch managed to talk to several victims of abductions and rape in the early days after the invasion. Salma M., a 49-year-old woman from Baghdad, was abducted in May 2003 from her home, as she was standing outside her door. Four men put guns to her head, pulled her hair and pushed Salma into the car:

> They made me put my head down between my legs and put a
> pistol to my head. They said that if I moved my head I'd be killed,
> so I don't know where they took me.... Then they took me into a
> building where they were hitting me on the head and the arms,
> and I still can't stretch because my whole body hurts. They used
> hot water on my head, my eyes still hurt from that and my arms.
> They raped me, in many, many ways. They kept me until the next
> day, I begged them, I said I have a young child, I said he might die
> if I leave him alone. And so then they left me alone. When I came
> home my appearance was so bad, my hair was a mess, my mouth
> was bloody and my legs too. They burned my legs with cigarettes.
> They bit me, on my shoulders and my arms. All of them raped me,
> there were five or six more than the four who kidnapped me, there
> were ten of them in total and I was raped by all of them.[8]

When Salma returned home, she was in shock and had a nervous breakdown. By the time she was interviewed, about a month after the attack, Salma was still not sleeping at night. She was scared that her abductors would return and refused to go outside the house. She wouldn't let her 18-year-old daughter leave the house anymore.

While Salma's husband and extensive family were supportive after her ordeal, many families of less educated backgrounds associate shame and the violation of family honour with rape. Incidents of so-called 'honour killings' have risen drastically. According to several women activists working with victims of violence, some women who have been abducted beg the police to keep them in the police station or in prison so that they won't be killed by their families. Some women's rights activists have been trying to set up safe houses for women survivors of abductions and kidnappings. Kidnappings, unlike abductions, involve the demand for a ransom and might or might not involve sexual violence. There are accounts of families not paying the ransom in the case of female family members, for fear of the shame attached to the perceived loss of honour.

In addition to abductions with the intent to sexually assault a woman, there has also been an increase in abductions in the context of sex trafficking. Although the number of trafficked women and girls is difficult to estimate, Iraqi NGO activists, and even the US State Department's June 2005 trafficking report,[9] confirm the growning scale of the problem, with young women abducted and sent to Yemen, Syria, Jordan and the Gulf countries for sexual exploitation.

None of the women I talked to had experienced sexual violence themselves, but all had heard stories or even knew someone who had been abducted or kidnapped. Despite the continuing climate of fear and the underlying dangers, many women and girls nevertheless started to venture out to schools, university and workplaces in the latter part of 2003. According to the Human Rights Watch report which refers to an assessment conducted by Save the Children UK, school attendance increased from 50 per cent in May 2003 to and estimated 75 per cent in June 2003. However, girls' school attendance was often dependent on the availability of male relatives to accompany the girls.[10] Several women told me that after several months they felt unable to sit at home anymore and so began to venture out. Although they lived in fear, many families tried to create a sense of normality, which meant a return to education, work and even political mobilization.

Yet abductions, kidnappings and sexual violence by criminal gangs were not the only causes of fear and concern. Seventeen-year-old Nesreen H. told me in the summer of 2005 in Amman about the circumstances in which she went back to school in the fall of 2003:

> There were many stories of kidnapping. We were scared all the time. Even when we were at home we did not feel safe. There were lots of new people on the street, people we did not see before. I don't know how to explain, but when I looked at their faces, I could tell that they were criminals. They were dressed badly, with long beards and hair. I started to go to a new school a few months after the war. My mother was worried about me all the time when I went to school. They found bombs in our school. Every morning there were security men searching for them. Before school ended at two, the police would close the street to make sure that no terrorist would attack the school. There were many stories of Iraqi women going inside schools wearing *abaya* and hiding a bomb under it. I was not scared of American soldiers. They looked friendly. They came to our school and brought books. I felt normal when I saw them. But sometimes I felt scared because they were ready to shoot. I was more scared of the terrorists. For me, I felt that if I do not hurt the Americans, they will not hurt me, but it is different with the terrorists. But I do know that Americans also kill innocent people.

At the time Human Rights Watch published its report in July 2003, most of the sexual violence experienced by women was carried out by criminal gangs taking advantage of the general situation of lawlessness and chaos. By the time Nesreen went back to school in the fall of 2003, more politically motivated groups, remnants of the past regime as well as Islamist militia and terrorist groups, also contributed to the general climate of fear through bomb attacks targeting Iraqi civilians as well as kidnappings. As I show later on, women and children, just like men, have not only been victims of bombings, including suicide bombings, but have been targeted by Islamist militias and extremist organizations as an expression of a radical break with the previous regime and resistance to the occupation. Women's dress codes, mobility, participation in political and public life, as well as legal rights, are all contested issues and used in the power struggle between the various forces within society.

Although Nesreen might come across as naive in her assessment of the occupying forces, she was not alone in initially feeling positive towards American and British soldiers. In the early days after the invasion, the campaign to win hearts and minds succeeded to some extent, especially since there was a fund of goodwill and hope among a large proportion of the population, who were grateful to have got rid of a ruthless dictator. However, the failure to improve everyday living conditions, combined with the deteriorating security situation, an array of human rights abuses and escalating violence by occupation forces, soon led to a shift in the general attitude towards American and British troops among the majority of women I talked to. The Human Rights Watch report mainly focuses on the failure of the occupying forces to prevent abductions and sexual violence against women, stating that many of the problems 'derive from the US-led coalition forces and civilian administration's failure to provide public security in Baghdad. The public security vacuum in Baghdad has heightened the vulnerability of women and girls to sexual violence and abduction' (Human Rights Watch, 2003: Summary). This resonates with Iraqi women's rights activists, who chided coalition forces for their failure to protect women in post-war Iraq.

The police have been unable to prevent the violence, including that which is gender-based. Due to the fact that the police force is relatively small and quite poorly managed, there is a limited street presence. The position has in fact worsened in the recent period as the newly established Iraqi police force has frequently been targeted by militant resistance and has itself been infiltrated by Islamist militias.

As time has passed, it has become obvious that Iraqi civilians are caught between many different sources of anguish, suffering and aggression. US and UK troops have not only failed to protect the population from escalating violence by criminal gangs, Islamist militias and terrorist groups, but have themselves been a major source of violence and lack of security inside Iraq. Occupation forces have been responsible for killing thousands of innocent Iraqi civilians, including women and children, as a result of their bombing attacks and random shootings. And they have also been implicated in abuse, torture and sexual violence against Iraqi men, women and children.

Increasing Death Rates

In March 2006, I was invited by Code Pink to participate in a series of events revolving around International Women's Day. Five Iraqi women from inside Iraq were going to join US peace activists, American mothers who lost their sons or daughters in Iraq, and war veterans who condemned the occupation, in a month's tour of the USA in protest against the occupation. I joined the delegation for the first week and spent time with the Iraqi and Code Pink women in New York and Washington DC. Throughout this week I listened to one horrific account after another as the Iraqi delegates spoke about the ordeals they had witnessed or heard about. The women who had just risked their lives to make the dangerous journey to join us in the USA were full of sad and shocking stories of families being wiped out by US bombing attacks, widows struggling to survive in rubble, young men who disappeared into the new prison system without any news of their whereabouts, and stories of torture and abuse.

I did not always agree with the analysis of the other Iraqi women delegates in terms of the historical sources of sectarianism, the attitude of Iraqis towards war and occupation, and the future outlooks. Having spoken to many other women, I knew that perspectives on the war and the occupation were more diverse than those presented by the women delegates. Others I had talked to felt much more

Widow Vivian Salim

ambiguous, although increasingly fed up with the occupation. I also contested the notion that sectarianism was simply a result of the occupation and that people had been living in peace and harmony before. Although this had been the case to some extent, especially among urban middle classes, it was only part of the story – as earlier chapters have revealed. Saddam Hussein had already played on sectarian differences, using, like so many other dictators, divide-and-rule tactics. I was also not convinced that everything would return to harmony once US and U.K troops withdrew. Pandora's box had been opened: it was not possible for things to revert to what many chose to remember as the 'glorious past'. Yet, despite my differences and arguments at times, I was deeply moved and impressed by the resolve of these women, whose stories about the human tragedies of the occupation resonated with the accounts of so many other women, not to mention the growing body of documentation on the atrocities committed by the occupation forces.

The Iraqi delegation was missing two members: Vivian Salim and Anwar Kadhim Jawad. They were denied visas by the US embassy in Amman on the grounds that they did not have 'sufficient family ties that would compel them to return'. Both women had lost their husbands and children to random shootings by American soldiers as they tried to flee in their family cars the heavy fighting in their neighbourhoods during the invasion. The irony and twisted logic of the visa refusal was hard to bear. It was chilling. Yet even more painful is the realization that Vivian's and Anwar's terrible loss during the invasion has been multiplied by tens of thousands as the death rate has risen steadily since the official end of combat operations.

According to Iraq Body Count (IBC), by July 2006 between 38,960 and 43,397 civilians had been killed as a result of military intervention inside Iraq. Figures released by IBC in March 2006, updated by statistics for the year 2005 from the main Baghdad morgue, show that the total number of civilians reported killed has risen year-on-year since 1 May 2003 (the date that President Bush announced 'major combat operations have ended').[11] However, many critics have questioned Iraq Body Count's methods and its ability to compile accurate statistics. Some have argued that IBC has greatly underestimated the number of casualties. Already in October 2004, even before the escalation of violence inside Iraq, a study published by the *Lancet* medical journal suggests that poor planning, air strikes by coalition forces and a 'climate of violence' have led to more than 100,000 extra deaths in Iraq.[12] In the study, a research team led by well-respected American researchers interviewed about 1,000 families in 33 locations throughout Iraq in September 2004. Families were interviewed about births and deaths in the household before and after the invasion.

Data collection was difficult in the context of ongoing violence. Yet the data the researchers managed to collect is extensive.[13] Using what they described as the best sampling methods that could be applied under the circumstances, they found that Iraqis were 2.5 times more likely to die in the seventeen months following the invasion than in the fourteen months before it. Before the invasion, the most common causes of death in Iraq were heart attack, stroke and chronic diseases. Afterwards, violent death moved far ahead of all other causes. Furthermore, the risk of violent death was 58 times higher than before the war, the researchers reported. In 15 of the 33 communities visited, residents reported violent deaths in their families since the conflict had started, mostly due to air strikes by American-led forces. And most of those killed were women and children (Roberts et al., 2004).

The 'climate of violence' described in the *Lancet* report in 2004 worsened considerably in 2005 and 2006. Increasingly, Islamist militants, militias linked to political parties, and various terrorist groups have been responsible for much of the bloodshed in Iraq, primarily the killings of Iraqi civilians. Bombings, including suicide missions, as well as targeted assassinations of individuals and, increasingly, collective killings based on sectarian affiliations have created an atmosphere of mayhem and unbearable living conditions. Sectarian violence has been on the increase and started to spill over from small extremist factions to larger parts of the population.

The death toll among Iraqis as a result of the US-led invasion has now reached an estimated 655,000 according to a study published in the *Lancet* (Roberts et al., 2006). While these figures have been debated, there is no doubt that hundred thousands of Iraqis have died as a consequence of the ongoing violence and that death rates have been on the increase, with figures up to a hundred a day in December 2006. Riverbend wrote in July 2006:

> At nearly 2 p.m., we received some terrible news. We lost a good friend in the killings. T. was a 26-year-old civil engineer who worked with a group of friends in a consultancy bureau in Jadriya. The last time I saw him was a week ago. He had stopped by the house to tell us his sister was engaged and he'd brought along with him pictures of latest project he was working on – a half-collapsed school building outside of Baghdad. He usually left the house at 7 am to avoid the morning traffic jams and the heat. Yesterday, he decided to stay at home because he'd promised his mother he would bring Abu Kamal by the house to fix the generator which had suddenly died on them the night before. His parents say that T. was making his way out of the area on foot when the attack occurred and he got two bullets to the head. His brother could only identify him by the blood-stained T-shirt he was wearing.

People are staying in their homes in the area and no one dares enter it so the wakes for the people who were massacred haven't begun yet. I haven't seen his family yet and I'm not sure I have the courage or the energy to give condolences. I feel like I've given the traditional words of condolences a thousand times these last few months, '*Baqiya bi hayatkum... Akhir il ahzan...*' or 'May this be the last of your sorrows.' Except they are empty words because even as we say them, we know that in today's Iraq any sorrow – no matter how great – will not be the last. There was also an attack yesterday on Ghazaliya though we haven't heard what the casualties are. People are saying it's Sadr's militia, the Mahdi army, behind the killings. The news the world hears about Iraq and the situation in the country itself are wholly different. People are being driven out of their homes and areas by force and killed in the streets, and the Americans, Iranians and the Puppets talk of national conferences and progress.

Violence by Occupation Forces

While aerial bombings of residential areas are responsible for a large number of civilian deaths, many Iraqis have lost their lives being shot at by American or British troops. Whole families have been wiped out as they were approaching a checkpoint or failed to recognize areas marked as prohibited. Hind G. has been working for many years as a doctor in al-Kindi teaching hospital in the north-east of the city. In 2006 she told me, full of desperation and anger in her voice:

> I have seen many things while working as a doctor. But what I am seeing these days is too much. I treated children with metal fragments all over their bodies because they played with unexploded bomblets that were part of cluster bombs. I saw men, women and children with no limbs, bleeding to death because they were victims of bomb attacks. Sometimes by the Americans and sometimes by terrorists. My colleague works in the maternity ward and we get lots of complications. Many women are too afraid to come to hospital, especially when they get their labour during the night. They are afraid they and their families will be shot by soldiers or attacked by gangs. So they stay at home and often it is too late when complications occur. A few weeks ago we had a badly injured pregnant woman whose husband had died when

the soldiers opened fire on the car. They had a white flag but the soldiers claim they did not see it. The husband drove a bit too fast because he was worried about his wife. She was in so much pain.

Some of the worst destruction and atrocities have taken place in and around the city of Fallujah in the province of Al-Anbar, about 70 km west of Baghdad on the Euphrates river.[14] According to a detailed analysis of 300 contemporary news reports by Iraq Body Count, at least 572 of the 800 or so reported deaths during the first US siege of Fallujah in April 2004 were civilians, with over 300 of these being women and children.[15]

US forces committed major war crimes during the assault: warplanes, fighter bombers, military helicopters and gunships were used to attack residential areas, killing many civilians. In one incident '16 children and eight women were reported to have been killed when US aircraft hit four houses' (Independent, 8 April).

British activist Jo Wilding was in Fallujah during the April 2004 siege of the city.[16] She recorded in her blog:

We wash the blood off our hands and get in the ambulance. There are people trapped in the other hospital who need to go to Baghdad. Siren screaming, lights flashing, we huddle on the floor of the ambulance, passports and ID cards held out the windows. We pack it with people, one with his chest taped together and a drip, one on a stretcher, legs jerking violently so I have to hold them down as we wheel him out, lifting him over steps. The doctor rushes out to meet me: 'Can you go to fetch a lady, she is pregnant and she is delivering the baby too soon?' Azzam is driving, Ahmed in the middle directing him and me by the window, the visible foreigner, the passport. Something scatters across my hand, simultaneous with the crashing of a bullet through the ambulance, some plastic part dislodged, flying through the window. We stop, turn off the siren, keep the blue light flashing, wait, eyes on the silhouettes of men in US marine uniforms on the corners of the buildings. Several shots come. We duck, get as low as possible and I can see tiny red lights whipping past the window, past my head. Some, it's hard to tell, are hitting the ambulance. I start singing. What else do you do when someone's shooting at you? A tire bursts with an enormous noise and a jerk of the vehicle. I'm outraged. We're trying to get to a woman who's giving birth without any medical attention, without electricity, in a city under siege, in a clearly marked ambulance, and you're shooting at us. How dare you?

After a brief period of ceasefire, Fallujah became once again the target of aerial attacks. On 8 November 2004, the USA – with British support – began its second major assault on Fallujah, presented and justified as counter-insurgency Operation Phantom Fury. Thousands of US solders and hundreds of Iraqi troops engaged in a concentrated assault on Fallujah with air strikes, artillery, armour and infantry. According to US military officials, between 1,000 and 6,000 insurgents were hiding in the city. Although the majority of residents managed to flee the city before the major assault, thousands remained trapped. According to a high-ranking Red Cross official, 'at least 800 civilians' were killed in the first nine days of the November 2004 assault on Fallujah (Inter Press Service, 16 November 2004).

Samira H. was living in Baghdad but had gone regularly to Fallujah in the aftermath of the attacks in 2004 in order to provide humanitarian assistance. She was clearly distressed by the images that came to her mind when describing her visits to the city. She started to cry as she told me about the numbers of injured and killed she saw when visiting Fallujah the first time. She gathered herself and said sadly: 'You know I do not want to hate Americans. But it is difficult after having seen what happened to Fallujah.' She continued:

> We used to go with an ambulance from Baghdad, but the Americans would stop us for half an hour. We had to pass several checkpoints. And they gave us a hard time. It was very scary. Every time we went to Fallujah, people asked us to come again and bring more food, medicine and blankets. The journey between Baghdad and Fallujah would take us over three hours. We always went inside an ambulance and we had a white flag. Some ambulances were shot at. It was very dangerous. Every time we managed to go to Fallujah, we heard more terrible stories about people dying, being injured, not enough medical facilities to treat the wounded,

not enough food. There was no electricity because the Americans
had bombed the power station. There were so many massacres.
Bombings, people being shot at. Even doctors were targeted when
they tried to look after injured people. We heard that many houses
were destroyed but we could not believe what we saw with our
own eyes. Over 2500 houses were destroyed.[17]

Half of the estimated 200,000 Iraqis who fled the assault have yet
to return to their homes. Those who managed to return have been
subjected to a draconian regime of curfews, iris scans and checkpoints. The vast majority of former residents of Fallujah are living in
makeshift camps in and around Baghdad under extremely difficult
conditions, and they are only a fraction of the increasing number
of internally displaced people inside the country.

Fallujah might have received more media attention than other
places, but similar US military offensives in Ramadi, Haditha, Qaim,
Tal Afar and elsewhere have killed many more civilians and created
thousands more refugees. These military assaults have been justified
as part of counter-insurgency measures to eliminate violent insurgents responsible for targeting not only US and UK troops but also
Iraqi civilians. While thousands of fighters might have been killed
in these military assaults, so have thousands of innocent civilians.
Those surviving these attacks have lost relatives, friends, neighbours.
They have lost their homes, their livelihoods. They have also lost any
sense of trust or confidence in the American and British forces and
might even have developed greater sympathy for the insurgents.

In addition to the killing of innocent women, men and children, the
occupation forces have also been engaged in other forms of violence
against women. There have been numerous documented accounts of
physical assaults at checkpoints and during house searches. Several
women I talked to reported that they had been verbally or physically threatened and assaulted by soldiers as they were searched at
checkpoints. American forces have also arrested the wives, sisters and
daughters of suspected insurgents in order to pressure them to sur-
render.[18] Female relatives have been literally taken hostage by US forces

and used as bargaining chips. Aside from the violence of the arrests themselves, those women who were detained by the troops might suffer as well from the sense of shame associated with such detention. As there has been mounting evidence not just of physical assaults and torture but also of rape, there is a risk that women who have been detained will become victims of so-called honour crimes.

According to Amal Kadhim Swadi, an Iraqi lawyer representing women detainees at Abu Ghraib, abuse, sexual violence, rape and torture of Iraqi women by occupation forces has been taking place all over Iraq. Several documents released on 7 March 2005 by the American Civil Liberties Union (ACLU) show thirteen cases of rape and abuse of female detainees. The documents also reveal that no action was taken against any soldier or civilian official as a result.[19] The most well known case of rape and murder is that of Abeer Qassim a-Janaby, a 14-year-old girl from Mahmudiyaha, which been widely reported in the Western media. But, as Riverbend reflects in her blog, there are many more unreported cases of rape:

Rape. The latest of American atrocities. Though it's not really the latest – it's just the one that's being publicized the most. The poor girl Abeer was neither the first to be raped by American troops, nor will she be the last. The only reason this rape was brought to light and publicized is that her whole immediate family were killed along with her. Rape is a taboo subject in Iraq. Families don't report rapes here, they avenge them. We've been hearing whisperings about rapes in American-controlled prisons and during sieges of towns like Haditha and Samarra for the last three years. The naiveté of Americans who can't believe their 'heroes' are committing such atrocities is ridiculous. Who ever heard of an occupying army committing rape??? You raped the country, why not the people? In the news they're estimating her age to be around 24, but Iraqis from the area say she was only 14. Fourteen. Imagine your 14-year-old sister or your 14-year-old daughter. Imagine her being gang-raped by a group of psychopaths and then the girl was killed and her body burned to cover up the rape. Finally, her parents and her five-year-old sister were also killed. Hail the American heroes... Raise your heads high supporters of the 'liberation' – your troops have made you proud today.... It fills me with rage to hear about it and read about it. The pity I once had for foreign troops in Iraq is gone. It's been eradicated by the atrocities in Abu Ghraib, the deaths in Haditha and the latest news of rapes and killings. I look at them in their armored vehicles and to be honest – I can't bring myself to care whether they are 19 or 39. I can't bring myself to care if they make it back home alive. I can't bring myself to care anymore about the wife or parents or children they left behind. I can't bring myself to care because it's difficult to see beyond the horrors. I look at them and wonder just how many innocents they killed and how many more they'll kill before they go home. How many more young Iraqi girls will they rape? (11 July 2006)

Violence by Islamist Militants

Islamist militants and terrorist groups pose a particular danger to Iraqi women. Many women's organizations and activists inside Iraq have documented the increasing Islamist threats to women, the pressure to conform to certain dress codes, the restrictions in move-ment and behaviour, incidents of acid thrown into women's faces, and even targeted killings. Early on in 2003, many women in Basra, for example, reported that they were forced to wear a headscarf or restrict their movements in fear of harassment from men. Female students at the University of Basra reported that since the war ended groups of men began stopping them at the university gates, shouting at them if their heads were not covered.[20]

In 2004, reports from several cities around Iraq stated that Islamist extremists were targeting universities by threatening and even attack-ing female students who were wearing Western-style fashions, setting off bombs on campuses and demanding that classes be segregated by sex. Thousands of female students decided to postpone their studies after bombs exploded in a number of universities. According to several women I talked to, pamphlets found on several campuses declared: 'If the boy students don't separate from the girl students, we will explode the college. Any girl student who does not wear a veil, we will burn her face with chemicals.' Female students have been abducted as they leave the campus, threatened that they would be killed if they didn't wear 'Islamic dress' and if they continued to mingle with male students. Even non-Muslim women, who are not normally expected to cover their heads, do not escape the threats, students said (*Washington Times*, 17 October 2004).[21]

Not only students, but women of all ages and walks of life are nowadays forced to comply to certain dress codes, as well as restrict their movements. Suad F., a former accountant and mother of four children who lives in a neighbourhood in Baghdad that used to be relatively mixed before the sectarian killings of 2005 and 2006, told me during a visit to Amman in 2006:

> I resisted for a long time, but last year also started wearing the *hijab*, after I was threatened by several Islamist militants in front of my house. They are terrorizing the whole neighbourhood, behaving as if they were in charge. And they are actually controlling the area. No one dares to challenge them. A few months ago they distributed leaflets around the area warning people to obey them and demanding that women should stay at home. I have been trying not to take them so seriously, but when they threatened to kill me in front of my house I got really worried. I stopped working as an accountant after the invasion because of the lack of security, but I have been helping out in the women's NGO in the neighbourhood. We are providing some basic training and humanitarian assistance to extremely poor women. I need to go out. What am I supposed to do now?

By 2006, the threat posed by Islamist militias as well as the mushrooming Islamist extremist groups went far beyond imposed dress codes and called for gender segregation at university. In the British-occupied south, where Muqtada' al-Sadr's Mahdi Army retains a stranglehold, the situation has been critical for some time, as women have been systematically pushed back into their homes. One Basra woman, known as Dr Kefaya, was working in the women and children's hospital unit at Basra University when she started receiving threats from extremists. She defied them. Then one day a man walked into the building and

murdered her (Judd, 2006).[22] Many other professional women have
been shot in Basra since the invasion. However, by 2006 the same
pressures and threats applied to women throughout Iraq, except for
the Kurdish-controlled areas in the north.

Aside from Shi'i Islamist militias, such as the Mahdi Army linked
to al-Sadr, and the Badr Brigade linked to the Supreme Council for
the Islamic Revolution in Iraq (SCIRI), numerous Sunni Islamist
groups have been mushrooming since the invasion. Among the many
different groups are Al-Faruq Brigades, a militant wing of the Islamic
Movement in Iraq (al-Harakah al-Islamiyya fi al-'Arak), the Mujahideen
of the Victorious Sect (Mujahideen al ta'ifa al-Mansoura), the Mujahideen
Battalions of the Salafi Group of Iraq (Kata'ib al mujahideen fi al-jama'ah
al-salafiyya fi al-'Arak), al-Qaeda in Iraq, and the Jihad Brigades.

Leaders in these groups issue fatawa (singular fatwa: legal pronouncements in Islam) banning women from leaving their homes,
from driving, and from working. According to several women's rights
activists I spoke to in 2006, incidents of women being killed on the
streets had risen over the past months and have started to become
a noticeable and extremely worrying pattern. 'Even veiled women
who are seen to be out alone or driving a car started to be targeted',
Zeinab G. told me. She continued:

> Women are being murdered, just because they are women. And we
> don't even know who to turn to. The police are themselves scared
> by the militias and many units are actually infiltrated by the Mahdi
> Army or the Badr Brigade. Others would like to help but are not
> in a position to do so because they are just not numerous enough
> and they are ill-equipped. The Islamists are targeting women who
> have a public profile even more, but they have started even to kill
> women who are not in any way politically active or who work in
> an NGO. Those of us who do, live in constant fear. Several of my
> colleagues have already been shot, and I have received several death
> threats.

A leading Iraqi women's rights activist told me during a visit to
London in July 2006 that she had to escape from Baghdad a few
weeks before:

I have been active for the past two years, but after I mentioned the targeted killing of women on television, I received a death threat via email. I was asked to stop all my activities or expect to be killed. I ignored this for some time, and then received another email, basically telling me that the group has noticed that I had continued with my political activism, and that I had ten days to leave the country. One of my close affiliates was shot a few days after that, and I realized that this was really serious. I left Iraq the following night. I really want to go back, but I am not sure that it would be safe for me.

In addition to the violence aimed at women who are perceived to diverge from the Islamists' specific narrow interpretations of Islam, women are also falling victim to the increasing sectarian violence that has increasingly taken hold over Iraq. The main perpetrators of sectarian violence and killings are the militias and Islamist groups. Both the Badr Brigade and the Mahdi Army, effectively, have taken over several ministries and infiltrated the security and police apparatus, and have used their positions to target, attack and kill Sunni Iraqis. Sunni Islamist groups, on the other hand, have been involved in the targeted killing of Shi'i. By 2006, whole neighbourhoods had been 'ethnically cleansed', as militias and militant groups took hold over particular areas. Although sectarian violence has so far largely been limited to extremist groups, sectarian sentiments have spilled over into the general population as the tit-for-tat killings increased and hatred began to grow. Accounts were heard of neighbours and former friends turning against each other, as well as violence between ordinary civilians.

Riverbend reports, exasperated, on one incident of sectarian killing that took place in July 2006:

The day before yesterday was catastrophic. The day began with news of the killings in Jihad Quarter. According to people who live there, black-clad militiamen drove in mid-morning and opened fire on people in the streets and even in houses. They began pulling people off the street and checking their ID cards to see if they had Sunni names or Shia names and then the Sunnis were driven away and killed. Some were executed right there in the area. The media is playing it down and claiming 37 dead but the people in the area say the number is nearer 60. The horrific thing about the killings is that the area had been cut off for nearly two weeks by Ministry of Interior security forces and Americans. Last week, a car bomb was set off in front of a 'Sunni' mosque people in the area visit. The night before the massacre, a car bomb exploded in front of a Shia *husseiniyya* in the same area. The next day was full of screaming and shooting and death for the people in the area. No one is quite sure why the Americans and the Ministry of Interior didn't respond immediately. They just sat by, on the outskirts of the area, and let the massacre happen. (11 July 2006)

Changing Gender Ideologies

Reports about Islamist groups and activists restricting women's mobility, dress code and public spaces, and of targeted assassinations, are symptomatic of wider conservative trends and the various ways in which women are being used in Iraq – as in many other conflict-ridden societies – to demarcate boundaries between 'us' and 'them'. Everywhere in the world, women are used to mark difference between people, between cultures, between religious groups, and so on. It is not only in Muslim societies, but equally in Western countries, that statements such as 'Your women dress this way and are not behaving properly' are deployed to discredit other communities, nations or cultures. A shift to more conservative and restricted gender ideologies and relations framed as Islamization fulfils two objectives in the context of Iraq: first, a break with the previous, largely secular, regime of Saddam Hussein; and, second, resistance to the occupying forces. Unfortunately women are being squeezed between the attempt to start a new Iraq that diverges from the policies of the previous regime and the attempt to challenge the imposition of western cultural norms and morals generally, as well as more specifically US and UK occupation.

As was shown in the previous chapter, more conservative norms and ideas relating to men and women and their respective roles and relations became obviously appparent during the period of economic sanctions. But in the current climate of fear and violence there has been an even greater push towards conservative social norms, partly responding to threats and risks, and partly due to actual changing social values. Yet, processes related to the Islamization of society and Islamist politics are not only leading to increasing conservatism in gender relations, but are also dominating Iraqi political power struggles in the post-Saddam era. One early example of the growing impact of Islamist tendencies was the attempt in December 2003 to scrap the Personal Status Code (family laws) in favour of shar'ia-based jurisdiction by the Iraqi Governing Council under its chair Abdel Aziz al-Hakim, head of the Supreme Council for the Islamic Revolution in Iraq (SCIRI). The established unified code was once considered the most progressive in the Middle East, making polygamy difficult and guaranteeing women's custody rights in the case of divorce.

Since 1959, Iraq has had a unified family law based on a relatively liberal reading of Islamic law. It codified all laws and regulations related to marriage, divorce, child custody and inheritance. This set of laws combined Sunni and Shi'i regulations and applies to all Iraqis, contributing to a sense of unity. It facilitated mixed marriages between Sunni and Shi'i Iraqis, as well as between Arabs and Kurds. Amendments to the family laws were made under the Ba'th regime in 1978. The amended Personal Status Code widened the conditions under which a woman could seek divorce, outlawed forced marriage, required the permission of a judge for a man to marry a second wife, and prescribed punishment for marriage contracted outside the court.

Although unsuccessful at the time, the attempt to change the law and the discussion around it was evidence of the current climate and the dangers that lay ahead. The debate about the personal status laws in particular and Islamic law in general emerged again in the context of the constitution. Whilst not the only source of legislation, Islam is the official religion and a basic source of legislation. Moreover, no law can be passed that contradicts the 'undisputed rules' of Islam.[23] Neither the previous Transitional Administrative Law (TAL) nor the current constitution explicitly mentions women's rights in the context of marriage, divorce, child custody and inheritance. Instead, Article 41 states that 'Iraqis are free in their adherence to their personal status according to their own religion, sect, belief and choice, and that will be organized by law.'

In other words, Article 41 of the new Iraqi constitution stipulates that the existing family laws, which apply equally to all members of society, will be replaced by family laws pertaining to specific religious and ethnic communities. This would give authority to conservative religious leaders to define laws according to their belief and particular interpretation. It provides no safeguards against extremely regressive and discriminatory interpretations of Islamic law, such as under the Taliban in Afghanistan, for example. And Article 41 doesn't only point to the likely future erosion of women's rights but also threatens to increase sectarianism inside the country. It will make new mixed marriages virtually impossible and will threaten already existing ones. Most significantly, it will further the cause of communalism as opposed to egalitarian unified citizenship, and may well fuel sectarian violence.

Because of several unresolved issues related to the constitution, including federalism, the status of Kirkuk, and opposition to Article 41, it was agreed that once the new government was formed a three-month window of opportunity would exist in which to amend the proposed new clauses. At the time of going to press a constitutional committee has been established, but Iraqi women's organizations are demanding that the period to discuss amendments be extended to one year, as the current security situation does not allow for proper campaigning and debate.

Increasing Poverty and Humanitarian Crisis

Most Iraqi women are oblivious to debates related to the constitution or the personal status law. Everyday survival is a priority in a context where lack of security goes hand in hand with incredibly difficult living conditions. The Iraqi infrastructure, already severely debilitated as a result of economic sanctions and war, has deteriorated even further since 2003. Electricity shortages, lack of access to potable water, malfunctioning sanitation systems and a deteriorating health system are part of everyday life in post-2003 Iraq. Intisar K., a doctor in a teaching hospital in Baghdad, summed up a situation that has been documented in several UN-related documents: 'We only have electricity for three to a maximum of five hours a day. There is not enough clean drinking water. Lack of sanitation is a big problem and continues to be one of the main causes of malnutrition, dysentery and death among young children.' Sawsan H., who previously worked as an accountant but has been unemployed since 2003, describes a scene in her everyday life:[24]

> The alarm clock woke me at 6.30 in the morning. There was no electricity. I wanted to take a shower but there was no water – so I said to myself 'Well, hallelujah, no water, no electricity.' I took a jug and went to get water from the emergency tank, washed, gathered my things and went out. The air was cool, lovely. I felt very happy. You see how simple things can make you happy? Suddenly something disturbed my joy – I heard a loud car honk and spun around, fearful. I saw no reason why anyone should be honking so loudly, and especially at that time in the morning, when there were so few cars on the street. There was no explanation, but we've become used to things without an explanation, and used to cars honking for no reason. The traffic in Baghdad is very bad and there are long stationary queues of cars, and people just honk their horns endlessly. What makes me very afraid on the streets, though, is hearing the faraway sound of gunshots, which then move increasingly closer. I begin to ask myself, 'is this the gunfire of people chasing terrorists, or gunshots at a funeral procession, or something else entirely?' Riding in a taxi, I see queues of cars waiting to fill up with petrol, winding down one street after another, and I ask myself 'will the petrol run out before the last car in the queue gets to the station?' Ah, how patient you have to be, oh Iraq. No electricity, no water, no petrol. No peace, no security. But despite all this crisis around me, I used to be pleased to see traffic policemen doing their jobs with energy, trying to

Children in an impoverished neighbourhood of Baghdad, 2004

control so many cars – the number of cars has increased incredibly.
I feel safer when I see Iraqi policemen doing their job and I think
'God help them.' I think about the efforts of the good people here,
good Iraqis. Suddenly I hear the voice of the taxi driver saying
'Here we are madam.'

It is not only lack of electricity, clean water and petrol that af-
fects the lives of Iraqi civilians. According to reports published by
the United Nations Children's Fund (UNICEF) and the British-based
charity organization Medact, the 2003 invasion and ongoing occupation have led to the deterioration of health conditions, including
an increase in malnutrition, a rise in vaccine-preventable diseases,
and higher mortality rates for children under 5. Iraq's mortality
rate for children under 5 rose from 5 per cent in 1990 to 12.5 per
cent in 2004.[25] One in three Iraqi children are malnourished and
underweight, according to a UNICEF report published in Amman
in May 2006. An earlier study states that about a quarter of Iraqi

children between six months and 5 years old suffer from either acute or chronic malnutrition.[26] The report shows that some 400,000 Iraqi children are suffering from 'wasting' and 'emaciation', conditions of chronic diarrhoea and protein deficiency.[27] The survey also records the growing drop-out rate among pupils less than 15 years of age – 25 per cent of students, who live mostly in rural areas and were identified as extremely poor. The main reasons given are the inability of families to afford the schooling and schools being located too far away from home.[28]

University students are also dropping out as a consequence of poverty. Hana G., a university professor at Baghdad University, told me in June 2005:

> I want my country back. Why do I have to pay the price for their bad government? Since the occupation, I do not feel safe to go to university. The university is no longer the place I used to know. I cannot socialize. I cannot visit my friends. I cannot even read when I want, because there is no electricity. I cannot even attend an exhibition. My salary has increased, but I cannot buy things anymore, because prices have risen. I do not know if I will come home alive if I go into the university. Many people I know from our university have been murdered. Everyday life is hell because we have to queue for everything, even petrol. Imagine, we are one of the countries with the largest oil reserves and we have a shortage of petrol. And my students are dropping out all the time. It is not only that they are scared to come; many are simply too weak because they are too poor to eat. Others have no money to buy shoes.

An increasing proportion of the Iraqi population are in dire need of humanitarian aid, including food. Similar to the humanitarian crisis during the sanctions period, women suffer particularly as they are often the last ones to eat after feeding their children and husbands. But they are also having to stand by as their often sick and malnourished children do not obtain adequate health care.

Despite incredibly difficult circumstances, Iraqi women have been at the forefront of trying to cope with and improve the exceedingly difficult living conditions and humanitarian crisis since 2003. There has been a flourishing of locally based women's initiatives and groups, mainly revolving around practical needs related to widespread poverty, lack of adequate health care, lack of housing, and lack of proper social services provided by the state. Women have also pooled their resources to help address the need for education and training, such as computer classes, as well as income-generating projects. Many of the initiatives filling the gap in state provision of welfare and healthcare are related to political parties and religiously motivated organizations and groups. However, independent nonpartisan professional women have also been mobilizing.

In the early days after the invasion, initiatives were mainly directed towards the most immediate needs of people. Ameena R. and other women in her social circle and neighbourhood organized themselves to feed patients left in a local hospital with no care after the violence and looting had scared away most doctors and nurses:

> We started to get organized after the invasion. We went to a hospital where there were fifty people and no one was taking care of them. We took turns to cook for the patients. We organized the clean-up of our local schools. When I went with a group of women to clean up a school in our neighbourhood, there was an American soldier and he tried to prevent us, but we managed to clean the school anyway. We were still afraid to send our children to school though.

A few months after the invasion, women got together to address humanitarian needs and to play an active role in both education and income generation. Hala G. told me how she and a number of her friends and colleagues started a charity for extremely poor women, widows and orphans in Baghdad:

> Bremer started to speak about civil society being open to all people. At that moment, we decided to start something, to start an organization. In the beginning, we wanted to help women. It was difficult for women to get outside their houses. We gathered women in our neighbourhood and told them about our idea.

We started with the project in May 2003. By July everything was settled. We knew what we wanted to do. We looked for a place. We wanted to help poor women in different ways: help them to learn something, to be skilful, help those who lost their husbands, help women to get some work. We rented a big house for three years. The owner was a doctor living outside Iraq. We used the money from our own savings and individual contributions. We only had money for two computers. Some people helped with their own means. We opened a small clinic and a small computer centre. We brought some young women who were skilled in computing and they started computer classes for girls. The centre is in the middle of a residential area. We recognized those who were extremely poor. We asked women to show us their documents to prove that they were widows.

Although few reliable statistics are available on the total number of widows in Iraq, the Ministry of Women's Affairs says that there are at least 300,000 in Baghdad alone, with hundreds of thousands more throughout the country (UN Office for the Coordination of Human Affairs, April 2006).

Saddam Hussein was responsible for the killing of thousands of men during his dictatorship: political repression and the series of wars created a demographic imbalance, with the female population making up between 55 and 65 per cent of the population of some 24 million Iraqis. The situation has become much more critical since the US-led invasion in 2003, as the daily violence and killing of innocent civilians goes hand in hand with an ineffective government that fails to provide the necessary financial and social support for the growing numbers of widows. Left with virtually no government support, no income due to the economic crisis and high unemployment rates, collapsed family networks due to the ongoing humanitarian crisis and lack of security, many widows are left with no choice but to beg on the streets or even to engage in prostitution.

Hala's charity, like several others that have emerged over the past years, is trying desperately to fill the gap left by the lack of government provision and welfare. When asked what her organization was doing in concrete terms to help poverty-stricken women, she replied:

> We gave them 25,000 dinars (about US$ 17) monthly to help them. Before we gave them the money, we told them of the importance of helping themselves and not depending on charity. We spoke about the need to work. So women came to us asking us to help them find work. We bought them cheap cloth, and taught them how to sew. We sold the clothes in a charity market. Some women did not like sewing, so we thought about cooking. We had a big kitchen in the house. We thought about letting them make *kubbah*, *burek* and other Iraqi foods, which was a very good project. Some girls asked for lectures in English. We have one member who graduated in languages, who volunteered to teach English. Some women did not like sewing, cooking or learning English, so we gave them lessons in memorizing the Qur'an. Then they started to bring children. So we opened a kindergarten. We have nine rooms, and each room has a different function.

After the siege and attacks on Falujah in 2004, Hala and her colleagues visited the city several times with medicine and food. But she wanted to help in a more systematic way:

> I spoke to my friends in Fallujah and we opened a branch there. We asked people to bring documents proving that their houses had been destroyed. They asked for compensation from the Iraqi government not from the USA. The first payment was for rebuilding the house and the second payment for furniture. People started rebuilding their houses. The numbers of widows and orphans started to increase dramatically. In this environment in Fallujah, there are no women's groups or organizations. Women started coming to us. They did not even have a glass of water. We tried to organize kitchen sets for families. When the heat started, they needed electric fans and small generators for electricity. We also distributed water containers. We started to develop good relations between the members of our organization and the women there. They asked for courses similar to those in our centre in Baghdad. We have nine women on the *majlis al-adara* [administration]. When we gathered together for discussion, we registered the fact that there was not enough money to buy new computers and sewing

machines, so we took two computers and two sewing machines from our centre in Baghdad and moved them to Fallujah. Then we started computer classes and sewing classes. We also started Qur'anic classes for older women. There was a problem with child-care, so we started a nursery. We did not give them much money, but they had enough to survive. We try to visit them once in a while but it is still very dangerous. Sometimes you feel so hopeless, so tired, but when you see the love and happiness in the eyes of the women, then we can continue. They are very grateful to us.

It became obvious throughout my interviews with Iraqi women who continue to live inside Iraq that women have been particularly hard hit by poverty, lack of adequate health care, malnutrition, lack of electricity and clean water, on top of the daily violence and lack of security. However, women have also been at the forefront of trying to cope with and improve their difficult living conditions, sharing scarce resources, expertise and professional skills to help those in even greater need.

Women's Political Participation

Since April 2003, women's organizations and initiatives have been mushrooming all over Iraq, although their mobility and political spaces have been severely impeded by the security crisis, especially since 2005. Many of these organizations, like the National Council of Women (NWC), the Iraqi Women's Higher Council (IWHC), the Iraqi Independent Women's Group, and the Society for Iraqi Women for the Future, have been founded either by members of appointed interim governments, such as the Iraqi Governing Council (IGC) or by prominent professional women with close ties to political parties. Many of the organizations were initiated by returnees, Iraqi women activists who were part of the diaspora before 2003.

While the organizations have mainly been founded and represented by elite women, some have a broad membership, with branches throughout the country. The Iraqi Women's Network (Al-Shabaka), for example, consists of thirty-seven women's grassroots organizations across the country. Their activities revolve around humanitarian and practical projects, such as income generation, legal advice, free health care and counselling, as well as political advocacy and lobbying. Women's rights activists work across political differences, in terms of party political ties or lack thereof, and regardless of attitude vis-à-vis the occupation – while some demand an immediate withdrawal of troops, others call for a concrete timetable for a handover of power; some would prefer the US and UK troops to remain until there is security, out of fear of Islamist militancy and terrorism.

The main issues that have politically mobilized women, mainly of an educated middle-class background, throughout Iraq are: (1) the attempt to replace the relatively progressive personal status law governing marriage, divorce and child custody with a more conservative law (Article 137 in 2003, and Article 41 of the new constitution 2005/06); (2) the issue of a women's quota for political representation – although women were unsuccessful in obtaining a 40 per cent quota in the transitional administrative law (TAL), they managed to negotiate a 25 per cent quota; (3) the struggle against sectarianism and for national unity; (4) the struggle against Islamist encroachment both from political parties and from militias and terrorist organizations; (5) the debate over the Iraqi constitution, mainly with respect to the role of Islam, the personal status laws and the demand to include an article covering international conventions, such as CEDAW,[29] and (6) the targeted murders of professional women and women's rights activists.

Several Iraqi diaspora organizations and individual activists based in the USA and the UK were initially instrumental in facilitating and encouraging Iraqi women's political mobilization. A flurry of conferences and the establishment of several women's centres marked the early phase of post-Saddam Iraq. Diaspora women involved themselves in charity organizations, humanitarian assistance, training programmes, advocacy around women's issues, democracy and human rights, and wider political issues both inside Iraq and in their countries of residence. Yet, due to the deteriorating security situation, women's activism in Iraq has been seriously impeded. As middle-class professionals as well as foreign passport holders have been key targets in both the frequent kidnappings for ransom and targeted murders, Iraqi women returnees have been particularly vulnerable. Moreover, the lack of credibility of the large number of previously exiled Iraqi politicians who have been disproportionately represented in the various interim governments and held key positions has also contributed towards a growing resentment against women returnees involved in women's organizations, and in political processes and reconstruction in general.

Some women, such as Najwa, whom I quoted in Chapter 1, understand the causes of resentment and anger towards returning Iraqis by those who have stayed inside Iraq during all those years. Others were much less understanding in their assessment and their accounts of their experience inside Iraq. Widad M., a doctor and activist in her fifties, who has lived in London for the past twenty-five years and worked for the Coalition Provisional Authority (CPA) in 2003 and 2004, said:

> It was very shocking, even my family had problems accepting me as I am. The characters changed, they seem to have closed up. At one time, I organized a meeting between students and the Ministry of Education. They wanted to discuss things. The first thing they wanted to discuss was young girls turning up at the university with short sleeves or short skirts or dresses. The mentality went so wrong. Why is this so important to them? They do not know how to run an organization. They are not used to taking any initiative. And everyone has this strong sense of entitlement, which is not very constructive if you want to rebuild a country.

Widad, like many other women I spoke to, feels very disillusioned. She was not the only one who told me that she was giving up because her efforts were not appreciated by people inside Iraq and also because things had just gone from bad to worse.

In the context of the specific debate about the Iraqi constitution, it became obvious that some of the discrepancies between diaspora women's attitudes and those of women 'from the inside' had more to do with lack of actual information about the content of the constitution as well as inadequate understanding of its implications rather than deeply entrenched political differences. On several occasions women from inside Iraq who were just visiting Amman told me that they were happy with the call for the implementation of the *shar'ia* (Islamic law). Azza A., for example, said: 'We are Muslims. Of course we want Islamic law.' The moment I started to discuss the possible implications, such as the right to unilateral divorce, restrictions on freedom of movement, increased polygamy, changes in existing child custody laws, and so on, most women I talked to expressed shock and acknowledged that they had been unaware of these implications.

Political transition in the form of two elections and a referendum on the constitution has not resulted in a credible and widely accepted government. Despite the 25 per cent women's quota stipulated by law, the steady exclusion of women from the public sphere that began in the 1990s during the sanctions period has accelerated under the occupation. Leila H., a women's rights activists still living inside Iraq, told me while visiting Amman for a short respite during the hot summer months of 2005:

> Initially many of us were very hopeful. We did not like foreign soldiers on our streets, but we were happy Saddam was gone. Once the general chaos and the looting settled down a bit, women were the first ones to get organized. Women doctors and lawyers started to offer free services to women. We started to discuss political issues and tried to lobby the American and British forces. But the Americans, especially, sent people to Iraq whose attitude was: 'We don't do women.' Bremer was one of them. Iraqi women managed to get a women's quota despite the Americans, who opposed it. Their interpretation of women's issues was to organize big meetings and conferences and to build modern women's centres. Do you think anyone went to visit these centres? What we need is more women in all aspects of governance. But the problem is that some of the women that are appointed are actually very conservative and are against women's rights.

There has been a debate over the benefits and problems of stipulating a women's quota, especially in light of the fact that many of the conservative Islamist political parties have obviously appointed conservative Islamist women who might not necessarily be interested in the promotion of women's rights. However, in a general political climate of social conservatism and increased patriarchal power, a quota ensures at least some female presence in public life and might also allow those more committed to women's issues and social justice to enter government institutions. Moreover, in the case of a conservative Islamist majority, it is still important to include conservative women who might or might not add to existing discourses and debates. The chances are that some women would challenge prevailing opinions and politics, and might also develop and change in the course of being involved in politics.

The mainstreaming of gender, as stipulated by UN resolution 1325, would have to involve the appointment of women to the government, and to all ministries and committees dealing with systems of local and national governance. However, appointing women within political parties and government institutions constitutes only one element of political transition. More significant in the context of reconstruction, social change and political transition is women's presence and activism within the judiciary, policing, human rights monitoring, allocation of funds, free media development, and all economic processes. Also important is the creation of independent women's groups, NGOs and community-based organizations. Female illiteracy rates and the general deterioration of the education system need immediate and urgent attention.

Unfortunately, any discussion about women's rights and women's inclusion in reconstruction processes remains a theoretical exercise as long as the condition on the ground does not change dramatically. For the majority of women, the basic survival of themselves and their families overshadows any other concerns. Iraqi men and women nowadays when they leave their houses say goodbye to their loved ones as if they will never return. Depending on where you live in Iraq, in which town or which part of a city like Baghdad, the chances of being killed by a US sniper or missile will be greater or lesser; in other places, the risk of a suicide bomb or militant attack might be greater. For women, the lack of security often results in severely restricted mobility, generally only in the company of at least one male guardian.

What Kind of Liberation?

Despite – or even partly because of – US and UK rhetoric about liberation and women's rights, women have been pushed back even further into the background and into their homes. They suffer both in terms of the ongoing and worsening humanitarian crisis and through lack of security on the streets. They are experiencing different forms of violence from many sides: the occupation forces, Islamist militias and organizations, criminal gangs, and even, in some case, from their own relatives, who are determined to protect the 'honour' of their families in cases of abduction and rape. Reconstruction processes have been seriously impeded, if not entirely stopped, by the escalating violence and chaos. Women who have a public profile, either as doctors, academics, lawyers, NGO activists or as politicians, are systematically threatened and have become targets for killings.

In June 2006, I visited Cairo once more for a conference, but also to catch up with friends. I met with my friend Mona again, both of us feeling shattered and depressed about the course of events. In Egypt, several of our common friends had been imprisoned for months without trial, simply because they were part of a pro-democracy movement demanding fair and transparent elections with a proper opposition. Yet Hosni Mubarak, one of the closest allies of the USA in the region, got away with the systematic repression of people who took the rhetoric about democracy and human rights seriously. We also discussed the fact that Cairo had become one of the many destinations of yet another wave of 'brain-drain' as thousands of Iraqi professionals have fled the deteriorating conditions and the escalating violence since 2003.

The conference on 'Gender and Empire' I was attending in Cairo was focusing mainly on Iraq and Palestine, but examples from different parts of the region very clearly revealed how empires, historically and in present times, use women and gender ideologies. In Iraq, all political actors have been guilty of instrumentalizing women and women's issues: the USA and the UK to legitimize their invasion and ongoing occupation; Islamist political parties and militias to signal a break with the past regime of Saddam Hussein, generally associated with secular policies; and Islamist militias and insurgents using women's dress, movement and wider gender ideologies and relations to resist American and British occupation and the imposition of Western values and norms.

The moment it became clear that no weapons of mass destruction were to be found, the legitimacy of the 'war on terror' in Iraq became linked to the struggle for democracy, human and women's rights. Ironically, the alleged link between Saddam Hussein and al-Qaeda has become a reality post-2003, as remnants of the previous regime fight side by side with Islamist extremists despite their inherent ideological differences. Women have not been mere passive victims of unfolding events, but have continued to try to hold together communities, families, neighbourhoods, to reject violence, to aid humanitarian assistance, and to resist not only occupation but also Islamist conservative gender ideologies and extremist violence. By the time of finishing this book, however, all forms of violence have escalated to unprecedented levels, particularly sectarian violence, making it more or less impossible for women even to venture outside their homes.

Conclusion

Thinking about my Aunt Salima triggers mixed feelings in me. I still get angry about her death, wondering whether it could have been prevented had she been able to make it to hospital that night when the curfew stopped my relatives from taking her. If only she had been granted a visa to enter Germany, where my father could have made sure that she received proper health care. If economic sanctions had not destroyed much of Iraq's previously excellent health-care system, her cancer might have been contained. If depleted uranium had not been used by US and British troops during the Gulf War in 1991, maybe she would not have suffered from cancer in the first place. And if only Iraq hadn't been ruled by the megalomaniac Saddam Hussein, long-term ally of 'the West'. If only... Yet, knowing my aunt, I suspect her heart would have broken if she had known what was to follow. During her lifetime, she would often sigh in great sadness: 'I am glad I cannot see.' But she still 'saw' clearly what was happening around her in all those years.

The stories retold in this book are full of 'if onlys', as women reflect on the past. A sense of nostalgia for better times and a melancholy linked to lost opportunities and potential pervade many of the accounts I heard. On one level, each historical period appears to have been preceded by better times and followed by greater difficulties, more disasters and increased hardship. Yet I also became acutely aware of the tendency to elevate and even glorify the past as it was seen through the filter of the present. When Iraqi women speak about better times and point to Saddam Hussein, for example, it is not because they enjoyed living in a repressive dictatorship with wars and, in later years, sanctions. Any positive nostalgia for the period before the invasion is largely a measure of the extent to which living conditions have deteriorated since 2003.

Plurality and Difference

In doing the research for this book, I recognized that while some women might have experienced a certain historical period as 'the golden age', for others it was a rather different story. Whether it was the pre-revolutionary era, the years immediately following the revolution in 1958, the period of economic boom and the expanding middle class in the 1970s, the time of the Iran–Iraq war (1980–88), or even the thirteen years of economic sanctions (1990–2003), there were always diverse experiences and memories. And such memories contain both the experience of harmonious living together within a multi-ethnic and multicultural national entity, a prospering economy and rapid modernization, and the history of repression, discrimination, deterioration in living conditions, sectarian tensions, and divide-and-rule tactics by the government.

One of the many problems in the post-invasion era, to my mind, is the failure by many sectors of society to acknowledge these different experiences, thereby alienating those parts of the population that do not see themselves represented in a particular narrative. In reference to the present situation, I always feel uneasy when I hear people say 'Iraqi women think...' or 'Iraqi women want...', generalizing from what is inevitably a wide variety of opinions, views and visions. What arguably has emerged from this book, however, is that difference is historically based on a complex set of variables and cannot simply be reduced to ethnicity and religion, as is often construed nowadays.

The chapter focusing on the 1950s and 1960s demonstrates that political divisions were not solely or even substantially based on sectarian or ethnic affiliation. Women of all backgrounds were attracted to either of the two main political trends: communism or Arab nationalism. Of course Kurdish nationalism is more clearly linked to Kurdish ethnicity, but Kurds were also attracted to communism and played an important role within the Iraqi Communist Party. Moreover, political divisions within the Kurdish movement have been linked to social class and to urban or rural background. The political establishment prior to the revolution in 1958 was largely dominated by Sunni Arabs, while the government of 'Abd al-Karim Qasim was more inclusive of ethnic and religious groups. Outside politics, women's social and cultural lives were also not solely dictated by ethnicity or religion; social class and political and intellectual orientation influenced people's social circles, cultural production and consumption.

Although most of the women I interviewed for this book were of urban background, their narratives and historical documentation give evidence of the sharp disjuncture between urban and rural lives during the 1950s and 1960s. Women in the countryside benefited neither from the expanding education system nor from the dynamic cultural and intellectual movements and events that made this period exhilarating and inspiring for the older women I interviewed. The other immense rupture, as explained earlier, existed between social classes, with the majority of girls and women belonging to impoverished classes with no access to education or adequate health-care facilities. The revolutionary changes and relatively liberal social values and norms experienced by educated middle- and upper-middle-class women stood in harsh contrast to the tribal and traditional patriarchal values shaping the lives of the majority of Iraqi women at the time.

In the accounts of the women presented in this book, the period after the first Ba'thi coup (1963) is generally associated with increased political violence, greater sectarianism and a reversal of progressive laws and reforms. Yet many women I interviewed spoke about the relative social freedom and cultural vibrancy during the rule of the 'Arif brothers (1963–68) and the early Ba'th period (1968–78). The experiences of these periods differ again most significantly in terms of class and political orientation. Many secular and apolitical middle-class Shi'i, Sunni, Kurdish and Christian women concurred in their appreciation of the achievements of the early Ba'th in education, modernization of infrastructures and welfare provision. However, the memories of those who were politically active in opposition to the regime are filled with accounts of political repression, mass arrests, torture and executions. Yet even some of those women who had first-hand experiences of the regime's repressive practices retrospectively appreciate its developmental policies.

Since Saddam Hussein's assumption of the presidency in 1979, divide-and-rule tactics increased the polarizing of sectarian divisions inside Iraq. There is no doubt that Kurds and Shi'is bore the brunt of the atrocities committed by the regime, especially in terms of the Anfal campaign in the 1980s, the deportations of Shi'is in the late 1970s and throughout the 1980s, and the brutal repression of the uprisings in the north and south after the Gulf War in 1991. Yet Sunni Arabs in political opposition parties and, increasingly, even within the Ba'th Party were also subjected to arrest, torture and executions, as were members of other minorities such as Chaldeans, Assyrians, Turkmen and Mandeans if they were part of opposition groups, or suspected of being so.

At the same time, the accounts of Iraqi women reveal that an urban middle-class identity, especially the more cosmopolitan Baghdadi identity, continued to subsume ethnic and religious differences even throughout the period of the sanctions. In other words, a middle-class Shi'i family in Baghdad had more in common with its Sunni Arab and Kurdish middle-class neighbours in mixed neighbourhoods than the impoverished Shi'is living in Madina al-Thawra (renamed Saddam city and now called Sadr city), or the majority of Shi'is in the south. Indeed, Baghdadi families have frequently been multi-religious and multi-ethnic and mixed marriages amongst urban Baghdadi middle classes were quite common.

Since the late 1970s, differences along the lines of secular and Islamist political positions started to assume greater significance and influence women's experiences of the regime. Members or sympathizers of the Islamist Shi'i Dawa Party, for example, were targeted not so much because of their religious affiliation but because of their opposition to the regime and their aim to establish an Islamic state. Without wanting to diminish the suffering and hardship that members of the Shi'i Islamist opposition parties endured, it must be accepted that the narrative that perceives them as the main recipients of state repression plays down not only the suffering of Kurds but also that of other segments of the population, including those Sunni Arabs who actively resisted the regime. Moreover, the claim that the Shi'is were singled out as a group because of their religious affiliation rather than political convictions contributes to the current atmosphere in which rights, privileges and power are linked to sectarian divisions and contestations over who suffered most. This is not to suggest that specific atrocities committed by the previous regime should be swept under the carpet for the sake of national unity. Quite the contrary; in my view, the show trial of Saddam Hussein has been a missed chance to initiate a more credible and serious truth and reconciliation process.

Saddam Hussein, Women and Gender Relations

Whilst fully acknowledging the magnitude of the crimes and atrocities committed by the previous regime, my study suggests that a closer and more nuanced analysis is needed to comprehend the various ways the former state impacted on women, gender relations and society more generally. This is not only because state policies towards women were complex and often contradictory, but also because the Ba'th regime itself radically changed both its rhetoric and it policies towards women in response to changing economic, social and political conditions. Despite their limitations and pragmatic nature, the regime's initial policies of pushing women into the public sphere, especially in the educational system and the labour force, certainly had an impact on the position of women in society and on relations between men and women. This was particularly the case within the expanding urban middle classes, but even women of other socio-economic backgrounds benefited from literacy programmes, improved health care and welfare provisions.

From 1968 to the late 1980s, the Iraqi state attempted to shift patriarchal power away from fathers, husbands, brothers, sons and uncles, in order to establish itself as the main patriarch and patron of the country. Many middle-class men and women welcomed the relatively progressive social policies of the state that held sway while the economy prospered. Yet, among the more religious and conservative forces in Iraqi society, such as tribal leaders and Islamists, there was considerable resentment at the state's attempt to interfere in people's traditions and sense of propriety. The limitations of 'state feminism', witnessed in the easy reversal of reforms and changes imposed from above, became apparent as conditions on the ground changed. The historically ambivalent position towards women, as educated workers on the one hand and mothers of future citizens on the other, was acutely apparent during the Iran–Iraq war, when Iraqi women were expected to be 'superwomen': they had to contribute in even greater numbers to swell the ranks of the depleted labour force, the civil service and all public institutions while men fought at the front. At the same time, women were pressured to produce more children – ideally five, according to Saddam Hussein – and contribute to the war effort by providing future generations of Iraqi soldiers.

As we saw in Chapter 4, the regime used women to demarcate boundaries between communities and carry the heavy burden of honour in a society that was becoming more and more militarized. Their bodies became increasingly the site of nationalist policies and battles. Iraqi men were encouraged to divorce their 'Iranian' wives during the war with Iran. On the other hand, Iraqi Arab men were encouraged to marry Kurdish women as part of the regime's Arabization policies in the north. At the same time, Islamist, Kurdish nationalist, communist and other women affiliated with political opposition were tortured and sexually abused, not only humiliating the women but 'dishonouring' their male relatives as well.

After the Gulf War and the uprisings in 1991, there was a radical shift away from Saddam Hussein's previous policies of centralization and suppression of tribal powers. Weakened by another war and a deteriorating economy, one of Saddam Hussein's strategies to maintain power was to encourage tribalism and revive the power of loyal tribal leaders. Central to the co-option of tribal leaders, and a bargaining chip to obtain loyalty, was the issue of women and women's rights. The regime accepted tribal practices and customs, such as 'honour killings', in return for loyalty.

Based on this more in-depth reading of the previous regime's gender policies and its attitudes to the position of women in society, I argue that within the general context of political repression, many Iraqi women gained in terms of socio-economic rights during the 1970s and 1980s. Living conditions improved for the majority of the population as the state not only relied on force and its power to control and co-opt, but also devised generous welfare programmes and opened up opportunities for investment and capital accumulation which were of great benefit to a large number of people within the expanding middle classes. It would also be too simplistic to state that the General Federation of Iraqi Women (GFIW) was merely a mouthpiece of the regime, as there was a level of tension and a degree of debate between the male political leadership and women activists throughout the 1970s and 1980s.

However, political repression, a series of wars and the militarization of society seriously affected women, families and gender relations, not only in terms of the loss of loved ones but also in terms of a deteriorating economy, changing government policies, and shifting norms and increasingly conservative values surrounding women and gender. After the end of the war, and under the sanctions in the

1990s and early 2000s, a radical shift took place in terms of women's diminishing participation in the labour force, restricted access to education, inadequate health care and other social services, as well as greater social conservatism and restrictions. Women were increasingly pushed back into their homes as unemployment rates skyrocketed, the economy faltered and the infrastructure collapsed.

There is a tendency to write out of the narrative the devastating impact of the most comprehensive sanctions system ever imposed on a country. Again, I do not suggest that everything was fine prior to the sanctions period, but would stress that dramatic changes with respect to women's position in society, social values and living conditions characterized the 1990s. But it is obvious that the changes and developments triggered by sanctions and changing state policies provide an important part of the immediate context of the current situation in post-2003 Iraq. It is a measure of the desperate straits to which the country has been reduced over the past four years that many Iraqi women now refer even to the sanctions period in nostalgic terms and compare it favourably with the current situation.

Alternative Histories

Telling the stories of Iraqi women is one way to uncover more layers of Iraq's multiple and shifting narratives. As I have tried to show throughout this book, Iraqi women have been involved in shaping all aspects of society and making up its very fabric. They have not merely been passive victims but have had agency and have reacted resourcefully to, adopted and coped with changing living conditions, state policies, laws and wars. Some women have even been part of oppressive political and social structures, whether as Ba'th functionaries, leading members of the GFIW, Islamist activists or within their professions, such as teachers and professors. Women have been part of political movements across a wide political spectrum; they have played an important role within the expanding economy and labour market; they have contributed to a rich and diverse culture, including literature, the arts and music; they have held together families and society; and they have been at the heart of the everyday attempts by ordinary people to resist political repression, occupation and extremist Islamist encroachment in nonviolent ways.

Yet, examining the experiences of women also makes it painfully clear that Iraqi women have not only suffered as the rest of society from repression, wars, sanctions and occupation. They have also been subjected to gender-specific forms of oppression, poverty and violence. A growing number of Iraqi women have been carrying the burden of being the main breadwinner while having to care for children and other dependants, as thousands of Iraqi men lost their lives through political persecution, wars, occupation and, more recently, sectarian violence. Women have more and more been used as symbols to demarcate boundaries and 'authentic' culture. In the process, women's dress codes, mobility, participation in public life and moral conduct have become subject to public scrutiny and control. Under the previous regime and, increasingly, since 2003, Iraqi women have experienced gender-based violence, such as sexual harassment, rape, domestic violence and honour killings. They are targeted by Islamist militants groups linked to the insurgency as well as by Islamist militias linked to the government.

My book shifts the focus away from the top-down approaches prevalent in most modern histories of Iraq and contributes to a small yet hopefully growing body of social histories which places greater emphasis on personal narratives and the voices of ordinary citizens. These more anthropologically and sociologically rooted histories point to agency, diversity and the everyday impact of political events, economic developments and military operations. Life stories and oral histories humanize what all too easily is construed in schematic generalization and stereotyping. This is not to take issue with the excellent existing modern histories of Iraq, but with the tendency to neglect the impact of historical developments on different parts of the population and the contribution of non-political elites to social, economic, cultural and political developments.

Memory, as I argued in the introduction, is subject to change and is both selective and fluid. History and memory are not merely about the past but are dialectically linked to the present. The individual memories presented in this book are complex constructions based on personal experiences, world-views (political, religious and ethical) and collective narratives. The women's stories, accounts and experiences are their own and certainly not devoid of particularities, personalities and idiosyncrasies. Yet the stories are also reflective of wider narratives positioning an individual in terms of her gender, class, political orientation, ethnicity, religious affiliation and places of origin and residence.

The issue of 'truth' is a tricky one. The aim of this book has not been to present the unvarnished truth of what has been happening to Iraqi women, but to show how different women have experienced specific historical events and periods and how they have chosen to represent them in their memories. Throughout the book, I have tried to present varying narratives, sometimes more congruent, sometimes contesting. It was obvious throughout the process of meeting and interviewing women that certain forms of knowledge and experiences are privileged over others: at the very least, a woman's own personal experience is often privileged over that of others. But often collective memories and histories creep into these personal accounts. Although there is a difference between remembering a personal experience and interpreting it, memories are often constructed in the context of interpreting, analysing and making sense of particular situations, events and developments. My strategy has been to try to keep a balance between presenting different accounts and contesting narratives and intervening as the author with my own views and interpretations.

Future Perspectives

Every chapter in this book could have filled volumes, and I see my book only as a beginning. I hope that my work will be built on, expanded and taken in new directions. The voices of peasants and

Iraqis of low-income backgrounds, for example, need to be heard in order that we gain a fuller picture of the social history of Iraq. It is also important to try to document the contributions of particular Iraqi women intellectuals, artists, professionals and political activists to the rich and exciting history of intellectual writings and cultural production. For my own part, I am interested in further exploring the way Iraqi women artists have contributed to the development of modern Iraqi art and how modern Iraqi art, in turn, has represented women, 'the feminine' and gender relations. My more immediate concern, however, is the present situation and the need to document the role of women and gender in political, social and economic developments since 2003.

It is impossible to predict the future either for Iraqi women or for Iraqi society more generally. However, more than three years after the invasion, all indications point to the painful reality that women are among the biggest losers in the new Iraq. They have been used by all political parties and actors concerned to score points and get across specific messages and signals. They have been pushed back into their homes. They are targeted not only because of what they wear or do not wear, their activities, their politics, even their driving, but often simply for being women. Yet, despite the gloomy picture of reality that I paint in the last chapter of this book, I do feel that Iraqi women continue to carry and embody the seed of hope for a more secure, peaceful and dignified time.

I will finish this book by sharing a poem by the Iraqi poet Dunya Mikhail; her 'Inanna' – the Sumerian goddess of love, fertility and war – captures the spirit in which I have written this book.

> Inanna
> I am Inanna.
> And this is my city.
> And this is our meeting
> round, red and full.
> Here, some time ago,
> someone was asking for help
> shortly before his death.

Houses were still here
with their roofs,
people,
and noise.
Palm trees
were about to whisper something to me
before they were beheaded
like some foreigners in my country.
I see my old neighbors
on the TV
running from bombs,
sirens
and Abu Al-Tubar.[1]
I see my new neighbors
on the sidewalks
running
for their morning exercises.
I am here
thinking of the relationship
between the mouse and the computer.
I search you on the Internet.
I distinguish you
grave by grave,
skull by skull,
bone by bone.
I see you
in my dreams.
I see the antiquities
scattered
and broken
in the museum.
My necklaces are among them.
I yell at you:
Behave, you sons of the dead!
Stop fighting
over my clothes and gold!
How you disturb my sleep
and frighten a flock of kisses
out of my nation!
You planted pomegranates and prisons
round, red and full.
These are your holes in my robe.
And this is our meeting...

Notes

Introduction

1. For a detailed analysis of British colonial rule, see Dodge, 2003. While some of the parallels between the two operations have resonance, most of the principal differences result from American unwillingness to commit the United States to 'nation-building' in the broadest sense, a project which, in spite of their paternalism and condescension, the British always considered would bring the most favourable returns.

Chapter 1

1. Economic and political pressures as well as persecution and massacres prompted many Iraqi Assyrians to leave (Al-Rasheed, 1998: xv–xvi) to Western Europe and the US. As British influence was diminishing, Assyrians felt increasingly insecure and became more subject to persecution. Iraqi Assyrians had not only felt protected by the British colonizers but some had also been enlisted in the army, and were therefore perceived as traitors by Arab nationalist forces inside Iraq.
2. Women's groups affiliated to political parties – i.e. the Iraqi Communist Party (ICP), the Iraqi Worker's Communist Party, the Kurdish Democratic Party (KDP), the Patriotic Union of Kurdistan (PUK), the Dawa Party, the Iraqi National Congress (INC), the Iraqi Democratic Party – exist side by side with independent groups, such as the Iraqi Women's Rights Organization, the Iraqi Women's League, Iraqi Women for Peace and Democracy, and Act Together: Women's Action for Iraq. Women activists also work through mixed groups like the Iraqi Prospect Organization, mainly comprising young professional Shi'i based in and around London. Women are also active within their ethnic and religious communities, such as the Assyrian Club of London, Kurdish Community Associations and the Shi'i Al-Khoei

Foundation. These various groups and organizations represent a wide range of activism – from charity to advocacy and direct involvement with the British government as well as the main political actors inside Iraq.

3. Act Together: Women's Action for Iraq has been trying to raise awareness about the plight of Iraqi women and highlight changing gender relations as a result of political repression, economic sanctions, war and occupation.

4. I discuss the emergence of the Iraqi Women's League inside Iraq in the following chapter.

5. Halabja is the name of the town that was gassed with chemical weapons as part of the wider Anfal campaign of the previous regime. Some 5,000 people died in this attack; many more live with lasting injuries and birth defects.

6. I was particularly shocked by the degree of segregation and racism with respect to African Americans, who are linked to high rates of poverty, unemployment, drug use, burglaries and homicide.

7. ACCESS (Arab Community Center for Economic and Social Services) provides social services, basic social and health care, English and computer classes, and assists in immigration matters for the Arab community in Dearborn.

8. Shi'i places of worship.

9. Mandaeans, also known as Sabeans and Subbi, originate in Iran and the south of Iraq. Only a few survive, some near the Tigris and Euphrates rivers, others in the area of Shushtar, in Iran, and in cities of Asia Minor. Their customs and writings indicate early Christian, perhaps pre-Christian, origin. Their system of astrology resembles those of ancient Babylonia and the cults of the Magi in the last centuries BC. Their emanation system and their dualism suggest a Gnostic origin, but unlike the Gnostics they abhor asceticism and emphasize fertility. Although some of their practices were influenced by Christianity, Judaism and Islam, they reject all three religions. The Mandaeans respect St John the Baptist because of his baptizing, since their principal concern is ritual cleanliness and their chief rite frequent baptism.

10. For detailed analyses of Iraqi refugees in Jordan, see Chatelard 2002, 2003.

11. Business and residential areas in Amman are located in relation to a number of roundabouts and crossroads along Zahran Street, the main road from downtown to the Queen Alia International Airport. These are referred to as 'circles' and are numbered one to eight.

12. ECRE, *Guidelines on the Treatment of Iraqi Asylum Seekers and Refugees in Europe*, March 2006.

13. UNHCR speaks of at least 580,000 IDPs in the three northern governorates; see UNHCR, *Guidelines Relating to the Eligibility of Iraqi Asylum Seekers*, October 2005, pp. 56–7.

14. UNHCR states that shelter is one of the most pressing concerns for IDPs, who return to their place of origin, only to find themselves in search of a new region to move to in search of protection. See UNHCR, *Country of Origin Information – Iraq*, October 2005, p. 97.

15. See IRIN, *Iraq: Year in Brief 2005 – Chronology of Humanitarian Events*, 9 January 2006; UNAMI, *UN–Iraq Humanitarian Update*, September 2005, p. 2; UNAMI, *UN–Iraq Humanitarian Update*, October 2005, pp. 1–3; and UNAMI, *Human Rights Report 1 November–31 December 2005*, 18 January 2006.

Chapter 2

1. By 1958, 2,480 individuals, about 1 per cent of the population, owned over 55 per cent of all land in private hands (Farouk-Sluglett and Sluglett, 2001: 33).

2. Since King Faisal II was still a minor after the death of King Ghazi in an automobile accident in 1939, his uncle 'Abd al-Ilah was appointed regent.

3. Muhammad Mahdi al-Jawahiri (1903–1999) was a famous poet and sympathizer with the influential Iraqi Communist Party.

4. Now known as al-Sadr City.

5. Black traditional loose head-to-toe garment.

6. Nuha is referring to the Shi'i rituals associated with 'Ashurah, the tenth day of the Islamic month of Muharram. For Shi'i Muslims, the day commemorates the martyrdom of Husayn ibn 'Ali, the grandson of the Prophet Muhammad at the Battle of Karbala' in the year 61 AH (680 AD) and is a day for mourning. Plays re-enacting the martyrdom are frequently staged and many take part in mourning rituals. Some Shi'is observe 'Ashurah with a traditional flagellation ritual called *zanjeer zani* or *zanjeer matam*, involving the use of a *zanjeer* (a chain with a set of curved knives at the end). The practice is not universal – many Shi'is enact the ritual by beating their chests symbolically.

7. Jawad Salim, the most famous Iraqi artist even long after his premature death in 1961, was a pioneer in the modernist movement. Salim worked as a painter, graphic artist, illustrator and sculptor. He created the Monument of Freedom, one of Baghdad's most recognizable icons in Tahrir Square.

8. *Mahr*, marriage gift by the bridegroom to the bride, is a symbolic expression of the groom's economic responsibilities within marriage and of his readiness to assume these. The general principle is that *mahr* should be estimated according to circumstances. In this context, *Ras al-shahar maku mahar* ['at the end of the month there will be no more gifts to the bride'] is interpreted by my respondent as the promotion of sexual relations outside of marriage.

9. For an account of the history of the women's movement in the first part of the twentieth century, see Efrati, 2004.

10. The Arab Socialist Ba'th Party (Ba'th) was founded in 1947 by the Syrian Christian Michel 'Aflaq as a radical, secular Arab nationalist political party. *Ba'th* means 'resurrection' or 'renaissance'. Ba'thist beliefs combine pan-Arabism, socialism and Arab nationalism. The motto of the party is 'Unity, Freedom, Socialism' (*wahda, hurriya, ishtirakiya*). 'Unity' refers to Arab unity, 'freedom' emphasizes freedom from foreign control and interference in particular, and 'socialism' refers to what has been termed Arab socialism rather than to Marxism, mainly standing for the nationalization of property and wealth. It functioned as a pan-Arab party with branches in different Arab countries, but was strongest in Syria and Iraq. In 1966, the Syrian and Iraqi parties split into two rival organizations. Both Ba'th parties retained the name and maintain parallel structures in the Arab world.

11. Al-Bazzaz was the first civilian prime minister since the overthrow of the monarchy in 1958.

12. One of the five pillars of Islam: giving charity to the poor.

Chapter 3

1. Small white flower with sweet smell, type of gardenia.
2. Ahmed Hasan al-Bakr suddenly announced his resignation in July 1979, officially for health reasons. Saddam Hussein was sworn in as president within hours.
3. Michel 'Aflaq (1910–1989) was the ideological founder of Ba'thism. Born in Damascus to a middle-class Greek orthodox Christian family, he studied at the Sorbonne in Paris, where he first developed his Arab nationalist ideals, attempting to combine socialism with the vision of a pan-Arab nation. In his political pursuits, 'Aflaq became committed to Arab unity and the freeing of the Middle East from Western colonialism. While considered an 'ideological founder' of the pan-Arab movement, 'Aflaq had little connection to the government that took power in Syria under the name of the Ba'th Party in 1963. Eventually, the government and he had a falling out and he was forced to flee to Iraq, where another Ba'th Party had taken power. While this party also failed to follow most of 'Aflaq's teachings, his presence gave symbolic support to the Saddam Hussein regime's claim that Iraq was in fact the true Ba'thist country. In Iraq he was given a token position as head of the party; his objections to the regime were silenced and ignored.
4. The main opposition parties were the Communist Party (ICP), the Kurdish Democratic Party (KDP), the Nasserists, and the pro-Syrian Ba'this.
5. For a detailed account, see Farouk-Sluglett and Sluglett, 2001: 107–206.
6. See Davis, 2005.
7. The Museum of Popular Heritage is a collection of traditional old Baghdadi houses, and contains displays of traditional crafts, such as basketwork, carpets, woodwork and metalwork.
8. Originally designed as an inn for travelling merchants, and the dwelling place of many university scholars in the fourteenth century, the building was in a state of disrepair for over two centuries, sometimes with waist-high flood water from the Tigris in the famous hallway. By the mid-1980s, the building had been restored and was in use as a restaurant.
9. This expression is borrowed from the main character of Betool Khedairi's novel *Absent* (2005).
10. See Al-Ali, 2000: 73–84.
11. The Iraqi currency consists of dinar and fils. Fils is the equivalent to cents and pence.
12. Title of speech delivered by Saddam Hussein at the Third Conference of the General Federation of Iraqi Women, on 17 April 1971, trans. K. Kishtainy, Baghdad: Translation and Foreign Languages Publishing House (1981).
13. Amal al-Sharqi's chapter 'The Emancipation of Iraqi Women' is clearly biased in favour of Ba'th propaganda and relies heavily on official government statistics.
14. For a detailed analysis, see Rohde, 2006.
15. See Farouk-Sluglett, 1993; Joseph, 1991; and Rassam, 1992.
16. For a detailed and in-depth discussion on the debates about the Personal Status Laws of 1959 and 1978, see Efrati, 2005.

Chapter 4

1. Saddam Hussein played on the historical battle of Qadisiya, fought near Hira in 637 AD, during which Arab-Muslim armies defeated Sasanid Persia.
2. Regional and international forces, such as the Gulf countries and the USA, played an important role in encouraging Saddam Hussein as well as prolonging the war.
3. For an in-depth analysis of the Iraqi regime's ambivalent attitude towards women's roles in the 1980s, see Efrati, 1999.
4. Iraq was conquered by the Ottomans in 1424 winning over the Persian Safavid Empire. Aside from a brief interlude of a second Persian conquest, the Ottomans divided Iraq into three provinces of Mosul, Baghdad, and Basra to 1918.
5. Anfal is the title of the eighth sura (chapter) of the Qur'an, meaning 'the spoils of war'. In the context of the genocide against the Kurds, Anfal is a blasphemous and cynical abuse of a Qur'anic term.
6. For more details, see Human Rights Watch (1993) Genocide in Iraq, the Anfal Campaign Against the Kurds; and www.womenwarpeace.org/iraq/iraq.htm.

Chapter 5

1. See http://news.bbc.co.uk/onthisday/hi/dates/stories/august/2/newsid_2526000/2526937.stm; Abdullah, 200.
2. For further details, see MacArthur, 1992.
3. SCR 661 (6 August 1990) imposed a complete ban on trade to and from Iraq, exempting only 'supplies intended strictly for medical purposes, and in humanitarian circumstances, foodstuffs' (PARA. 3C).
4. See http://news.bbc.co.uk/2/hi/middle_east/2754103.stm for further details.
5. Line south of Irbil. The safe haven was later extended to include Sulamaniyya and Halabja.
6. Economic sanctions significantly limited Iraq's ability to earn the foreign currency needed to import sufficient quantities of food. As a consequence, the state of nutrition changed from adequate before the Gulf War in 1991 to a situation where food shortages and malnutrition became the norm. An even greater humanitarian crisis in terms of malnutrition was only avoided by the government's programme of food rations in south-central Iraq and the presence of NGOs and foreign aid in the north (Pellet, 2000: 156).
7. For a detailed, in-depth analysis of the sanctions regime, see Brown, 1999.
8. One of the most reliable studies on sanctions in Iraq is the 1999 report 'Morbidity and Mortality among Iraqi Children' by Richard Garfield, Professor at Columbia University (Garfield, 1999b). Garfield, an expert on the impact of sanctions on public health, conducted a comparative analysis of the more than two dozen major studies that have analysed malnutrition and mortality figures in Iraq during the 1990s. He estimates the most likely number of excess deaths among children under 5 years of age from 1990 through March 1998 to be 227,000. Garfield's analysis shows that child

mortality rates were double those of the previous decade. He has recently recalculated his numbers, based on the additional findings of another study by Mohamed Ali and Iqbal Shah in *The Lancet* (May 2000) to arrive at an estimate of approximately 350,000 through 2000. Most of these deaths are associated with sanctions, according to Garfield, but some are attributable to the Gulf War, which destroyed eighteen of the twenty electricity-generating plants and disabled vital water-pumping and sanitation systems. Untreated sewage flowed into rivers used for drinking water, resulting in a rapid spread of infectious disease (for further information see Cortright, 2001).

9. The UN initially determined that 53 per cent of the oil revenue would be allocated to the humanitarian programme in the areas under the control of the Iraqi government, 30 per cent to pay for compensation claims arising out for the Gulf War, 13 per cent to the UN programme in the Kurdish regions of Northern Iraq, and the remainder spent on further administrative costs of the UN. The programme was organized in six-month 'phases': every six months the Iraqi government proposed a list of import contracts for scrutiny and, if judged adequate, was approved by the UN Sanctions Committee. However, the politicization of the programme and the bureaucracy involved caused severe delays in both the approval and the processing of contracts. For further details, see www.casi.org.uk/guide/off.html.

10. In September 1998, UN Assistant Secretary General and Humanitarian Coordinator of the Oil-for-Food Programme for Iraq, Dennis Halliday, resigned his post in protest at the continuing economic embargo against Iraq. He asserted that 'We are in the process of destroying an entire society. It is as simple and terrifying as that. It is illegal and immoral.' On 26 October 1998, and after Halliday's resignation, Hans Graf Sponeck was named UN Humanitarian Coordinator for Iraq. Sponeck was as outspoken as Halliday in his condemnation of the economic sanctions. He was highly critical of the US bombing in the southern and northern 'no-fly' zones, saying that they interfered with the implementation of the UN humanitarian programme. On 15 February 2000, Sponeck resigned his post in protest at the failure of the United Nations' Oil-for-Food Programme. He urged an end to UN sanctions on Iraq, calling them 'a true human tragedy'. He observed that 'the humanitarian programme has failed to meet the needs of Iraq's 22 million people.' He added: 'As a UN official, I should not be expected to be silent to that which I recognise as a true human tragedy that needs to be ended.' In less than a week after Sponeck's resignation, a third senior UN humanitarian official in Iraq, Jutta Burghardt, head of the World Food Programme (WFP) in Iraq, had resigned, citing the same reasons as Sponeck and Halliday. See www.geocities.com/iraqinfo/sanctions/sarticles9/whytop.htm.

11. According to a United Nations report in 1999: 'In addition to the scarcity of resources, malnutrition problems also seem to stem from the massive deterioration in basic infrastructure, in particular in the water-supply and waste disposal systems. The most vulnerable groups have been hardest hit, especially children under five years of age who are being exposed to unhygienic conditions, particularly in urban centres' (Report of the second panel established pursuant to the note by the president of the

Security Council of 30 January 1999 (S/1999/100), concerning the current humanitarian situation in Iraq; see www.casi.org.uk/info/panelrep.html.).

12. 1999–2000 Country Report, Iraq Country Office, June 2000.

13. UNICEF, "Iraq: Facts and Figures", 2004, www.unicef.org/media/media_9788.html.

14. UNIFEM, Gender Profile, Iraq 2004, www.womenwarpace.org/iraq/iraq.htm.

15. According to a study carried out by an Iraqi sociologist, polygamy had decreased from 8 per cent in 1940 to 2 per cent in 1980 in Baghdad (Al-Janabi, 1983: 16). However, during the Iran–Iraq war polygamy increased as the government encouraged Iraqi men to marry war widows.

16. www.unicef.org/emerg/files/IraqOct.pdf.

17. www.irinnews.org/report.asp?ReportID=35434&SelectRegion=Iraq_Crisis &SelectCountry=IRAQ.

18. See www.womenwarpeace.org/iraq/iraq.htm.

19. Traditional black loose garment worn by Iraqi women.

20. City in south of Iraq, known for its Shi'i shrines and cemetery.

21. New York Times, Letter to the editor, 13 September, 1999. See www.casi.org.uk/discuss/1999/msg00450.html.

22. FAO, Assessment of the Food and Nutrition Situation: Iraq, 2000. See www.reliefweb.int/library/documents/iraqnutrition.pdf.

23. The term 'gendercide' refers to systematic patriarchal violence against women that cannot be reduced to the action of a single male person, but involves policies and actions by the state, non-state communities, religious establishments, and/or by the military at war. Mojab, 2003: 25.

24. Depleted uranium, DU, is radioactive waste used to coat shells and ammunition because of its capacity to penetrate heavy armour and tanks. It is both chemically and radiologically toxic to humans and other forms of life. 'Upon impact, DU penetrators oxidize rapidly, spreading toxic uranium oxide particles. If a person inhales or ingests DU, it enters into the bloodstream and then can circulate throughout the whole body. Prolonged internal exposure to radiation may cause severe health problems, including cancers (mainly leukaemia and lung and bone cancer); pulmonary and lymph node fibrosis; pneumoconiosis; inhibition of reproductive activities; chromosomal changes; depletion of the body's immune system; and finally death' (Ammash, 2000: 169–70).

25. Back in 1999, major US newspapers ran front-page investigative stories revealing that the CIA had covertly used UN weapons inspectors to spy on Iraq for the USA's own intelligence purposes. 'United States officials said today that American spies had worked undercover on teams of United Nations arms inspectors', the New York Times reported (1 July 1999). According to the Washington Post (3 February 1999), the USA 'infiltrated agents and espionage equipment for three years into United Nations arms control teams in Iraq to eavesdrop on the Iraqi military without the knowledge of the U.N. agency.' www.fair.org/activism/unscom-history.html.

26. 'Smart sanctions' referred to a reformed sanctions regime with two major changes. First, the tightening of sanctions by pressurizing Iraq's neighbours

to stop the smuggling of oil from Iraq. It was suggested that Iraqi neighbours losing smuggling revenue would be compensated, probably from Iraqi oil revenues held in the UN escrow account. The second main change was that the UN Sanctions Committee would play a reduced role in processing contracts for export to Iraq. A list of items with potential 'dual use' would be drawn up; this became known as the Goods Review List (GRL). All goods not on that list could be imported by Iraq without the approval of the Sanctions Committee, under procedures similar to the 'fast track' in place since March 2000 for a variety of civilian goods: items on these lists only required that the secretary-general be notified in order to import them; the Sanctions Committee did not have to get involved. www.casi.org. uk/newslet/0207reform.html.

Chapter 6

1. CBS News, 2002.
2. Colin Powell, 5 February 2003. 'US secretary of State Colin Powell Addresses the U.N. Security Council', www.whitehouse.gov.
3. The United Nations Monitoring, Verification and Inspection Commission was created through the adoption of Security Council resolution 1284 of 17 December 1999. UNMOVIC replaced the former UN Special Commission (UNSCOM) with the mandate to verify Iraq's compliance with its obligation to be rid of its weapons of mass destruction (chemical, biological weapons and missiles with a range of more than 150 km), and to operate a system of ongoing monitoring and verification to ascertain that Iraq does not reacquire the same weapons prohibited it by the Security Council. The Secretary General of the United Nations appointed Dr Hans Blix of Sweden as the Commission's Executive Chair. He served from 1 March 2000 to 30 June 2003. www.unmovic.org.
4. See Left, '2003. Also 'Transcript of Blix's U.N. presentation', www.CNN.com, 7 March 2003.
5. Under international humanitarian law, or the laws of war, an occupying power has a duty to restore and ensure public order and safety in the territory under its authority. Military commanders on the spot must prevent and where necessary suppress serious violations involving the local population. Ensuring local security includes protecting people from reprisals and revenge attacks, such as those directed against members of minority populations or government officials. This may require that occupying forces be deployed to secure public order until the time police personnel, whether local or international, can be mobilized for such responsibilities. See ICRC, 2003.
6. Ibid.
7. The title of the Human Rights Watch Report on sexual violence and abductions of women and girls in Baghdad, vol. 16, no. 7, July 2003.
8. Human Rights Watch, 'Climate of Fear: Sexual Violence and Abduction of Women and Girls in Baghdad', vol. 15, no. 7, July 2003, p. 5.
9. See Bennett, 2006.
10. Human Rights Watch, 2003.

11. See Iraq Body Count, 2006.
12. See Roberts et al., 2004.
13. See Rosenthal, 2004.
14. For details about the events at Fallujah, see http://iraqbodycount.org/resources/falluja/index.php. For an analysis, see Rai, 2005.
15. For further details, see www.rememberfallujah.org/why.htm and http://www.iraqbodycount.org.
16. For an eye witness account of the atrocities committed in Fallujah, see, for example, Jo Wilding's blog Wildfirejo, www.wildfirejo.blogspot.com/.
17. Ibid.
18. Those suspected of being involved in both the resistance and terrorist activities are regularly detained without their families being informed of their whereabouts and their well-being. People disappearing, random arrests, torture and abuse in prison are, ironically, common phenomena is post-Saddam Iraq.
19. Hassan, 2005.
20. IRINNews.org, 004.
21. http://washingtontimes.com/world/20041017–013506–9889r.htm.
22. Judd, 2006.
23. Article 2. Nathan Brown translates 'undisputed rules' as 'the fixed elements of the ruling of Islam'. Brown, 2005: 2.
24. I am grateful to Ibtesam Al-Tahir and Act Together: Women's Action for Iraq for allowing me to use several accounts of women describing their everyday realities. Ibtesam had gathered these accounts during a visit to Iraq in 2006. Act Together has been reading out some of these accounts at public events to raise consciousness about the lives of Iraqi women under occupation.
25. See www.unicef.org/infobycountry/iraq_statistics.html; and www.medact.org/content/wmd_and_conflict/Medact per cent2oIraq per cent202004.pdf.
26. The study, entitled Iraq Living Conditions Survey 2004 (ILCS), was organized by the UN Development programme (UNDP) in collaboration with the Iraqi Ministry of Planning and Development Cooperation and conducted by a Norwegian-trained team from the Central Organization for Statistics and Information Technology in Baghdad. It drew its conclusions from interviews carried out between April and August 2004 with members of 21,688 households in Iraq's eighteen provinces.
27. Ibid.
28. See UN World Food Programme/Government of Iraq: 'Food Security and Vulnerability Analysis in Iraq', survey of May 2006, with the support of UNICEF.
29. The Convention on the Elimination of All Forms of Discrimination against Women (CEDAW); see www.un.org/womenwatch/daw/cedaw/.

Conclusion

1. 'The hatchet man': a serial killer in Baghdad during the 1970s, who was later discovered to be an evil hand of the Ba'th regime.

References

Abraham, N., and A. Shryock (eds) (2000) *Arab Detroit: From Margin to Mainstream*, Wayne State University Press, Detroit.

Abdul-Jabar, F., and H. Dawod (2003) (eds) *Tribes and Power: Nationalism and Ethnicity in the Middle East*, Saqi Books, London.

Abdullah, T. (2003) *A Short History of Iraq*, Pearson-Longman, London.

Al-Ali, N. (2005) 'Gendering Reconstruction: Iraqi Women between Dictatorship, Wars, Sanctions and Occupation', *Third World Quarterly*, vol. 26, no. 4–5, pp. 739–58.

Al-Ali, N. (2003) 'Women and Economic Sanctions in Iraq', in S. Inati (ed.), *Iraq: Its History, People and Politics*, Prometheus Press, Philadelphia.

Al-Ali, N. (2000) 'Sanctions and Women in Iraq', in Campaign Against Sanctions on Iraq, *Sanctions on Iraq: Background, Consequences, Strategies*, CASI, Cambridge.

Al-Ali, N., and N. Pratt (2006) 'Women in Iraq: Beyond the Rhetoric', *MERIP*, June 2006.

Al-Ali, N., and Y. Hussein (2003) 'Between Dreams and Sanctions: Teenage Lives in Iraq', in Akbar Mahdi (ed.) *Teenagers in the Middle East*, Greenwood, Westport CT.

Al-Janabi, A'ida (1983) *Al-Mutghirat al-ijtima'iya wal thqafiya li dhaherat ta'adud al-zawjat fi al-irak*, Dar Al-Huriya, Baghdad.

Al-Khamis, U. (2001) 'An Historical Overview: 1900s–1990s', in M. Faraj (ed.), (2001) *Strokes of Genius: Contemporary Iraqi Art*, Saqi Books, London.

Al-Khayat, S. (1990) *Honour and Shame: Women in Modern Iraq*, Saqi Books, London.

Al-Radi, N. (1998) *Baghdad Diaries*, Saqi Books, London.

Al-Rasheed, M. (1998) *Iraqi Assyrian Christians in London: The Construction of Ethnicity*, Edwin Mellen Press, Lewiston NY/Queenston ON/Lampeter.

Al-Rasheed, M. (1994) 'The Myth of Return: Iraqi Arab and Assyrian Refugees in London', *Journal of Refugee Studies*, vol. 7, no. 2/3, pp. 199–219.

Al-Rasheed, M. (1993) 'The Meaning of Marriage and Status in Exile: the Experience of Iraqi Women', *Journal of Refugee Studies* vol. 6, no. 2, pp. 89–104.

Al-Sharqi, A. (1982) 'The Emancipation of Iraqi Women', in T. Niblock (ed.), Iraq: The Contemporary State, Croom Helm, London.

Al-Windawi, T. (2004) Thura's Diary: My Life in Wartime Iraq, Viking, New York.

Ammash, H. S. (2000) 'Toxic Pollution, the Gulf War, and Sanctions', in A. Arnove (ed.) Iraq under Siege: The Deadly Impact of Sanctions and War, Pluto Press, London.

Amnesty International (2005) 'Iraq: Decades of Suffering, Now Women Deserve Better', 22 February, web.amnesty.org/library/index/eng-mde 140012005?open&of+eng-irq.

Amnesty International (2001) Amnesty International Report: Iraq, http://web.amnesty. org/web/ar2001.nsf/webmepcountries/iraq.

Arnove, A. (ed.) (2000) Iraq Under Siege: The Deadly Impact of Sanctions and War, Pluto Press, London.

Baram, A. (1997) 'Neo-Tribalism in Iraq: Saddam Hussein's Tribal Policies 1991–96', International Journal of Middle Eastern Studies, vol. 29, no. 1, pp. 1–31.

Batatu, H. (2004) The Old Social Classes and the Revolutionary Movement of Iraq, 3rd edn, Saqi Books, London.

Bengio, O. (1998) Saddam's Word: Political Discourse in Ba'thist Iraq, Oxford University Press, Oxford.

Bennett, B. (2006) 'Stolen Away', Time Magazine, 1 May, http://205.188.238.109/ time/archive/preview/0,10987,1186558,00.html, accessed 12 July 2006.

Black, J. (2005) Using History, Hodder Arnold, London.

Brown, N. (2005) 'The Final Draft of the Iraqi Constitution: Analysis and Commentary', Carnegie Endowment for International Peace, New York, August.

Cainkar, L. (1993) 'The Gulf War, Sanctions and the Lives of Iraqi Women, Arab Studies Quarterly, vol. 14, no. 2: 14–49.

CASI (Campaign Against Sanctions on Iraq) (2000) Sanctions on Iraq: Background, Consequences, Strategies, proceedings of the conference hosted by the Campaign against Sanctions on Iraq, 13–14 November 1999, CASI, Cambridge, www. casi.org.uk/conf99/proceedings.pdf.

CBS News (2002) 'Plans for Iraq Attack began 9/11', 4 September, www.cbsnews. com/stories/2002/09/04/september11/main520830.shtml.

Chatelard, G. (2002) 'Jordan as a Transit Country: Semi-protectionist Immigration Policies and their Effects on Iraqi Forced Migrants', Working Paper no. 61, New Issues in Refugee Research, Robert Schuman Centre for Advanced Studies, European University Institute, Florence.

Chatelard, G. (2003) 'Iraqi Forced Migrants in Jordan: Conditions, Religious Networks, and the Smuggling Process', Discussion Paper no. 2003/34, WIDER, United Nations University, April.

Chatelard, G. (2004) 'Jordan: A Refugee Haven', Migration Policy Institute, Washington DC, www.migrationinformation.org/Profiles/display.cfm?id=236

Cobbett, D. (1986) 'Women in Iraq', Saddam's Iraq: Committee against Repression and for Democratic Rights in Iraq, Zed Books, London.

Cohen, R. (1995) 'Rethinking Babylon: Iconoclastic Conceptions of the Diasporic Experience', New Community, vol. 21, no. 1, pp. 5–18.

Cortright, D. (2001) 'A Hard Look at Iraq's Sanctions', The Nation, 3 December.

Davis, E.(2005) Memories of State: Politics, History, and Collective Memory in Modern Iraq, University of California Press, Berkeley.

Dodge, T. (2003) Inventing Iraq: The Failure of Nation Building and a History Denied, Columbia University Press, New York.

Dodge, T., and S. Simon (eds) (2003) Iraq at the Crossroads: State and Society in the Shadow of Regime Change, Adelphi Paper 354, International Institute for Strategic Studies, London.

Efrati, N. (2005) 'Negotiating Rights in Iraq: Women and the Personal Status Law', Middle East Journal, vol. 59, no. 4, August, pp. 577–95.

Efrati, N. (2004) 'The Other Awakening in Iraq: The Women's Movement in the First Half of the Twentieth Century', British Journal of Middle Eastern Studies, vol. 31, no. 2, pp. 153–73.

Efrati, N. (1999) 'Productive or Reproductive? The Roles of Iraqi Women during the Iran–Iraq War', Middle Eastern Studies, vol. 35, no. 2, pp. 27–44.

Faraj, M. (ed.) (2001) Strokes of Genius: Contemporary Iraqi Art, Saqi Books, London.

Farouk-Sluglett, M., and P. Sluglett (2001) Iraq since 1958: From Revolution to Dictatorship, 4th edn, I.B. Tauris, London and New York.

Farouk-Sluglett, M. (1993) 'Liberation or Repression? Pan-Arab Nationalism and the Women's Movement in Iraq', in D. Hopwood, H. Ishow and T. Koszinowski (eds) Iraq; Power and Society, Ithaca Press, Reading.

Fischer-Tahir, A. (2004) '"Ich war eine, die keine Angst hatte": Biografische Annäherungen an Frauen im organisierten Widerstand im irakischen Kurdistan der 1980er Jahre', in S. Hajo, C. Borek, E. Savelsberg and S. Dogan (eds), Gender in Kurdistan und der Diapora, Unrast Verlag, Münster.

Food and Agriculture Organization of the United Nations (FAO), Assessment of the Food and Nutrition Situation: Iraq, 2000, www.reliefweb.int/library/documents/ iraqnutrition.pdf, accessed 12 September 2006.

Garfield, R. (2000) 'Changes in Health and Well-being in Iraq during the 1990s: What Do We Know and How Do We Know It?', in Campaign Against Sanctions on Iraq, Sanctions on Iraq: Background, Consequences, Strategies, CASI, Cambridge.

Garfield, R. (1999a) 'Mortality Changes in Iraq, 1990–1996: A Review of Evidence', Occasional Paper, Fourth Freedom Forum, Gashen IN.

Garfield, R. (1999b) 'Morbidity and Mortality among Iraqi Children from 1990 through 1998: Assessing the Impact of the Gulf War and Economic Sanctions', www.casi.org.uk/info/garfield/dr-garfield.html.

Graham-Brown, S. (1999) Sanctioning Saddam: The Politics of Intervention in Iraq, I.B. Tauris, London.

Gunter, M. (1999) The Kurdish Predicament in Iraq: A Political Analysis, St. Martin's Press, New York.

Gunter, M. (1992) The Kurds of Iraq: Tragedy and Hope, St. Martin's Press, New York.

Hassan, G. (2005) 'Iraqi Women Under Occupation', 9 May, www.counter-currents.org/iraq-hassan090505.htm.

Hajo, S., C. Borek, E. Savelsberg and S. Dogan (eds) (2004) Gender in Kurdistan und der Diapora, Unrast Verlag, Münster.

Haynes, K. (2006) 'Other Lives in Accounting: Critical Reflections on Oral History Methodology in Action', Working Paper no. 21, Department of Management Studies, University of York.

Hazelton, F. (ed.) (1994) Iraq since the Gulf War: Prospects for Democracy, Zed Books, London.

Helms, C.M. (1984) *Iraq: Eastern Flank of the Arab World*, Brookings Institution, Washington DC.

Human Rights Watch (2003a) *The Anfal Campaign Against the Kurds*, Middle East Watch Report, Human Rights Watch, New York, Washington, Los Angeles and London, www.hrw.org/reports/1993/iraqanfal/

Human Rights Watch (2003b) *Climate of Fear: Sexual Violence and Abduction of Women and Girls in Baghdad*, vol. 15, no. 7, July.

Husein, Y. (2005) 'International Sanctions, Gender and the State: The Impact of the United Nations Sanctions on Iraqi Women', Ph.D. thesis, University of Exeter.

Hussein, S. (1981) *The Revolution and Woman in Iraq*, trans. Khalid Kishtany, Translation and Foreign Languages Publishing House, Baghdad.

Hussein, S. (1979) *Social and Foreign Affairs in Iraq*, Croom Helm, London.

ICRC (2003) 'Iraq: ICRC Calls Urgently for Protection of the Civilian Population and Services and of Persons No Longer Fighting', Press Release 03/28, 11 April, www.icrc.org/Web/eng/siteeng0.nsf/iwpList581/C53DC80C5FEF5290C1256D05004D817E.

Inati, S. (ed.) (2003) *Iraq: Its History, People, and Politics*, Humanity Books, Amherst.

Iraq Body Count (2006) Press Release 13, 'Iraq Death Toll in Third Year of Occupation is Highest Yet', March, www.iraqbodycount.net/press/pr13.php.

IRINNews.org (2004) 'Iraq: Female Harassment from Religious Conservatives', 14 April, http://washingtontimes.com/world/20041017-013506-9889r.htm.

Ismael, J. (1980) 'Social Policy and Social Change: the Case of Iraq', *Arab Studies Quarterly*, vol. 2, no. 3, pp. 235-48.

Ismael, J., and S. Ismael (2000) 'Gender and State in Iraq', in S. Joseph (ed.), *Gender and Citizenship in the Middle East*. Syracuse University Press, New York.

Jabar, F. (2003) *The Shi'ite Movement in Iraq*, Saqi Books, London.

Jabar, F. (2002) 'Sheikhs and Ideologues: Deconstruction and Reconstruction of Tribes under Ba'th Patrimonial Totalitarianism', in F. Jabar and H. Dawod (eds) *Tribes and Power: Nationalism and Ethnicity in the Middle East*, Saqi Books, London.

Jabra, I.J. (2005) *Princess Street: Baghdad Memories*, trans. I. Boullata, University of Arkansas Press, Fayetteville.

Joseph, S. (ed.) (2000) *Gender and Citizenship in the Middle East*, Syracuse University Press, New York.

Joseph, S. (1991) 'Elite Strategies for State Building: Women, Family, Religion and the State in Iraq and Lebanon', in D. Kandiyoti (ed.), *Women, Islam and the State*, Temple University Press, Philadelphia.

Judd, T. (2006) 'For the Women of Iraq, the War is Just Beginning', *Independent*, 8 June.

Kamp, M. (2003) 'Organizing Ideologies of Gender, Class and Ethnicity: The Pre-Revolutionary Women's Movement in Iraq', in S. Zuhur (ed.), *Women and Gender in the Middle East and Islamic World Today*, University of California Press, Berkeley.

Kamp, M. (1997) 'Abschied von der Abaya? Eine historische Interpretation zur politischen und sozio-ökonomischen Situation irakischer Frauen während der Monarchie', 1921–1958, M.A. thesis, University of Hamburg.

Kandiyoti, D. (ed.) (1991) *Women, Islam and the State*, Temple University Press, Philadelphia.

Khedairi, B. (2005) *Absent*, trans. M. Jamil, American University in Cairo Press, Cairo.

Khedairi, B. (2001) *A Sky So Close*, trans. M. Jamil, Anchor Books, New York.

Laizer, S. (1996) *Martyrs, Traitors and Patriots: Kurdistan after the Gulf War*, Zed Books, London.

Lasky, M. (2006) *Iraqi Women under Siege*, Codepink: Women for Peace and Global Exchange, www.codepinkalert.org/downloads/IraqiWomenReport.pdf.

Left, S. (2003) 'Blix Wants More – and Straw Offers 10 Days', *Guardian Unlimited*, 7 March. Also 'Transcript of Blix's U.N. Presentation' , CNN.com, 7 March.

MacArthur, J. (1992) 'Remember Nayirah, Witness for Kuwait?', *New York Times*, op-ed, 6 January.

McDowall, D. (2000) *A Modern History of the Kurds*, I.B. Tauris, London.

Mahdi, A. (ed.) (2003) *Teen Life in the Middle East*, Greenwood Press, Westport CT.

Mahdi, K. (1999) 'The Iraq Sanctions Debate: Destruction of a People', *Middle East International* 615, 24 December.

Marr, P. (1985) *The Modern History of Iraq*, Westview Press, Boulder CO.

Mikhail, D. (2005) *The War Works Hard*, trans. E. Winslow, New Directions Books, New York.

Mohsen, F. (1994) 'Cultural Totalitarianism', in F. Hazelton (ed.), *Iraq since the Gulf War: Prospects for Democracy*, Zed Books, London.

Mojab, S. (2004) 'No "Safe Haven": Violence against Women in Iraqi Kurdistan', in W. Giles and J. Hyndmann (eds), *Sites of Violence: Gender and Conflict Zones*, University of California Press, Berkeley.

Mojab, S. (2003) 'Kurdish Women in the Zone of Genocide and Gendercide', *Al-Raida*, vol. 21, no. 103, Fall.

Mojab, S. (ed.) (2001) *Women of a Non-State Nation: The Kurds*, Mazda, Costa Mesa.

Mojab, S. (2000) 'Vengeance and Violence: Kurdish Women Recount the War', *Canadian Women's Studies*, vol. 19, no. 4, winter.

Mojab, S. (1996) 'Nationalism and Feminism: The Case of Kurdistan', in *Simone de Beauvoir Institute Bulletin: Women and Nationalism* 16, Concordia University Printing Services, Montreal.

Neshat, S. (2003) 'A Look into the Women's Movement in Iraq, *Farzaneh* vol. 6, no. 11, pp. 54–65.

Niblock, T. (2001) '*Pariah States' and Sanctions in the Middle East: Iraq, Libya, Sudan*, Lynne Rienner, Boulder CO.

Omar, Suha (1994) 'Honour, Shame and Dictatorship', in F. Hazelton (ed.) *Iraq since the Gulf War: Prospects for Democracy*, Zed Books, London.

Orfalea, G. (2006) *The Arab Americans: A History*, Olive Branch Press, Northampton MA.

Ouzgane, L. (ed.) *Islamic Masculinities*, Zed Books, London.

Pellet, P. (2000) 'Sanctions, Food, Nutrition and Health in Iraq', in A. Arnove (ed.), *Iraq under Siege: The Deadly Impact of Sanctions and War*, Pluto Press, London.

Pina, A. (2006) *Women in Iraq: Background and Issues for U.S. Policy*, Congressional Research Service, Library of Congress, March.

Pratt, N. (2005) 'Reconstructing Citizenship in post-Invasion Iraq; The Battle over Women's Rights', conference paper, MESA, Washington DC, pp. 12–13.

Rai, M. (2005) 'Turning Point Fallujah: How US Atrocities Sparked The Iraqi

Resistance', *Electronic Iraq*, 4 May, http://electroniciraq.net/news/1947.shtml.

Rassam, A. (2003) 'Iraq', in *Women's Rights in the Middle East and North Africa: Citizenship and Justice*, Freedom House, Washington.

Rassam, A. (1992) 'Political Ideology and Women in Iraq: Legislation and Cultural Constraints', in J. Jabbra and N. Jabbra (eds), *Women and Development in the Middle East and North Africa*, E.J. Brill, Leiden.

Rassam, A. (1982) 'Revolution within the Revolution? Women and the State in Iraq', in T. Niblock (ed.), *Iraq: The Contemporary State*, Croom Helm, London.

Rejwan, N. (2004) *The Last Jews in Baghdad: Remembering a Lost Homeland*, University of Texas Press, Austin.

Riverbend (2006) *Baghdad Burning*, http://riverbendblog.blogspot.com/2006_07_01_riverbendblog_archive.html, accessed July 2006

Riverbend (2005) *Baghdad Burning: Girl Blog from Iraq*, New York: The Feminist Press at the City University of New York.

Riverbend (2004), *Baghdad Burning*, http://riverbendblog.blogspot.com/2004_04_01_riverbendblog_archive.html.

Roberts, L., R. Lafta, R. Garfield, J. Khudhairi and G. Burnham (2004) 'Mortality before and after the 2003 Invasion of Iraq: Cluster Sample Survey', *The Lancet*, vol. 364, no. 9448, pp. 1857–64.

Rohde, A. (2006) 'Facing Dictatorship: State Society Relations in Ba'thist Iraq', Ph.D. thesis, Freie Universität Berlin.

Rohde, A. (2006) 'Opportunities for Masculinity and Love: Cultural Production in Iraq during the 1980s', in L. Ouzgane (ed.), *Islamic Masculinities*, Zed Books, London.

Rosenthal, E. (2004) 'Study Puts Civilian Death Toll in Iraq at over 100,000', *International Herald Tribune*, 30 October, www.iht.com/articles/2004/10/30/1second_19.php.

Saghieh, Hazim (2000) 'Saddam, Manhood and the Image', in M. Ghoussoub and E. Sinclair-Webb (eds), *Imagined Masculinities: Identity and Culture in the Middle East*, Saqi Books, London.

Salam Pax (2003) *The Baghdad Blog*, Atlantic Books, London.

Salbi, Z. (2006) *Between Two Worlds: Escape from Tyranny: Growing Up in the Shadow of Saddam*, New York, Gotham Books.

Saleem, H. (2005) *My Father's Rifle*, trans. C. Temerson, Atlantic Books, London.

Salim, R. (2001) 'Diaspora, Departure and Remains', in M. Faraj (ed.), *Strokes of Genius: Contemporary Iraqi Art*, Saqi Books, London.

Salucci, I. (2005) *A People's History of Iraq: the Iraqi Communist Party, Workers' Movements, and the Left 1924–2004*, Haymarket Books, Chicago.

Sassoun, J. (2003) *Mayada: Daughter of Iraq – One Woman's Survival under Saddam Hussein*, Dutton, New York.

Save the Children (2003), 'Assessment in Three Schools', Baghdad, 18 May.

Shiblak, A. (2005) *Iraqi Jews: A History of Mass Exodus*, London, Saqi Books.

Shurdom, J.A. (2001) 'Why Top UN Humanitarian Coordinators in Iraq Resign Their Posts', *Jordan Times*, www.geocities.com/iraqinfo/sanctions/sarticles9/whytop.htm.

Simons, G. (1998) *The Scourging of Iraq: Sanctions, Law and Natural Justice*, 2nd edn, Macmillan, London.

Smiles, S. (2005) 'Over Their Dead Bodies: War, Women and Honor in Saddam's Iraq', M.A. thesis, American University of Beirut, December.

Sponeck, Hans-C. von (2005) *Ein anderer Krieg: Das Sanktionsregime der UNO im Irak*, Hamburger Edition, Hamburg.

Tripp, C. (2000) *A History of Iraq*, Cambridge University Press, Cambridge.

UN World Food Programme–Government of Iraq (2006) 'Food Security and Vulnerability Analysis in Iraq,' survey, May, with UNICEF, Amman.

UNICEF (2001) *UNICEF Humanitarian Action: Iraq Donor Update*, New York.

UNICEF (1993) *Children and Women in Iraq: A Situation Analysis*, Amman.

Van Hear, N. (1988) *New Diasporas: The Mass Exodus, Dispersal and Regrouping of Migrant Communities*, University of Washington Press, Seattle.

Wahlbeck, Ö. (1998) *Transnationalism and Diasporas: The Kurdish Example*, Institute of Migration, Turku.

Waite, L. (2000) 'How is Household Vulnerability Gendered? Female-headed Households in the Collectives of Suleimaniyah, Iraqi Kurdistan', *Disasters*, vol. 24, no. 2, pp. 153–72.

Yildiz, K. (2004) *The Kurds in Iraq: The Past, Present and Future*, Pluto Press, London.

Zubaida, S. (2002) 'The Fragments of the Nation: the Case of Iraq', *International Journal of Middle East Studies*, vol. 34, no. 2, pp. 205–15.

Zubaida, S. (1991) 'Community, Class and Minorities in Iraq Politics', R. Fernea and R. Louis (eds), *The Iraqi Revolution of 1958: the Old Social Classes Revisited*, I.B. Tauris, London.

Websites

BBC News, 21 March 2003, 'Flashback: 1991 Gulf War', news.bbc.co.uk/2/hi/middle_east/2754103.stm.

BBC News – On This Day '2 August 1990', http://news.bbc.co.uk/onthisday/hi/dates/stories/august/2/newsid_2526000/2526937.stm.

Campaign Against Sanctions on Iraq (CASI), www.casi.org.uk.

Fair Action Alert, www.fair.org/activism/unscom-history.html.

Iraq Body Count, www.iraqbodycount.org, accessed 4 August 2006.

Iraq Body Count, Fallujah http://iraqbodycount.org/resources/falluja/index.php.

Jo Wilding, *Wildfirejo*, www.wildfirejo.blogspot.com/.

MEDACT, www.medact.org/content/wmd_and_conflict/Medact per cent20Iraq per cent202004.pdf, accessed February 15 2006.

UNICEF, 'Iraq: Facts and figures', 2004, www.unicef.org/media/media_9788.html.

Remember Fallujah, www.rememberfallujah.org/why.htm.

UNICEF Iraq Programme Update, 1–31 October 2003, www.unicef.org/emerg/files/IraqOct.pdf; Iraq Country Statistics, www.unicef.org/infobycountry/iraq_statistics.html.

UNIFEM, Gender Profile, Iraq 2004, www.womenwarpace.org/iraq/iraq.htm.

UNMOVIC, www.unmovic.org/.

WomenWarPeace.Org, www.womenwarpeace.org/iraq/iraq.htm.

Index